ENDORSEMENTS

"When we think of the 'hero,' we are drawn to images of success — wealth, strength, prestige, recognition, excellence. Too often, our society encourages us to seek heroes only in the most obvious places and overlooks great heroes that toil outside the spotlight of mainstream America. But this book, *African-American Heroes & Heroines*, has a different message. It is that despite the persistent racism in our culture and the overwhelming odds stacked against many African-Americans, heroes and heroines are plentiful. Frequently, these role models are not just "successful" in their capacity to earn money or fame; more importantly, they represent stories of the greatest human virtues: perseverance, courage, moral determination, and even love. That is why I am so proud my heroine, Special Olympics athlete Loretta Claiborne, is included in this volume."

—Timothy Shriver, President & CEO, Special Olympics International

"I am thrilled that such a book is available. These biographical entries are right on target: crisply written and engaging."

—Carolyn Kingcade, Editor, *St. Louis Post-Dispatch*

"After reading this book I found the material to be educational in addition to entertaining. The audience will no doubt attract youth and adults. It makes learning quick and fun."

—Thyra Echols-Starr, President,
Urban League of Palm Beach County

"Mrs. Bel Monte breathes life into the known and little known valiant stories of persons of color. This book will continue to capture the reader's interest."

—Isa Bryant, President, Florida Black Historical Research Project

"To succeed in today's world, our young people must know the roles played by their ancestors. For too long, the textbooks have either left us out, or portrayed us as non-players in the important developments in American history. Your book should help dispel those notions, and help our young people to understand that America is far bigger and better than a European enclave. Congratulations, and you can count on my support."

—Charles B. Rangel, Member of Congress

"Brilliance, courage, determination, vision, and commitment to the concept of human freedom and dignity — these are the definitive characteristics of the men and women whose lives are presented in *African-American Heroes and Heroines*. Most especially, their refusal to submit to the tyranny of realities that sought to humiliate, degrade, and even destroy them is surely an inspiration to all who are seeking ways to 'keep on, keeping on.'"

—Joanne M. Martin, Executive Director, Great Blacks in Wax Museum

"Thanks for giving me the opportunity to acknowledge a professional who realized the importance of introducing African-American heroes and heroines to our youth."

—Addie L. Greene, Florida State Representative

"This book will give readers of all ages a chance to understand and appreciate the many accomplishments that have been made and that are being made by our own heroes and heroines. *African-American Heroes & Heroines* will be a welcomed addition to all markets that are interested in knowing the truth."

**—Edward Golson, President,
100 Black Men of Palm Beach County**

"Kathryn Bel Monte has written an informative and inspirational book. The brief biographies give an outstanding overview of the lives of some great Americans. The book would be on my 'must-read' list."

—Sandy Whelchel, Director, National Writers Association

"*African-American Heroes & Heroines* documents more of the true history of the people of this great nation. This book sheds more light on the fallacy of racism."

**—Gloria Atkins, Director,
The Institute for the Healing of Racism of Palm Beach County**

"Bel Monte's book brings to light for all Americans the contributions of many African-Americans to our nation's growth — heroes whose impact has heretofore been hidden or forgotten."

—Dana Cassell, President, Cassell Network of Writers

"The candor and perception used in this work should prove enlightening and image-enhancing to its readers as well as to those who might feel they have no place in our current social system."

—Dr. B. Carleton Bryant, Chairman,
Black Citizens Coalition of Palm Beach County

"*African-American Heroes & Heroines* is a wonderful compilation of past and modern day pioneers, documenting their strength, contribution and place in America's history."

—Mary Butler Hooks, West Palm Beach City Commissioner

"Bel Monte's book is a long overdue, factual account of the great contributions that African-American citizens have made in America."

—Diana Dee Cattaneo, Accredited Genealogist

"Kathryn Bel Monte's book on African-American Heroes and Heroines in America is a must for every home, library, school and office."

—The Honorable Melvin E. Clark, Jr.,
President, Metroplex Corporation

AFRICAN-AMERICAN HEROES & HEROINES

150 True Stories of African-American Heroism

Written & Illustrated by
Kathryn I. Bel Monte

Lifetime Books, Inc.
Hollywood, Florida

Purchased with
Allegheny Regional Asset
District Funds

This publication is designed to provide accurate and authoritative information in regard to
the subject matter covered. It is sold with the understanding that the publisher is not engaged
in rendering legal, accounting, or other professional service. If legal advice or other assistance is required, the services of a competent professional person should be sought. *From A
Declaration of Principles jointly adopted by a Committee of the American Bar Association
and a Committee of Publishers.*

Library of Congress Cataloging-in Publication Data
Bel Monte, Kathryn I.
    African-american heroes & heroines : 150 true stories of African-American heroism
    / Kathryn I. Bel Monte
        p. cm.
    Summary: Profiles Afro-American men and women who have succeeded in fields
such as politics, medicine, law, science, education, art, sports, business, and the military.
    ISBN 0-8119-0869-0
    1. Afro-Americans--Biography. 2. Heroes--United States-Biography. 3. Women
heroes--United States--Biography. [1. Afro-Americans--Biography. 2. Heroes--
Biography. 3. Women heroes--Biography. 4. Women--Biography.] I. Title.
E185.96.B377   1998
920' .009296073--dc21   97-39569
                                                                CIP
                                                                AP

10 9 8 7 6 5 4 3 2 1
Interior Design by Vicki Heil
Cover Photos by AP/Wide World Photos
Author Photo by The Photography Studio©, Maximilian Kaufmann
Printed in Canada

TABLE of CONTENTS

Foreword xiii

Preface by Seymour "Sy" Brody xv

Introduction xix

CHAPTERS

1   **Henry "Hank" Aaron:** Baseball Player 1

2   **Abraham:** Diplomat, Interpreter 3

3   **Alvin Ailey:** Dancer, Choreographer 5

4   **The Tuskegee Airmen:** World War II Bombardment Group ... 7

5   **Ira Frederick Aldridge:** Actor 9

6   **Muhammad Ali:** Prize Fighter 11

7   **Richard Allen:** Church Founder, Bishop 13

8   **Bishop Barbara Amos:** Evangelist 15

9   **Caroline Virginia Anderson:** Physician 17

10   **Marian Anderson:** Opera Singer 19

11   **Russell L. Anderson:** Physician 21

12   **Maya Angelou:** Poet, Educator, Actress, Director 23

13   **Louis Armstrong:** Jazz Musician 25

14   **Arthur Robert Ashe, Jr.:** Tennis Champion 27

15   **Crispus Attucks:** Freedom Martyr 29

16   **Josephine Baker:** Dancer, Humanitarian 31

17   **James Baldwin:** Essayist, Novelist, Playwright 33

18   **Edward M. Bannister:** Artist 35

19   **Ida B. Wells Barnett:** Civil Rights Advocate 37

20   **James P. Beckwourth:** Explorer, Pioneer 39

21   **Lerone Bennett, Jr.:** Historian, Lecturer 41

22   **Mary McLeod Bethune:** Educator 43

23 **James A. Bland:** Composer, Musician 45
24 **Carleton Bryant:** Educator, Historian 47
25 **Isa Hamm Bryant:** Black Historical & Trainer Director 49
26 **Ralph Johnson Bunche:** United Nations Official 51
27 **George Bush:** Pioneer 53
28 **William Harvey Carney:** Civil War Hero 55
29 **George Washington Carver:** Botanist 57
30 **Loretta Claiborne:** Distance Runner, Advocate 59
31 **Nat "King" Cole:** Singer, Entertainer 61
32 **Bessie Coleman:** Aviator 63
33 **William "Bill" Cosby:** Comedian, Actor, Businessman 65
34 **Rebecca Lee Crumpler:** Pioneering Medical Doctor 67
35 **Paul Cuffe:** Colonizationist 69
36 **Dorothy Dandridge:** Actress 71
37 **Benjamin Oliver Davis, Sr.:** United States Army Officer 73
38 **Sammy Davis, Jr.:** Entertainer 75
39 **Thomas Day:** Cabinetmaker 77
40 **Frederick A. Douglass:** Abolitionist 79
41 **Charles R. Drew:** Physician 81
42 **William Edward Burghardt Du Bois:** Civil Rights Leader ... 83
43 **Paul Laurence Dunbar:** Poet 85
44 **Todd Duncan:** Opera Singer 87
45 **Robert S. Duncanson:** Artist 89
46 **Katherine Dunham:** Dancer, Choreographer 91
47 **Lee Elder:** Golfer 93
48 **Ralph Ellison:** Essayist, Novelist 95
49 **Medgar Evers:** Civil Rights Activist 97
50 **Ella Fitzgerald:** Jazz Singer 99
51 **Curtis Charles "Curt" Flood:** Baseball Player, Activist 101
52 **James Forten:** Inventor, Abolitionist 103

53 **Edward Franklin Frazier:** Sociologist 105

54 **Marcus M. Garvey:** Colonizationist 107

55 **Willie Edward Gary:** Attorney-at-Law 109

56 **Berry Gordy, Jr.:** Music Executive 111

57 **Earl G. Graves:** CEO Earl G. Graves, Ltd. 113

58 **Addie L. Greene:** Government Official 115

59 **Alex Haley:** Journalist, Lecturer, Historical Novelist 117

60 **George Cleveland Hall:** Physician, Educator 119

61 **Fannie Lou Hamer:** Civil Rights Activist 121

62 **William Christoper (W.C.) Handy:** Musician 123

63 **Lemuel Haynes:** Minister, Minuteman 125

64 **James Augustine Healy:** Catholic Bishop 127

65 **Josiah Henson:** Abolitionist 129

66 **Matthew Alexander Henson:** Explorer 131

67 **William Augustus Hinton:** Physician, Educator 133

68 **William Meredith Holland, Sr.:** Civil Rights Advocate 135

69 **John Hope:** Educator 137

70 **Lena Horne:** Singer 139

71 **James Langston Hughes:** Author 141

72 **Frederick S. Humphries:** Educator, Chemist 143

73 **Zora Neale Hurston:** Anthropologist, Novelist 145

74 **Jesse Louis Jackson:** Politician 147

75 **Nell Cecilia Jackson:** Olympic Track Star, Coach 149

76 **Bishop Thomas D. Jakes:** Evangelist 151

77 **Caterina Jarboro:** Opera Singer 153

78 **Mae Carol Jemison:** Astronaut, Physician 155

79 **John H. Johnson:** Publisher, Entrepreneur 157

80 **Malvin Gray Johnson:** Artist 159

81 **Barbara Jordan:** Congresswoman 161

82 **Michael Jordan:** Basketball Player 163

ix

83   **Percy L. Julian:** Research Chemist 165

84   **Jackie Joyner-Kersee:** Heptathlon Olympian 167

85   **Everett A. Kershaw:** Educator, Radio Personality 169

86   **Coretta Scott King:** Human Rights Leader 171

87   **Martin Luther King, Jr.:** Civil Rights Leader, Orator.......... 173

88   **Theodore K. Lawless:** Dermatologist, Philanthropist 175

89   **Jacob Lawrence:** Artist.. 177

90   **Lewis Sheridan Leary:** Anti-Slavery Fighter 179

91   **Carl Lewis:** Olympic Track and Field Athlete 181

92   **Mary Edmonia Lewis:** Sculptor 183

93   **Joe Louis:** Prize Fighter... 185

94   **Mary Eliza Mahoney:** Pioneer in Nursing 187

95   **Thurgood Marshall:** U.S. Supreme Court Justice 189

96   **Joanne M. & Elmer P. Martin:** Wax Museum Founders 191

97   **Jan Matzeliger:** Inventor 193

98   **Hattie McDaniel:** Actress 195

99   **Ronald E. McNair:** Astronaut, Laser Physicist 197

100 **Oscar Deveraux Micheaux:** Filmmaker, Author 199

101 **Abbie Mitchell:** Singer, Actress 201

102 **Garrett A. Morgan:** Inventor 203

103 **Constance Baker Motley:** Lawyer, Judge 205

104 **Isaac "Ike" Murphy:** Jockey 207

105 **James Cleveland "Jesse" Owens:** Olympic Athlete 209

106 **Rosa Parks:** Civil Rights Activist 211

107 **Bill Pickett:** Cowboy, Wild West Showman 213

108 **Sidney Poitier:** Actor.. 215

109 **Alvin Poussaint:** Psychiatrist....................................... 217

110 **Colin L. Powell:** Four Star General, U.S. Army 219

111 **Leontyne Price:** Opera Singer 221

112 **Asa Philip Randolph:** Labor Leader, Rights Advocate....... 223

113 **Harold Calvin Ray:** Evangelist, Businessman 225

114 **Garth C. Reeves, Sr.:** Editor, Community Activist 227

115 **Paul Robeson:** Actor 229

116 **Jack Roosevelt "Jackie" Robinson:** Baseball Player 231

117 **Luther (Bill) "Bojangles" Robinson:** Dancer, Actor 233

118 **Augusta Savage:** Sculptor 235

119 **Philippa Duke Schuyler:** Musician 237

120 **Eric O. Simpson:** Newspaper Publisher 239

121 **Naomi Sims:** Fashion Model 241

122 **Benjamin "Pap" Singleton:** Colonizationist 243

123 **Moneta Sleet, Jr.:** Photographer 245

124 **Mabel Keaton Staupers:** Nurse, Activist 247

125 **Bessie B. Stringfield:** WWII Motorcycle Courier 249

126 **Henry Ossawa Tanner:** Artist 251

127 **Susan L. Taylor:** Editor 253

128 **Mary Church Terrell:** Civil Rights Advocate 255

129 **Debi Thomas:** Olympic Figure Skating Champion 257

130 **Adah Belle Samuels Thoms:** Nursing Pioneer 259

131 **Channing H. Tobias:** Relations Leader, Clergyman 261

132 **William Monroe Trotter:** Journalist, Civil Rights Leader 263

133 **Sojourner Truth:** Abolitionist, Civil War Heroine 265

134 **Harriet Tubman:** Underground Railroad Conductor 267

135 **Walter Turnbull:** Choirmaster, Vocalist 269

136 **Madame C.J. Walker:** Businesswoman 271

137 **Booker T. Washington:** Educator 273

138 **Phyllis Wheatley:** Poet 275

139 **Isaac "Bogue" White:** Soldier 277

140 **Lawrence Douglas Wilder:** Activist, Politician 279

141 **Roy Wilkins:** Civil Rights Leader 281

142 **Daniel Hale Williams:** Surgeon 283

143 **Paul R. Williams:** Architect 285

144 **Oprah Winfrey:** Talk Show Host 287

145 **Eldrick "Tiger" Woods:** Golf Champion 289

146 **Granville T. Woods:** Inventor 291

147 **Carter G. Woodson:** Educator, Historian 293

148 **Louis T. Wright:** Physician, Activist 295

149 **The Wrought Iron Men:** Artisans 297

150 **Malcom X (El-Hajj Malik El-Shabazz):** Nationalist. 299

FOREWORD

What makes a hero?

The definition must be shaded by time, circumstances, and locale. To select one requires that we eliminate external qualities: a heroine's looks may inspire no poetry, a hero's pedigree may not qualify him for inclusion among the well-born.

Because heroes and heroines generally wear the face of the conqueror, the triumphs and contributions of African-Americans and other minorities have, historically, been ignored by mainstream America. This resulted in a "ghetto-izing" of history: one for the Euro-American, another for the black. The contributions of African-American soldiers during the Civil War have been woefully underplayed. The bond between Native Americans and black Americans has been under-explored by both white and black historians. Many African-Americans, though aware of their Indian ancestry, have little knowledge of these ancestors, creating a different kind of diaspora; a kind of spiritual as well as physical separation from part of themselves.

To dispel feelings that have alienated cultural and racial groups in America — inferiority in black Americans, and arrogance in whites — a conscious effort must be made to seek those areas that are common to all. One way is to bring to light those contributions that benefit all, and those that exemplify what is loftiest in the spirit of man.

The heroes and heroines in this volume come from all walks of life, and range from the Colonial era to the present. Only wisps and fragments remain of some lives, yet they are worthy of inclusion. Others, we feel we know well: Harriet Tubman, Frederick Douglass, Mary McLeod Bethune, Dr. Martin Luther King, Jr. But you will also meet some "new" friends. Among them is one of my ancestors, Isaac "Bogue" White, a fugitive slave who became a Union soldier. There is a Special Olympics athlete, born legally blind, and with mental and physical handicaps, who largely overcame her limitations and now holds an honorary Ph.D. You will also meet a share-cropper's son who became one of the nation's top trial attorneys and who won a five hundred million dollar judgment in a Jackson, Mississippi courtroom.

They are heroic for different reasons. Some fought gallantly in wars. Others risked or sacrificed their lives because of their political beliefs. And though their profiles do not appear in this book, white Americans who saw wrong and tried to right it deserve to be acknowledged: John Brown, however misguided, gave his life for the black man's freedom. Quakers and other white abolitionists saw the evils of slavery and refused to obey unjust laws. Contemporary heroes such as Morris Dees of the Southern Poverty Law Center defend the rights of oppressed minorities through the courts.

Down through the ages, men and women of conscience have dared to speak out against unspeakable wrongs. The fortunate lived to see change. Others could only view the "promised land" from afar. Yet, through their sacrifice, they ensured it as a heritage for those who followed.

Though the eras in which they lived and the circumstances of their lives may differ, the men and women in this book are united in a common struggle for positive change. Each made a unique contribution to the betterment of the great family of man.

And that is what made them heroes and heroines.

—Kathryn I. Bel Monte

"God has made of one blood all peoples of the earth."
Motto, Berea College, Berea, Kentucky
From Acts 17:26, New Testament

PREFACE

America is the greatest country in the world because of its people. It has taken the best of the many ethnic, racial and religious groups that live within its borders to help make it "number one" in the world with regard to economics, democracy, health and the military.

Yet, the recognition of the achievements, contributions and sacrifices made for our country by the various ethnic, racial and religious people has been obscured.

African-American Heroes & Heroines helps us redefine the importance of African-Americans in our history.

African-Americans have fought in every major battle, war and expedition in which America has been involved, from Colonial times to the present. It is only recently that six of them, 52 years after their service, were finally recognized and honored for their bravery in World War II and were awarded the Congressional Medal of Honor.

In peace time, African-Americans have made many outstanding contributions in science, medicine, arts, literature, entertainment, etc. They have improved the quality of our lives with their innovations, inventions and creativity.

The time has come to recognize and document the American heroes and heroines of all ethnic, racial and religious people so that our children will have these positive role models to emulate.

— **Seymour "Sy" Brody, author of**
Jewish Heroes and Heroines of America

Suggested Reading

The African-American Encyclopedia, New York, 1993

The Ebony Picture History of Black America, Vols I-III, Tennessee, 1971

The Ebony Success Library, Tennessee, 1973

Christian, Charles M., *Black Saga, The African-American Experience,*
New York, Boston, 1995

The Encyclopedia of African-American Culture and History,
New York, 1996

Harley, Sharon, *The Time Tables of African-American History,*
New York, 1995

The International Library of Negro Life and History, Vols. I-V,
New York, 1967

Low, W. Augustus, and Clift, Virgil A., Editors, *The Encyclopedia
of Black America*, New York, 1981

Mahon, John K., *History of the Second Seminole War 1835-1842,*
Florida, 1985

Oates, Stephen B., *Let the Trumpet Sound,* New York, 1982

Parks, Rosa with Reed, Gregory J., *Quiet Strength,* Michigan, 1994.
New York, 1994

Potter, Joan, with Claytor, Constance, *African-American Firsts,*
New York, 1994

Acknowledgments

Writing a book such as *African-American Heroes & Heroines* was an enlightening as well as humbling experience. Even though I thought my knowledge in the area was fairly extensive, once I became involved in the research, I discovered the actual thread of history, the continuum on which we all exist. I felt so small. Flesh and blood, men and women, bigger than life, were no longer mere words on paper, but actual people who entered and exited life's stage. Contemporary heroes and heroines are the "movers and shakers" of today. Whether artist, inventor, performer, healer or educator — all risked possible rejection by offering something of themselves to society; each risked the humiliation that we all dread when faced with the possibility of failure. And yet, each accepted the challenge. Each endured, and performed great deeds whether spectacular or quiet, that impacted the world. With the help of many who assisted in the selection process, it is my greatest pleasure to present these one hundred fifty heroes and heroines.

I take this opportunity to express my gratitude to those special people whose assistance and support helped to make *African-American Heroes & Heroines* possible.

To my husband, Joseph, I say "thanks so much" for understanding when I spent long days and nights rooted in front of the word processor. I thank my daughters, Angela and Cynthia, for their assistance and moral support. I express my appreciation to the Palm Beach County Association of Black Journalists, especially C.B. Hanif and Catherine Rambeau, for their assistance.

I acknowledge the enthusiastic support of Dr. Patricia A. Mulvey, Professor of History, Bluefield State College, Bluefield West Virginia, and her class for submitting rosters of heroes and heroines.

My sincere thanks to Frederick H. Stephens, MSW, ACSW, Assistant Professor of Social Work, the University of North Carolina at Pembroke, Pembroke, North Carolina, and his students, for submitting biographies, lists, news clippings, and other data.

I thank Roschelle Mears, Counselor and Coordinator of Minority Student Programs, Cleveland State Community College, for her efforts, and her willingness to assist on future projects.

A special thanks is extended to my former classmate, Dollie Lewis Franklin, Tallahassee, Florida, for supplying lists of area schools.

I also acknowledge the tenacious efforts of NiNi Smiley, of Florida Community College, Jacksonville, Florida, for coordinating the students that assisted with the project.

Thanks, also, to Mike Janes and Dr. Timothy Shriver of Special Olympics International for supplying crucial information.

I extend my sincere thanks to Linda Nevarez of the United States Olympic Committee for assisting with locating Olympic athletes; to Julia Rather, Archivist II, Tennessee State Library and Archives, and Dee Cattaneo, genealogist, for their assistance in historical and genealogical research of my ancestor, Issac White, whose biography appears in this book.

To Monique Fortin, who so faithfully assisted with research, editing, and proofreading, I extend my heartfelt thanks. To Carolyn Kingcade of the *St. Louis Post-Dispatch*, I express my sincere gratitude for editorial and other assistance; Tanya Burke for contacting persons who played key roles in the success of the production of this book. Thanks to my selection committee, especially Drs. B. Carleton Bryant and Gerald Burke, Dr. A. Thomas White, Mr. John Howard, and to Carolyn Fredericks for reading the galley proofs and other assistance.

I also thank my mother and my sister for their support in all that I have ever attempted to do; and I thank God for sustaining me during the grueling days and nights when the "Deadly Deadline" was staring me down, and I was tempted to blink.

Special Acknowledgments

The story goes that late author Alex Haley kept a picture of a turtle perched on a fence in his office. It never failed to evoke the visitor's inevitable query, "How did it get up there?" Haley would respond, "Obviously, with somebody's help."

As another turtle on the fence, I sincerely thank Mr. Donald Lessne, publisher of Lifetime Books, for directing this project. For her assistance of inestimable value, a profound thank you is extended to Ms. Callie Rucker, editor. Her expertise rescued me from the quagmires I encountered while writing and illustrating under such a tight deadline. Without the help and encouragement from these two exceptional people, it would not have been possible for me to produce *African-American Heroes & Heroines*.

Introduction

The late Barbara Jordan, Congresswoman from Texas, said that when the original Constitution of the United States was written, African-Americans were not included as part of "We the People." This was not a simple oversight, but a policy of the American government, buttressed by its social and economic thought. Most black Americans, in 1790, were held as property and each was only considered as 3/5 of a person, for purposes of representation in the federal Congress. Although America later freed its African citizens, complete civil and political rights were dealyed for a full century. Notwithstanding this legacy, through slavery, segregation, separation and subjugation, African-Americans have achieved in every aspect of American life. Their deeds and accomplishments have served to better their own condition and the condition of all Americans.

African-Americans are the only group of Americans who did not come to this country voluntarily. Brought here as chattel property and systematically stripped of all cultural ties to their place of origin, African-Americans have nevertheless realized accomplishments consistent with and even exceeding those of almost any other group in this country. Though commonly associated with entertainment and athletics, African-Americans have participated with distinction in every war America has fought, and have written and published significant contributions to American literature. African-Americans have created and invented many of the appliances and everyday useful devices we think of as important to our standard of living and have led the fight for this country, to live out its credo, for all of its citizens, that "all men are created equal."

It has been difficult, however, for America to acknowledge the greatness of her black sisters and brothers. Partly out of racism and partly out of ignorance, African-Americans have been, and continue to be, marginalized in American history and American social thought. Even black Americans themselves knew much about their oppression and losses, but little about their successes and winners until Carter G. Woodson began the tradition of "Black History Week," following his publication of the classic book, *Miseducation of the Negro*.

Although much of the record has been, and is being, corrected, much still is required before African-Americans of distinction are accepted as great Americans, along with their fellow citizens, whose backgrounds are primarily European. More importantly, access to this information and knowledge must be enhanced so that Americans and others of all backgrounds, are familiar with these meaningful contributions.

Kathryn Bel Monte contributes significantly, with this book, to the effort to help Americans, particularly young people, know about and appreciate the high achievements of African-Americans in American life. While she includes well-known African-American men such as the reverend Dr. Martin Luther King, Jr., Bel Monte also highlights lesser recognized black achievers and women such as Dr. Mae Jemison, astronaut, physician and eminent scientist. Bel Monte's list identifies African-American contributors in almost every area of human endeavor.

The significance of this book is not simply in the cataloging of men and women of African-American heritage who can be identified as role-models for African-American youngsters. Its real contribution is in pointing out to all children how these persons are important to the growth and the development of this country, so that they can serve as role-models to Americans of all hues and national origins.

— Walter J. Pierce, Ph.D.
Barry University
School of Social Work

"Aim at perfection in everything, though in most things it is unattainable; however, they who aim at it, and persevere, will come much nearer to it, than those whose laziness and despondency make them give it up as unattainable."

—Chesterfield

Henry "Hank" Aaron (b. 1934)
Baseball Player

On April 8, 1974, "Hammerin' Hank" Aaron did what many had once thought impossible. At 9:07 pm EST, as thousands watched from the stands at Atlanta's Fulton County Stadium, his bat cracked against Dodger Al Downing's pitch, sending the ball skyrocketing out of the ballpark. The suspense was broken for stadium fans and the millions watching on television; Aaron had hit his 715th home run, shattering the time-honored record of the great Babe Ruth.

Not everyone was happy about Aaron's accomplishment. What should have been his happiest year turned out to be his worst. While the majority of the world saluted the new hero, some of the worst elements of society surfaced to protest an African-American's eclipsing of an Anglo-American. For Aaron, that year was one of racial slurs and constant death threats.

1

For Henry "Hank" Louis Aaron, son of Herbert and Estella Aaron, of Mobile, Alabama, baseball was a passion. Having captured his heart early in life, he played the favorite sport every chance he had, in spots ranging from vacant lots to the racially restricted municipal diamond.

In 1952, after beginning his career earlier that year with the semi-professional Mobile Black Bears, he joined the American Negro League's Indianapolis Clowns. That same year, he caught the eye of the National League's Boston Bears. They sent him to Eau Claire, Wisconsin, where he played with their farm league, and was named Rookie of the Year.

In 1953, along with two other African-American players, he integrated the South Atlantic League in Jacksonville, Florida, by playing for the Braves' Class A farm team. By 1954, the Braves, who were by then in Milwaukee, promoted him to the major league. He led the team to a World Series Championship in 1957 and was named the most valuable player of the year by the National League. He led his team to the World Series play-offs in 1958 as well, and, in 1969, to the National League Championship series. Though he made history by toppling Babe Ruth's phenomenal record, he was traded in 1975, the same year he was awarded the Spingarn Medal, to the Milwaukee Brewers, after 21 seasons with the Braves. He retired the following year.

Still the "Home Run King," his lifetime record also included 2,297 runs batted in. Because of his sterling career, spanning over twenty years, he was inducted into the Baseball Hall of Fame in Cooperstown, New York, in 1982, his first year of eligibility.

After his retirement, Hank Aaron returned to the Braves as director of player development, and later became one of the organization's vice-presidents. He was also made vice-president of Turner Broadcasting Company.

In spite of his personal success, Aaron has criticized major league baseball for not hiring more minorities in positions of leadership. His concerns for others further establish him as a true American hero.

DID YOU KNOW?

- He began as a shortstop.
- By the end of the 1974 season, Aaron had hit 733 home runs.
- He earned two hundred dollars a month playing for the Indianapolis Clowns.
- He received 406 of 415 votes from the Baseball Writers Association when he was voted into the Baseball Hall of Fame.

"The only freedom which deserves the name is that of our purusing our own good, in our own way, so long as we do not attempt to deprive others of theirs, or impede their efforts to obtain it."   —*J.S. Mill*

Abraham (c. Early 1800s)
Diplomat, Interpreter

nown as "sense bearer" for Chief Micanopy, he is sometimes referred to as "Negro Abraham" in various historical accounts. An interpreter for the Seminoles, at peace parlays between the Indians and the United States government, during the era of the Second Seminole War (1835-1842), it is rumored that he secretly visited plantations at night and persuaded slaves to escape and join the Indians.

Although there are few historical accounts of Abraham's life, it is known that he played key roles in negotiations between two very different cultures occupying the same turf. On January 27, 1837, after a skirmish between U.S. troops and Seminoles, near the Great Cypress Swamp in Florida's Everglades, 25 Indians and African-Americans were captured. The following day, one of the African-American captives was sent to give the Seminoles the United States government's offer of amnesty; the offer only stood if the chiefs complied with the removal treaties that would relocate the Seminoles west of the Mississippi River. Abraham played a prominent role by acting as interpreter between the Indians and the white troops. He was also included in the peace talks that followed between the Native American chiefs and the government troops, both having agreed to a suspension of hostilities pending on the outcome of the talks.

A humanitarian as well as an interpreter and diplomat, Abraham was concerned with the fate of African-Americans. He worried that they would be captured and re-enslaved during the trek west. Hence, he objected to settlement of the Seminoles with the Creek Indians, known African-American enslavers and enemies of the Seminoles.

One of 103 names on a report labeled "Registry of Negro Prisoners Captured by Thomas S. Jesup Owned (or claimed) by the Indians (1836-1837)," Abraham was listed as a fifty year-old Negro who claimed to be free, and who was supposedly friendly toward whites. General Jesup described him as a "principal Negro chief" as well.

Although historical accounts do not mention any formal education, Abraham demonstrated a high degree of intelligence, and possessed the ability to persuade and influence.

It is not clear where Abraham eventually settled. Some accounts state that he remained a key leader of the Seminoles until 1839, when he was shipped out of the territory.

HISTORY IN A CAPSULE

Osceola, the great Seminole freedom fighter, was the son of a white father and Indian mother. He was also of African ancestry, though accounts differ as to its source. He was a member of the anti-removal faction of the Creeks and Seminoles during the early days of the Second Seminole War. Because they had a mutual enemy, he relied upon fugitive slaves as allies. Since African-Americans had once lived among whites, they proved valuable to Osceola as intelligence agents, interpreters and sources of "inside" information, which was crucial to him and his warriors. For a brief period during the 1830's, the two groups controlled Central Florida. Many Florida cities (Pahokee), counties (Osceola), and waterways (Okeechobee) reflect the state's Seminole heritage.

"Perfection consists...in doing ordinary things extraordinarily well."
—Angelique Arnauld

Alvin Ailey (1931-1989)
Dancer, Choreographer

hen he appeared on Broadway as lead dancer in *Jamaica* and *House of Flowers*, he revolutionized modern dance. With the proceeds he earned from the two productions, he founded The Alvin Ailey Dance Company. *Revelations,* which became one of his signature pieces, was presented at his second concert, and was choreographed to music of African-American spirituals. Beautifully sculpted, moving in the message it portrayed, it rivaled any presentation by any company. Having moved with breath-taking magnificence, Ailey has been called the greatest male modern dancer.

He started his company in 1958 after completing high school and spending a short time in college. His troupe presented four annual concerts and toured Australia under the aegis of the State Department. Critiques from this time include a description of the troupe's performance as the most "devastating" dance presentation ever seen in the country.

In 1965, his group received sixty-one curtain calls in Hamburg, Germany, and was held over six weeks in London. It was one of the most successful tours ever made by an American dance company. In the words of a German critic, "One has never seen anything like it."

His dance company participated in the 1970's Bicentennial celebration by creating and presenting special jazz vignettes.

He has earned ovations at the Jacob's Pillow Dance Festival and the Boston Arts Festival, and choreographed the dance oratorio, *Mass*, in 1971, at the John F. Kennedy Center for the Performing Arts in Washington, D.C.

An Actor as well as a dancer-choreographer, he played opposite Claudia McNeil in a straight dramatic role in *Tiger, Tiger, Burning Bright*, and has performed with Harry Belafonte. Also a singer and a teacher, he played a leading acting role in *Call Me By My Rightful Name*, an off-Broadway play. With Carmen de Lavallade, he performed *Roots of the Blues*, which he choreographed specially for the two of them.

Born in Rogers, Texas, he was a star gymnast in high school who went to study at the Lester Horton Dance Theater in Los Angeles, and in New York City. When he died from a rare blood disease in 1989, more than four thousand people attended his funeral.

His dance troupe continued after his death and is currently a resident company of the City Center of New York and the Brooklyn Academy of Music.

DID YOU KNOW?

♦ Upon the death of Lester Horton, Ailey became the artistic director and choreographer of the Horton Theatre before moving to New York.

♦ His troupe has won acclaim for its use of popular dance patois and jazz music in its performances.

♦ Ailey choreographed the opera *Antony and Cleopatra* at the Metropolitan Opera House in 1966.

♦ Judith Jameson, once linked with the company, became its director after his death in 1989.

"If a thousand old beliefs were ruined in our march to truth, we must still march on."   **—Stopford A. Brooke**

The Tuskegee Airmen
World War II Bombardment Group

o the Americans who spoke of the Tuskegee Airmen with pride, they were the Black Eagles. To the German pilots who battled them in World War II, they were the Schwartze Vogelsmenschen — the Black Birdmen. The only unit with a record for having never lost one of the bombers they escorted, in over two hundred missions, they were a success story.

Referred to as "The Experiment," by the Pentagon, it wasn't until the NAACP threatened to file a lawsuit that the War Department appropriated 1.8 million dollars to form a school. Though a promise for funds was made on January 16, 1941, it wasn't until April of that year that the allotment came through. Though the student-pilots, named for the Alabama town where they were trained, were eager to serve their country, they opposed the War Department's plan to form a segregated school. During a three-day sympathy strike to protest the establishment of an all-black unit, forty-nine of the students were dismissed.

The first class, made up of ten members, was down to five by the time graduation day came on May 7, 1942. In spite of the conflict surrounding the school, it went on to produce some of the finest pilots that fought in the Allied War effort. On their first mission, Lt. Charles B. Hall of Indiana shot down a German plane and received a Distinguished Flying Cross. In 1943, they became a part of the 332nd Fighter Group and damaged or downed more than four hundred German aircraft during battles in the skies over Italy.

During the war, approximately six hundred African-Americans received their wings; sixty-three were killed; thirty-two were shot down and taken as prisoners of war. Though these pilots distinguished themselves continuously throughout WWII, the segregated society to which they returned refused to honor their heroism. Officers' clubs would not admit them; disciplinary actions, including court martials, made sure that they "stayed in their place." Some were transferred to obscure southern bases, where even German prisoners of war were allowed more privileges, such as the freedom to visit the commissary.

President Bill Clinton finally recognized the airmen, though more than a half a century late, for their part in WWII. He extended them the honor they earned, and deserved, in having served their country.

HISTORY IN A CAPSULE

In 1928, Charles Alfred "Chief" Anderson managed to scrape together two thousand five hundred dollars to buy himself an airplane. Because of his burning passion to be a pilot and because flying schools refused to take African-Americans, he studied on his own and taught himself how to fly. He became one of only four commercially licensed African-American pilots in the entire country, before WWII.

In 1940, he went to Tuskegee, Alabama, for the sole purpose of training African-American airmen Dr. Frederick Patterson, who was then president of Tuskegee Institute, welcomed the idea and tried to convince the War Department to train and use black combat pilots. Although the United States was woefully short of airmen, the prevailing thought that blacks did not possess the mettle to fly prevented the government agency from seriously considering them.

The intervention of First Lady Eleanor Roosevelt helped change the War Department's stand on this issue when she allowed Anderson to pilot one of her flights.

"All the world's a stage..." —**William Shakespeare**

Ira Frederick Aldridge (1807-1867)
Actor

ike many serious African-American performers of the day, Ira Aldridge found it impossible to perfect his craft in the United States. Wishing to develop his potential as a Shakespearean actor, he enrolled in the University of Glasgow in Scotland. There, he won several medals and prizes for his ability to master Latin.

In 1826, he began his acting career as Othello, in London's Royalty Theatre. He repeated the role in Ireland, playing opposite the great Edmond Kean's performance of Iago.

He received critical acclaim from European royalty. The Czar of Russia presented him with the Cross of Leopold and the city of Bern gave him the Maltese Cross. The monarchs of Sweden, Austria and Prussia also honored him, and his great skill was memorialized by the Ira Aldridge Chair at the Stratford-on-Avon Shakespeare Memorial Theatre.

9

His first role was at the African Free School in New York, where he received his early training. He played the role of Rolo in Sheridan's play, *Pizzaro*. After discovering that there were few opportunities for an African-American Shakespearean actor to develop and be appreciated in America, where the usual venue for African-American actors was a minstrel show, he began his voluntary exile to countries where the color line was not so rigidly drawn, or racial prejudices so intrinsically imbedded.

His portrayal of Othello the Moor was said to be so accomplished that the Europeans immediately hailed him as a great actor. Lovers of drama, in countries such as England, Ireland and Scotland did not seem to mind a black actor in lead roles that included King Lear and Shylock. Aldridge, they discovered, delivered the same high standard performance as did white actors.

So great was his acting that critics acclaimed each of his performances as his greatest. Because of its racism, America lost the opportunity to see him perform, and aspiring actors of his day missed having him as a mentor and role model.

After having finally decided to return to the United States, Aldridge died, tragically, on the eve of his departure from Lodz, Poland.

DID YOU KNOW?

♦ Ira Aldridge was reputed to have been the grandson of an African chief.

♦ Part of the reason for his immigrating to Europe, was the destruction of the Africa Company Theatre by white rowdies.

♦ The British did not initially accept Aldridge with open arms.

♦ He brought vitality to the craft for aspiring black actors.

♦ Aldridge was the first African-American to achieve international acclaim on the legitimate English-speaking stage.

♦ He was a former carpenter.

"Pursue not a victory too far. He hath conquered well that hath made his enemy fly; thou mayest beat him to a desperate resistance, which may ruin thee."

—Herbert

Muhammad Ali (b. 1942)
Prize Fighter

e wasn't gracious in victory and he wasn't humble in defeat, yet many thought his brash but good natured braggadocio amusing. This all changed when he converted to the Nation of Islam (NOI), a mysterious sect many considered militant and anti-white. It advocated self-defense by blacks against white aggresion, and was therefore feared by whites and some African-Americans.

Born Cassius Clay, in Louisville, Kentucky, he began boxing at age twelve, under Louisville Policeman, Joe Martin. Although he showed little interest in school, he demonstrated superior pugilistic skills and soon developed into one of the nation's most promising amateurs.

In 1959 and 1960, he won the National Amateur Athletic Championship. In Rome, at the 1960 Olympic games, he was a gold medal winner.

After going professional following the Olympics, young, handsome, and outgoing Clay, who had a penchant for coming up with snappy rhymes, dubbed himself "The Greatest" — becoming one of the most popular and infamous figures in boxing history.

Angelo Dundee was his mentor and trainer, while an association of white Louisville businessmen managed him. Although his first wins were against rather lackluster opponents, his roister and constant jabber attracted a large following of mostly agreeable fans and amused media, while his amazing hand and foot speed and unique boxing method attracted experts in the sport.

In 1964, he challenged the seemingly undefeatable Sonny Liston for the heavyweight title. Though Liston was known for his first-round demolition of Floyd Patterson, Clay defeated him in seven rounds. Immediately following the victory, Clay announced he was converting to Nation of Islam and changing his name to Muhammad Ali; Clay, he stated, was a slave name.

His conversion was a shock to the public, who had been unaware of his secret visits to mosques for over three years. Another point of consternation was his friendship with Malcolm X, whose militant rhetoric and confrontational stance both frightened and angered much of the nation.

Ali later won a rematch with Liston in 1965, this time demolishing his perpetually scowling challenger in the first round. Because he was so unpopular in the United States following his conversion, he fought abroad for most of 1966. During this period, he won against George Chuvalo, Ernest Terrell and Henry Cooper; it was during this period that he was drafted into the army to fight in the Vietnam War.

Although originally classified as 1-Y (unfit for service because of low scores on the Army intelligence tests), many believe that his conversion to Islam prompted government officials to reclassify him as 1-A (qualified for induction). In spite of his reclassification, Ali refused to serve, stating on one occasion that the "Viet Cong never did anything to me." He was convicted in federal court in 1967 of violating the Selective Service Act, stripped of his boxing title and sentenced to five years in prison. His sentence was eventually overturned in the Supreme Court.

In 1970, after nearly a four-year layoff, he made his comeback by knocking out Jerry Quary in the third round. However, in March of 1971, he lost to undefeated Joe Frazier in a close fifteen round battle. In 1975, Frazier and Ali came together again for what Ali dubbed the "Thrilla in Manila." In what would be their final match together, Ali prevailed; Frazier's trainer forbade his fighter to return to the ring for the fifteenth round of the bruising melee.

In a career that lasted perhaps too long, Ali lost only five times. Many speculate that it was the brutal fights of his later career that precipitated the palsy-like symptoms and slurred speech evident after his retirement in 1981.

One of the greatest boxers of all time, he was inducted into the Boxing Hall of Fame in 1987.

"If men are so wicked with religion, what would they be without it!"

—Franklin

Richard Allen (1760-1831)
Church Founder, Bishop

When Richard Allen and a group of African-Americans were asked to leave a white Methodist church congregation in Philadelphia because blacks were not welcome, his faith in God was not challenged; he merely focused his energy into the organizing of a new denomination. In 1816, he assembled sixteen independent black Methodist churches from around the country and founded the African-American Episcopal Church. Because of his leadership skills and personal qualities, he was elected its first bishop; this was quite a change in status for an ex-slave.

Born a slave in Philadelphia, he was purchased by a Delaware farmer and began preaching in 1777, after a religious conversion to Christianity. Allen's master was so affected by his zeal and power to persuade, that he allowed him to preside over services in his own home. So effective was the young slave's

13

preaching, he even converted his master, who allowed him to purchase his freedom. Allen returned to Philadelphia, settling there around 1786.

He attended St. George's Methodist Church, and, for a while, all went well. Friction began to rise after Allen brought so many African-American converts into the church. When the church sought to segregate itself by asking the African-American members to move to the gallery, Allen and Absalom Jones led a mass exodus of African-Americans from St. George's.

In 1787, Allen formed the Free African Society to promote advancement and self-improvement of African-Americans. It was the group's first official organization for African-Americans, and it was through it that Allen and Jones established St. Thomas' Free African Church within the Protestant Episcopal Church. In spite of the un-Christian manner in which he was treated by whites, Allen showed his inner conviction in 1793, when he and members of the society nursed victims of a Philadelphia yellow fever epidemic, regardless of their race.

In 1816, Allen assembled sixteen independent African-American Methodist churches from around the country and founded the Bethel African Methodist Episcopal Church (Mother Bethel). The AME Church expanded rapidly under Allen's leadership, and by 1826, it had nearly eight thousand members.

In addition to being a religious leader, Allen was also a patriot. With his friend, Absalom Jones, he was instrumental in recruiting more than 2,000 African-American soldiers to help defend Philadelphia during the War of 1812.

As a political activist, he opposed the ideology of the Colonization Society, a group formed in 1816 to send free blacks to Africa, their "ancestral homeland." In spite of all its social ills, Allen loved America. He did, however, support the relocating of African-Americans to Canada. As a result, many left the United States and settled north of the border.

In honor of his contributions to African-Americans, Payne Institute, established in Cokesbury, South Carolina (1870), and relocated to Columbia, was named Allen University.

In 1976, the Richard Allen Center for Culture and Art was founded in New York City, in the Empire Hotel opposite the Lincoln Center. The AME church was one of the major financial supporters of its establishment.

As an early church leader, Richard Allen's life reflected his belief in the Christian principles of love, forgiveness and service to mankind.

"My only aim and desire is to please the Lord and edify the body of Christ."
—Bishop Barbara Amos

Bishop Barbara Amos (b.1957)
Evangelist

T he church is known as "The Miracle on 26th Street," in Norfolk, Virginia. The members are armed and trained for combat; their weapon is the Word of God, their protection is the shield of faith. The over three thousand member-strong, predominately African-American, Faith Deliverance Christian Center (FDCC), situated in the heart of the inner city, is the safe haven and spiritual center for those who face a battlefield pockmarked with drug addiction, crime, unemployment and alcoholism; more than seventy percent of FDCC members are new converts. And, the field general of the congregation, and its source of inspiration is Barbara Amos.

As early as age sixteen, when she traveled with, and played the drums for, gospel singer Shirley Caesar's Caesar Singers, Amos knew that the ministry was her vocation. Her mother encouraged her desire to become a pastor, and Shirley Caesar, after recognizing Amos's "pulpit presence," became her mentor, helping her to develop her music and public speaking skills.

Entering a mostly male profession, Amos has delivered sermons from the floor, rather than the pulpit, on more than one occasion; many still believe women should teach and not preach, especially not from the pulpit. By not allowing barriers and negative experiences to bring her down, she believes she is paving the way for other women who want to enter the ministry.

One place where she always feels welcome is the FDCC; after assuming its pastorship on her thirtieth birthday, Amos earned the respect of both men and women members. She transformed the church, then consisting of four members and two kerosene heaters to ward off the unsympathetic cold of Norfolk's winters, by changing the lives of addicts, alcoholics and others through, "the power of Christ to work miracles in lives."

When the bite of winter brought the homeless, the unemployed, and the broken into the church for warmth, they found fellowship, and members who were ready, willing and able to provide clothing, food and other needs. The members also told these downtrodden about the love of God. Within six months, FDCC was filled to capacity. They moved to a YMCA and then to a Holiday Inn. By 1992, they were able to buy their own building. Once a member of the Church of God in Christ, Amos now belongs to the Mt. Sinai Holy Church of America, founded by Ida Robinson in 1924. In this denomination, she feels less of the sting of gender bias and oversees ministries in Virginia and North Carolina.

Though she strongly believes in women's parity in the ministry, she decries being labeled a feminist or anti-male. The men in her congregation, she states, are treated like men and do not feel threatened under her leadership.

Amos believes that only education will enable people to understand the role of women in the church, and she denies that there is anything scriptural that prohibits them from being pastors. She defends and encourages other women who pursue their call to preach and believes it "hypocritical" to advocate racial equality without gender equality.

A member of the National Congress of Black Women, she also serves on the board of directors of the Urban League of Hampton Roads, is a committee member of Mount Sinai Holy Church of America, Inc., and executive director of The Master's Touch Learning Center and the Faith Academy School of excellence. She holds a B.S. degree in criminal justice from Hampton University, and graduated Magna cum laude with a Master of Divinity degree from Virginia Union University. She is currently a graduate student in social work at Norfolk State University.

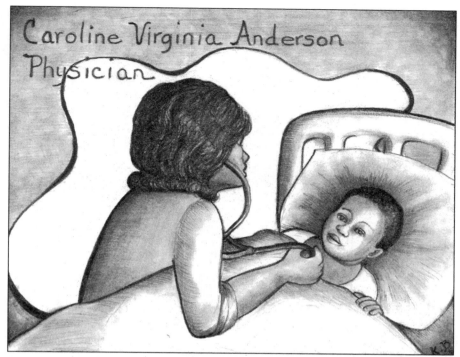

"A good physician is a John Baptist, who recognizes that his only mission is to prepare the way for a greater than himself — Nature." **— A.S. Hardy**

Caroline Virginia Anderson (1848-?)
Physician

S he was a female pioneer in the field of medicine, and like other African-Americans of her day, Caroline Virginia Anderson felt the sting of racism in her quest to enter a profession. After applying for an internship at the Boston New England Hospital for Women and Children, she was denied because she was a Negro. Because of a probable twinge of conscience, the board of directors later relented and unanimously accepted her.

Born in Philadelphia, she was the daughter of William Grant Still, the Underground Railroad conductor and secretary. Growing up, she attended the Institute for Colored Youth of Philadelphia. She also received private education at the Friends' Raspberry Alley School.

In 1829, Caroline graduated from Oberlin College in Ohio. She was only nineteen years old, the youngest in a class of forty-five students. She entered

Howard University School of Medicine in Washington, D.C., in 1875, where, in addition to her medical course of study, she also taught speech and drawing. She transferred from Howard the following year and entered the Women's Medical College of Philadelphia, where she received her medical degree in 1878. After her internship in Boston, she returned to Philadelphia, where she set up her practice.

Dr. Anderson was active in a number of civic and educational activities as well. She was president of the Women's Christian Temperance Union and treasurer of the Women's Medical Alumni Association. She was also a board member of the Home of the Aged and Infirm Colored of Philadelphia, a member of the Women's Medical Society, and one of the organizers of the first Colored YWCAs in the city. In addition to all this, she was a teacher and assistant principal at the Berea Church School for thirty years.

At a time when women largely did not seek professional careers, and in a time where racism often locked out many bright and talented minds, Caroline Virginia Anderson, as both a woman and an African-American, overcame the obstacles keeping her from her dreams, thereby opening the door for others to follow. She was an excellent role model for young women of her era and for ours today.

HISTORY IN A CAPSULE

In 1893, a group of white women were touched by the plight of New York City's African-American citizens, who, because of segregation, lacked proper medical facilities. These philanthropists founded Lincoln Hospital and Home. It soon became the area's major health provider for black citizens.

In 1898, the hospital opened a nursing school to train black nurses to care for their sick. Out of ten schools instituted during the 1890s, Lincoln ranked among the highest. In spite of the benevolence of the whites who instituted the hospital and school, the idea of blacks in high positions of leadership had not come yet. Adah Thoms, one of the most dedicated and talented nurses in the nation, could rise no higher than assistant superintendent. That position was held by a white.

The Lincoln facilities existed until 1961, when laws upholding segregation were no longer in effect in New York.

"Music is the harmonious voice of creation...one note of the divine concord which the entire universe is destined one day to sound." **—Mazzine**

Marian Anderson (1902-1993)
Opera Singer

On Easter Sunday, in 1939, Marian Anderson stood on the steps of the Lincoln Memorial Center in Washington, D.C., and sang before seventy-five thousand people. Her sweet voice washed over her audience, eliminating the bitterness surrounding the performance; the Daughters of the Revolution had denied her the opportunity to sing at Constitution Hall. Marian did not allow this to defeat her. She had faced adversity and racism before, and wouldn't allow it to bring her down.

Born to a poor couple in Philadelphia, Marian developed a love of music at an early age. Her family often gathered with friends to sing Negro spirituals. She made her debut at age six, at the Union Baptist Church and as she grew older, sang in both the junior and senior choirs. After her father died, Anna, Marian's mother, did other people's laundry to make ends meet. Marian, whose first pay, at age eight, was fifty cents, augmented her mother's earn-

19

ings by singing in church-sponsored concerts.

Marian attended elementary and secondary school in South Philadelphia. As a high school student at South Philadelphia High School for Girls, she sang in the Philadelphia Choral Society, an all black group. As a seventeen-year-old senior, master voice teacher Giuseppe Boghetti accepted her as a student, upon the urging of Marian's principal. Her lessons were paid for with coins collected by the members of her church.

A few months after studying under Boghetti, Marian entered a contest held at the Lewisohn Stadium, by the New York Philharmonic Society. Three hundred contestants vied, but Marian, singing *O Mio Fernando,* was the winner. Her prize was an appearance with the New York Philharmonic Orchestra. Dazzled by her contralto voice, the manager signed her to a contract.

Though she sang magnificently, because of the United States' rigid color barriers, engagements were hard to get. Her manager took her to London, where she was accepted and appreciated, and where she had many leading musicians working with her.

Although confronted with many barriers, Marian also scored her share of victories, in her fight to overcome the racial bias that could have deterred her singing career. In 1929, she was awarded the Julius Rosenwald Scholarship, and was able to travel and study. It was during her travels and performances in Europe that she received some of her greatest compliments and honors; in Salzburg, Austria, the world renowned musician Toscanini declared to her, "A voice like yours comes along only once in a Century." And, it was in Europe, that famous Finnish composer, Sibelius, dedicated a composition to her, and where she was decorated by the kings of Sweden and Norway. She was awarded the Order of African Redemption of the Republic of Liberia, the Bok Award (ten thousand dollars), and received a request for a command performance by the British crown as well.

Personally acquainted with the struggle of African-Americans in the fine arts, she established the Marian Anderson Award for young singers in 1942, clearing an easier path for those who were to follow.

In 1943, she was finally given the opportunity to sing in Constitution Hall, and in 1955, she became the first African-American to sing on stage at the Metropolitan Opera House. In 1957, the State Department sent her on a good-will tour of India and the Far East. The following year, 1956, she published her autobiography *My Lord, What A Morning.*

In 1963, she was the first black woman to receive the Presidential Medal of Freedom, awarded by President Lyndon Johnson. She gave her farewell concert in Carnegie Hall on Easter Sunday in 1965, and as one of the world's most esteemed contraltos, she was one of five artists to receive the first John F. Kennedy Center honors in 1978.

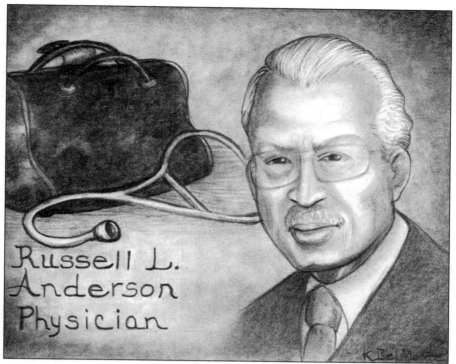

"The man who does his work, any work, conscientiously, must always be in one sense, a great man." **—Mulock**

Russell L. Anderson (1907-1991)
Physician

ike many of the early family physicians of African ancestry, who carried little black bags from house to house, Russell L. Anderson provided care for the sick, delivered the newborn and comforted the dying. Like thousands who are now gone, who were not "big" names, and whose healing intervention received only brief moments of gratitude, he labored quietly in his art.

Born in Pittsburgh, Pennsylvania, to Sylvestor Anderson and Virginia Gunn Anderson, Russell was one of seven children. Because Sylvestor recognized that without an education, only menial jobs would be open to his children, he always encouraged them to persist in their studies, and to persevere through the economic, social and spiritual challenges inherent in a segregated society.

While Russell was still very young, the family moved to Stockbridge, in western Massachusetts, where he finished both grade and high school. He became the first African-American to graduate from the city's Westinghouse High. He enrolled in the then tuition-free University of Pittsburgh, but dropped out when work and studies became too much. He took a job cleaning a drug store for ten dollars a week. Once he experienced the harshness of life as an African-American without an education, however, he returned to school.

In 1926, he married Celeste Johnson, and again considered dropping out of school, because of the hardships of maintaining a marriage while a full-time student. He would walk about while studying to keep from falling asleep. During these times, Dr. J.D. Avent, a dentist whom Russell met through one of his teachers, pumped up his spirits, by reminding him that the outcome would be worth the sacrifice. Avent would sometimes speak only Latin to him to keep him motivated.

Anderson received his B.S., M.S. and Ph.D. (1928) degrees in genetics at the University of Pittsburgh. From 1930 to 1943, he was head of the biology department at Johnson C. Smith University in Charlotte, North Carolina. He decided then that he would pursue a career as a medical doctor and enrolled in Howard University Medical School where he earned his M.D. degree in 1946. In the same year, he moved to Tallahassee, Florida, where he became head of the Biology Department at Florida A&M University and also established his medical practice. He eventually became director of student health at the university.

In 1957, he founded the Anderson-Brickler Medical Clinic with his son-in-law, Dr. Alexander D. Brickler. He practiced medicine there until his retirement in 1989. The clinic now has an integrated staff of seven full-time and twenty-four part-time employees, including his granddaughter, Dr. Celeste Brickler Hart.

In an age when other emerging professionals were distancing themselves from the black "underclass," Russell Anderson strongly identified with them. He rejected what he called "the illusion of wealth," spurned living above his means and was passionate about racial inequities.

He ran for a seat on the then all-white Leon County School Board in 1966. His candidacy spurred the largest voter turnout for a school board election in Leon County history, with Dr. Anderson receiving forty-one percent of the vote. He was ultimately defeated, but helped pave the way for future black candidates.

Anderson's many accomplishments are a tribute to his courage, intelligence and love for the medical arts in overcoming all obstacles placed before him.

"There's a world of difference between truth and facts. Facts can obscure the truth." **—Maya Angelou**

Maya Angelou (b. 1928)
Poet, Educator, Actress, Director

aya Angelou was born Marguerite Johnson in St. Louis, Missouri, and was the younger of two children born to Vivian and Bailey Johnson. When she was four years old, her parents divorced. She and her brother, Bailey Jr., were sent to live with Annie Henderson, their paternal grandmother, who owned the only black general store in Stamps, Arkansas. A pious woman, who was both strict and loving, she provided Maya with a sense of security.

When Maya was eight years old, she and her brother, Bailey Jr., moved to St. Louis to live with their mother, Vivian, and her boyfriend, Mr. Freeman, who later brutally attacked Maya. Required to testify in court, Maya lied out of fear and pity to protect him. He was sentenced to serve one year and a day in jail, but was somehow released the same day as his trial. That night, he was found dead, after having been kicked to death. Assailed by a melange of feelings, including guilt and the fear of not going to heaven for having lied under oath, Maya descended into a surreal world of muted sounds and colors. For five years, she did not speak to anyone but her brother.

She and Bailey Jr. were returned to Stamps, where a neighbor, Mrs. Bertha Flowers, whom Maya and the community highly esteemed, made Maya see that she mattered, and that communication was essential to being understood. Eventually, the young girl began to speak again. In 1940, she graduated eighth grade from the town's segregated Lafayette Training School. By then, Maya's mother had moved to San Francisco, and she and Bailey Jr., joined her.

Maya blossomed following her move to San Francisco. It was there that she studied drama and dance at the California Labor School. At age sixteen, however, she became an unmarried mother. By the time she was twenty-one, she was working two jobs to maintain a no-frills existence. To keep them well-clothed, she shopped at resale stores.

Maya danced professionally for sixteen years, having studied under distinguished performers Pearl Primus, Ann Halprin and Martha Graham. She performed in the musical *Porgy and Bess,* which began a twenty nation tour in 1954, played Kunta Kinte's grandmother in the blockbuster miniseries *Roots,* for which she received an Emmy nomination, and, in 1972, her screenplay, *Georgia, Georgia,* was the first by a black woman to be made into a film. She also taught for four years at the University of Ghana (1963-1967), where she wrote for the *African Review.* When she was in Cairo, Egypt, she wrote for the *Arab Observer.*

Maya's five autobiographical works include, *I Know Why The Caged Bird Sings* (1969), a chronicle of her childhood and youth in the racially polarized South; *Gather Together in My Name,* (1974), a description of the difficulties she overcame as an unwed mother; *Singin' and Swingin' and Getting' Merry Like Christmas*, a focus on her career in the theatre; *The Heart of a Woman* (1981); and *All God's Children Need Travelling Shoes.*

In 1993 she penned *Wouldn't Take Nothing For My Journey Now*, which was dedicated to talk show hostess Oprah Winfrey. This pithy volume shares her belief in the beauty of diversity, the importance of family and friends, of having faith, and the insidiousness of racism.

Her volumes of poetry include *Just Give Me A Cool Drink Of Water 'Fore I Die* (1971), *Still I Rise* (1978), and *I Shall Not Be Moved* (1990). In 1993, President Bill Clinton asked her to compose a poem for his inauguration. The result was *On the Pulse of the Morning.*

Describing all her work as being about survival, Maya reflects, "You may encounter many defeats, but you must not be defeated."

TLE: Seventh child : e family memoir o
RCODE: 34567003764774
 DATE: 01-20-09

LE: Turbulent years : the 60s
RCODE: 34567002929071
E DATE: 01-20-09

TLE: The African-American atlas : Blac
RCODE: 34567003143656
 DATE: 01-20-09

LE: A history of the African American
RCODE: 34567002188553
 DATE: 01-20-09

LE: African-American heroes & heroine
RCODE: 34567002541736
 DATE: 01-20-09

LE: Martin Luther King, Jr., spirit-l
CODE: 34567004821433
 DATE: 01-20-09

LE: Martin Luther King, Jr.
CODE: 34567005461817
 DATE: 01-20-09

LE: The 1960s
CODE: 34567005883358
 DATE: 01-20-09

LE: The 1960s : opposing viewpoints
CODE: 34567001320512
 DATE: 01-20-09

"Jazz is a heartbeat." **—Langston Hughes**

Louis Armstrong (1900-1971)
Jazz Musician

nown as "Satchmo" and referred to America's "Ambassador of Jazz," Louis Armstrong's brilliant technique and tones made him the first jazz soloist to receive international acclaim. Along with the beauty of his trumpet music, he is famous for his gritty singing voice, and was the first jazz artist to sing "scat" music, which, instead of using lyrics, uses cadenced gibberish.

Born into poverty, in the slums of New Orleans, he had a limited education. At the age of nine he left school to work, and, at the age of thirteen, was sent to the Colored Waif's Home, after being arrested for a prank he played. It was there that he was introduced to jazz.

While at the Colored Waif's Home, he learned to play the coronet, tambourine, drums and bugle. By the time he left a year and a half later, he played so well that he had become the band leader.

He received the big break that launched his career when a coronet player didn't show up for work in Henry Ponce's cabaret. Armstrong didn't own an instrument, so he had to use the missing player's.

King Oliver, a famous musician, gave Louis one of his old coronets and helped him with his technique. By 1918, he was living as a full-time musician, sailing up and down the Mississippi on a riverboat, playing with the *Fate Marable Orchestra*.

Louis had learned to read music, and had become so good that King Oliver invited him to play with his band in Chicago. It was there that he became famous for singing in his throaty, gravelly voice. By 1925, "Satchmo," an abbreviation of "Satchel Mouth," was going on world tours and composing music.

In 1938 Louis appeared in two movies, *Going Places* and *Everyday's A Holiday.* He went on to appear in *New Orleans* (1956), and *Hello, Dolly* (1969).

He performed with the *Fletcher Henderson Band*, and, between 1925 and 1928, recorded some of the greatest music in jazz history, with the three groups, The Hot Five, The Hot Seven, and The Savoy Ballroom Five. Some of his most famous music from that era is, *West End Blues, Potato Head Blues, Ain't Misbehaving* and *Coronet Chop Suey.*

Because he wanted to travel more, in 1947, he scaled down his group after being a bandleader in the 1930s and 1940s. While travelling, he performed several times for King George V of England.

When he was 65 years old, Louis "Satchmo" Armstrong, made his first million-seller record, *Hello, Dolly.* Without a doubt, he was one of the best-loved performers in the world.

DID YOU KNOW?

- Armstrong once worked as a coal deliveryman.
- David Jones, a melodeon player, taught Louis to read music.
- He was a member of the American Society of Composers, Authors and Publishers.

"...words cannot suffice to capture a career as glorious, a life so fully lived, or a commitment to justice as firm and as fair as was his."
—**David Dinkins, Former Mayor, New York City**

Arthur Robert Ashe, Jr. (1943-1993)
Tennis Champion

He was an officer in the United States Army, and he was a gentleman. He was also the first African-American to make the Davis Cup Tennis team (1968), to win the United States Open tennis championship (1968), and the Wimbledon singles in England (1975).

Born in Richmond, Virginia, Arthur Ashe was discovered and mentored by Ronald Charity, an African-American tennis player. His skills were further developed with the help of Dr. Walter Johnson, an African-American physician who trained young African-American tennis stars.

Upon entering the predominately white tennis circuit, Arthur felt the sting of racism. By the time he was fifteen years old, three major white tournaments in the region had rejected him. Young Arthur persevered, and, in 1961, at the age of eighteen — without losing a set — won the United States Lawn Tennis Association National Championship in Charlottesville, Virginia.

While a student at UCLA, he won the 1965 National Collegiate Athletic Association singles and doubles championship. In 1966, the same year he graduated college with a degree in business administration, he won the NCAA singles and doubles championships. The following year, he was clay court champion. In 1970, Arthur won the Australian Open. And, in 1973, although he became the first African-American to reach the South African Open Finals, he was unable to play; he was denied a visa by the South African government because of his anti-apartheid activism,

Arthur underwent quadruple bypass heart surgery in December of 1979, and, in less than two weeks, announced his comeback. In April of 1980, however, he suffered a post-operative setback and retired from competitive tennis. Unfortunately, more heart surgery was necessary in 1983. By 1985, though, he seemed the picture of health as, along with forty-six others, he was arrested at the South African Embassy in Washington, D.C., during an anti-apartheid demonstration.

He was inducted into the International Tennis Hall of Fame in 1985. Though he suffered more health problems, he bounced back again, and in 1991, with Quincy Jones and 31 other prominent African-Americans, he participated in a three-day political fact-finding visit in South Africa.

When he was named *Sports Illustrated* magazine's Sportsman of the Year in 1991, he became the first retired athlete to receive such an honor. Unfortunately, the honors he received, and the good he did, could not prolong his life. He died February 6, 1993, at the age of 49, due to complications with the AIDS virus he contracted during a blood transfusion administered during a heart surgery.

One of the greatest tennis players of his time, Arthur Ashe is not just remembered as a great athlete, but also as a hero and a humanitarian.

DID YOU KNOW?

♦ Arthur Ashe established the Arthur Ashe Foundation For The Defeat Of AIDS.

♦ He published *A Hard Road To Glory* (1988), a three-volume historical account of African-Americans in sports.

♦ He became the first African-American tennis player to become a millionaire.

"We cannot make a more lively representation and emblem to ourselves of hell, than by the view of a kingdom at war." **—Clarendon**

Crispus Attucks (c. 1723 - 1770)
Freedom Martyr

"**D**on't be afraid," he shouted. "They dare not fire." As spokesman and leader of the Boston citizens rebelling against the garrisoned British soldiers, Crispus Attucks uttered these words a few minutes before the British soldiers did indeed open fire. Hit in the chest, he fell back. The enraged citizens surged forth.

When the smoke and din of the 1770 melee settled, five citizens lay wounded and bleeding. Three were dead; Crispus Attucks, a forty-seven-year-old fugitive slave, was one of them. He was the first man to die in America's struggle for independence from British rule.

Of Afro-Indian decent, Attucks had managed to escape discovery for twenty years, having run away from his Framingham, Massachusetts, master. He became a merchant seaman and worker on the docks of Boston, and, later, answered Samuel Adams' call to the dockworkers, to protest the British troops' guarding of customs commissioners. Attucks, incensed, responded and showed up with a crowd of about fifty citizens.

Brandishing snowballs, sticks and clubs, the citizens approached the British soldiers who were armed with muskets. Apparently situated out in front, Crispus Attucks urged the mob on. As they approached King Street, where the Customs House was located, someone threw an object that hit one of the soldiers. As the crowd pressed on, the order, "FIRE," was heard.

Although only five citizens were killed in the attack, Samuel Adams called it a massacre and an example of the tyrannical use of power by the English.

It is ironic that a fugitive slave was willing to sacrifice his life, and was the first to die in a rebellion that ultimately led to the Revolutionary War, a war that secured freedom for Anglo-Americans, but not African-Americans.

DID YOU KNOW?

♦ The Boston Massacre was so widely publicized that it made the British reign in America increasingly unpopular.

♦ Part of the citizens' anger stemmed from the Townshend Acts, most of which were later repealed.

HISTORY IN A CAPSULE

Oliver Cromwell was seventeen years old when Crispus Attucks died in the Boston Massacre. Like Attcuks, he was of African heritage. Unlike Attucks, he is believed to have been born free in Columbus, Burlington County, New Jersey, in 1753. He stood with George Washington, when he crossed the Delaware River to surprise the British, on Christmas night in 1776.

Under the command of Colonal Israel Shreve, Cromwell enlisted in the Second New Jersey Regiment and served longer than many of the white soldiers, remaining in the military for 9 years and 6 months. He fought in the Battles of Trenton and Princeton in 1776, in Brandywine in 1777, Monmouth in 1778, and Yorktown in 1781.

After his discharge, he received a ninety-six-dollar-a-year-pension. He married, had six children, and loved retelling his adventures to his many avid listeners. He died in 1853, at the age of one hundred.

"There never was any heart truly great and gracious, that was not also tender and compassionate."   —South

Josephine Baker (1906-1975)
Dancer, Humanitarian

Dubbed the "Dark Star" of the Foiles-Bergere at the Casino de Paris, Josephine Baker's energetic dancing and colorful costumes made her one of show businesses most flamboyant and successful performers.

Born to a poor family in St. Louis, Missouri, she started working part-time at the age of eight, to support her family. When she was older, she moved to New York, where she began her career in *Shuffle Along,* an all-black musical. While in New York, she also danced at Harlem's Cotton Club and the New York City Old Plantation Club.

She traveled to Paris, France, in 1925, as part of *La Revue Negre* and became an overnight mega-star. Her sequined bodysuits and plumed head-pieces created excitement that reverberated across the Atlantic, earning her the title the "Toast of Paris." The French fell in love with Josephine, and she

31

with them. She became so well known that, by 1930, she was billed as simply, "Josephine," and became a nightly attraction at such places as the Foiles-Bergere, opera openers, clubs and theatres.

Also well known for her effervescent personality and attention-grabbing antics, she would stroll down the Champ-Elysees with two beautiful swans on leashes, while at other times with a pair of leopards.

As the headliner for the Ziegfield Follies, she returned to New York to perform on Broadway in 1936. She toured the United States and performed to packed houses, and played an acting role in *Siren of the Tropics*, a 1938 film by Jack Goldberg. Eventually, she began to miss Paris.

She returned to France, where she again performed at the Folies-Bergere and the Casino de Paris, and, in 1937, solidified her love for Paris by becoming a French citizen. She went on to perform in her long-running musical autobiography, *Paris, Mes Amours*, in France in 1958.

Josephine returned to the United States on occasion, where she often had a hand in more than just performing. In 1951, she refused to appear in a Miami, Florida club until blacks were allowed to attend her show. Ever conscious of racial prejudice in America, she flew to the United States in 1963 to participate in the March on Washington, and gave a civil rights benefit concert at Carnegie Hall. In 1973, she returned to New York to present *An Evening With Josephine Baker*. Although sixty-seven years old, she was still able to wear her old costumes to her benefit.

The French government also honored her for entertaining the Free French and Allied Forces during World War II. She received the Croix de Guerre and was the first African-American to receive France's highest commendation, the Legion of Honor. At her funeral in 1975, the French gave her a twenty-one gun salute, the first time such an honor was bestowed upon an American woman.

HISTORY IN A CAPSULE

Josephine Baker was an activist as well as a flamboyant entertainer and humanitarian. During WWII, she supported the Free French Resistance when the country was invaded by the Nazis in 1940. She also drove an ambulance on the Belgium front and served as an intelligence officer.

She and her French husband, Monsieur Bouillon, bought an estate in France in 1950. She adopted ten children of different races, calling them her "rainbow tribe." Children, she believed, could achieve equally, if treated equally and given the same opportunities.

"...this world is white no longer, and it will never be again."　　**—James Baldwin**

James Baldwin (1924-1987)
Essayist, Novelist, Playwright

T hough he never won the Pulitzer Prize or the National Book Award, James Baldwin was one of the most quoted African-American writers of the 1960s protest era. *The Fire Next Time* (1963), regarded as one of his most brilliant essays, soared to the best-seller list.

Born in New York City, he attended Frederick Douglass Junior High School, where he edited the school magazine. Before he became a household name, James was a storefront Pentecostal preacher in Harlem. He also waited tables and wrote books.

He won a Eugene Saxon Fellowship when he was only twenty-one years old and a Rosenwald Fellowship, that enabled him to travel to France. There he completed his first novel, in 1953, and his second work, a collection of essays titled *Notes of a Native Son*, in 1955. Both received favorable critical reviews.

He published *Giovanni's Room*, his second novel, in 1956, and his second collection of essays, *Nobody Knows My Name*, which chronicled his ten years of voluntary exile in France, his first trip to the South during the school desegregation years, and his return home to Harlem, in 1961. It was the publication of his second set of essays that put the spotlight of the literary world on him. The work was selected as one of the exceptional books of the year by the Notable Books Council of the American Literary Association.

Though his third novel, *Another Country* (1962), was a commercial as well as critical success, his plays *The Amen Corner* and *Blues For Mister Charlie* (based on the Emmett Till Murder), were only moderately successful.

Baldwin, who was once a Five College Professor for the University of Massachusetts at Amherst's W.E.B. DuBois Department of Afro-American studies, and whose articles were routinely published in major journals, continually received media attention for his appearances in racially troubled Southern cities.

Other works by Baldwin include the novels *Tell Me How Long The Train's Been Gone* (1968), *If Beale Street Could Talk* (1974), and *Just Above My Head* (1979). Baldwin's *Remember This House* includes biographies of Martin Luther King, Jr., Malcolm X and Medgar Evers, and *The Evidence Of Things Not Seen*, dealt with the early 1980s murders of twenty-eight African-American youths. *The Price Of The Ticket*, was a collection of non-fiction works from 1948 to 1985.

In 1986, the French government presented him their highest civilian award, the Legion of Honor. Baldwin, who lectured on race relations, brought the problems of a racially troubled society into sharp focus. James Baldwin, who is perhaps the most recognized of all the African-American protest writers of the modern era, is without a doubt, one of the major voices in the history of American Literature.

Edward M. Bannister
Painter
K BelMonte

"The mission of art is to represent nature, not to imitate her." **—W.M. Hunt**

Edward M. Bannister (1828-1901)
Artist

n the catalogue of the memorial exhibition of his work, the Providence Art Club stated that Edward Mitchell Bannister "...was par excellence as a landscape painter, and the best one our state has yet produced. Had early opportunity been more kind, he might easily have been one of America's greatest land-scape painters."

Born an impoverished orphan, in New Brunswick, Canada, he eventually made his way to Boston. By the age of ten, he was producing sketches, while also working odd jobs. He was later able to pay for private lessons and enrolled in the Lowell Institute in Boston for additional training.

Edward knew of the barriers he would face when deciding to become an artist. It was partly because of an 1867 *New York Herald* article stating that the Negro seemed to appreciate, but was incapable of producing art, that he took up painting. Over and over, he disproved the article's thesis wrong.

So commanding were his landscapes, that he won the Gold Medal at the 1876 Philadelphia Centennial Exhibition for his painting, *Under The Oaks.* The judges did not know, when they awarded the prize, that Edward was African-American. They wanted to reconsider the award after discovering that he was, but, to their credit, the losing competitors demanded that Edward be given the award. Another consolation was that a Mr. Duff, of Boston, purchased the painting for fifteen hundred dollars, a huge sum in Edward's day.

Although he was of African heritage, Edward chose to focus on landscapes, and marine subjects. He was able to live comfortably from the sales of his art. His works can currently be found at the Rhode Island School of Design, Howard University, Atlanta University, as well as the Providence Art club, which he helped to found.

Though society largely regarded African-Americans as incapable of the sensitivity and innate talent required to render fine art, Edward M. Bannister countered that notion with excellent paintings that are still preserved in museums and private collections. He did not allow racial prejudice to prevent him from developing his talent and producing some of America's greatest art.

HISTORY IN A CAPSULE

The style of William H. Simpson, some said, was reminiscent of the old European Masters Murillo, Raphael and Titian. Handling depth, richness of color and feeling with expertise, his special gift was in painting families and children.

He showed his talent at an earlier age. Often, his teacher would find him sketching and drawing when he should have been focusing on arithmetic and other subjects. After a rudimentary education, he was hired by Matthew Wilson, a local artist. Wilson spotted the boy's talent and gave him the training he needed to become an accomplished painter. In 1854, both moved to Boston, where Simpson became a successful and popular portrait artist.

Born in Buffalo, New York, William H. Simpson's paintings are in collections spread over California, Canada, and the New England States.

Southern
Horrors
by
Ida B
Wells

A Red
Record
by
Ida
Wells

Ida B. Wells Barnett
Activist

M. Belmonte

"He that lays down precepts for the government of our lives and the moderating of our passions, obliges human nature not only in the present, but in all succeeding generations." **—Seneca**

Ida B. Wells Barnett (1862-1931)
Civil Rights Advocate

fter a Yellow fever epidemic took the lives of both her parents when she was only fourteen years old, always precocious and headstrong, Ida B. Wells Barnett raised her seven siblings by becoming a teacher. Though her parents were former slaves, she had learned to read and write, and was determined to teach others to do the same.

Never accepting the second-class citizenship imposed on African-Americans, Ida protested the conditions she and others endured by writing fiery articles to newspapers. Her outspokenness catapulted her to national recognition, but did not please the Memphis, Tennessee Board of Education, where she taught. They fired Ida but did not silence her.

She continued to pursue her fight against the unfair treatment of African-Americans, targeting lynching in particular. When three of her colleagues were lynched, she campaigned as strongly as ever against the brutal practice by publishing articles and going on speaking tours.

She made two trips to England, in 1893 and 1894. Though she was enthusiastically received, and her campaign covered by the English and Scottish press, she drew sharp criticism from white newspapers and blacks urged her to temper her remarks. Ida's rhetoric, however, did not change.

Barnett worked with Frederick Douglass and Ferdinand Barnett, an Attorney, in formulating a booklet that criticized the Columbian Exposition for refusing to allow African-Americans to have a pavilion, and organized the first civic organization for African-American women in Chicago.

She eventually married Barnett, and the couple had four children. In 1895, she authored and published a publication that chronicled the cases of lynching entitled *A Red Record: Tabulated Statistics and Alleged Cases of Lynching in the United States, 1892-1894*. She presented it as evidence to condemn lynching in the United States.

When Ferdinand Barnett began the first African-American newspaper in Chicago, Ida served as editor. She went to Washington, D.C. in 1898, in a fruitless effort to impel the government to act in a case where an African-American postmaster was lynched in South Carolina.

Moderates such as Booker T. Washington stood in sharp contrast to Ida's militant stands. Out of frustration from the violence spreading further North, Ida found herself going wherever lynching and other acts of violence took place, and where other African-Americans were too afraid to protest.

Once, in Cairo, Illinois, Ida went to the statehouse and stood alone to protest against a sheriff who was about to be reinstated. The people there were so frightened by a lynching that had taken place, they wouldn't even protest against the sheriff who had done nothing to prevent it. Though it took her about a day and a half, she prevailed against Southern Illinois' best legal minds. Her courage and sharp intellect produced a record clear of lynching, for Illinois, from that point on.

In 1918 a virtual massacre of one hundred fifty African-Americans occurred when a group of whites went on a rampage. Again, Ida gathered data and met with the governor. This time, reason did not prevail. The white people involved were given no more than five year sentences, while fifteen African-Americans were given fifteen year sentences, with one man sentenced to life.

Ida ran unsuccessfully for the state Senate in 1930. Her autobiography, *Crusade For Justice*, was not published until 1970, with the help of her daughter and historian John Hope Franklin.

To honor a relentless warrior for justice, the city of Chicago recognized Ida as one of the twenty-five outstanding women in its history and named a housing project in her memory.

James P. Beckwourth

BECKWOURTH'S PASS

Explorer

C. Belmonte

"The truest courage is always mixed with circumspection, this being the quality which distinguishes the courage of the wise from the hardiness of the rash and foolish." **—Shaftesbury**

James P. Beckwourth (1798-1867)
Explorer, Pioneer

Credited with discovering the pass through the Sierra Mountains that now bears his name (located between what is now Reno and Sacramento), James P. Beckwourth was one of the leading African-American figures during the westward movement. Choosing to live among the Indians, he adopted Native American customs. He eventually rose to the position of chief of the Crow Indians, who named him "Bull's Robe," and with whom he lived between roughly 1826 and 1834.

Born as a slave in Fredericksburg, Virginia, to a mother of Afro-Indian heritage and a Revolutionary War officer father, he escaped bondage at the age of nineteen. In 1823, James moved to St. Louis to become a fur trader, and, in 1824, joined Colonel William H. Ashley's Rocky Mountain Fur Company. While traveling with him, Beckworth learned to be deft with the Bowie knife, the gun and the hatchet.

He joined Kearney's forces in California in 1844 and participated in the war with Mexico. In 1852, he opened a trading post in the Sierra Valley and sold horses and provisions to travelers. He worked in many positions, including functioning as a scout for the army, a mail carrier, and even as a prospector during the gold rush.

James P. Beckwourth's life and exploits are proof of the participation of African-Americans in the Westward expansion.

DID YOU KNOW?

♦ Beckwourth "married" into the Blackfeet and Crow tribes.
♦ He was adopted by the Crow Indians and died among them while on business for the United States Government.
♦ He explored many parts of the Western United States.
♦ Beckwourth's Pass became the chief passageway for those moving west.

HISTORY IN A CAPSULE

Some African-Americans found life easier among the Native Americans and chose to live among them, because most tribes were known to give asylum to runaway slaves. Many African-Americans intermarried with the Native Americans as well, and reared their offspring in the traditions and customs of the various tribes.

Many historical and contemporary figures of African-American heritage are also of Native American ancestry. Frederick Douglass, Paul Cuffe, Edmonia Lewis (Wildfire), Crispus Attucks, Dr. Martin Luther King, Jr., Redd Foxx and Leslie Uggams are just a few of these figures.

What Manner of Man

Wade in the Water

Before the Mayflower

Lerone Bennett

Historian Lecturer Editor

K•B

"In this world of change naught which comes stays, and naught which goes is lost." **—Swetchine**

Lerone Bennett, Jr. (b. 1928)
Historian, Lecturer

O ne of America's most prolific writers on the history of black people, his books include *Before The Mayflower: A History Of Black America* (1962), *The Negro Mood And Other Essays* (1964), and *The Shaping of Black America* (1975).

Regarded as Johnson Publishing Company's "resident historian," Lerone Bennett joined the company in 1953 as associate editor of *Jet* magazine. He was associate editor of *Ebony* magazine (1954-1957), and became *Ebony's* first executive editor in 1987, a position he presently holds. His prior experience includes work as a reporter for the *Atlanta Daily World* (1949-1952), as well as work as its city editor from 1952-1953.

Born in Clarksdale, Mississippi, to Lerone Bennett, Sr., and the late Alma Reed Bennett, he was reared in an environment that taught respect for tradition and family. After graduating from the area's schools, he went on to earn his A.B. degree from Morehouse College (1949), while supporting himself by "moonlighting" as a musician in nightclubs. He became proficient enough on the saxophone to earn the nickname "Duke" while still a young teenager.

His first series of historical articles for *Ebony* was published in 1961. Basing his writings on archaeological finds and anthropological studies, Bennett reinstructed the world on the contributions to society made by people of African ancestry. Because a positive sense of self was instilled in him at a young age, he desired to work for the African-American media, bringing the passion of his beliefs and scholarship to his work.

A schoolmate of Dr. Martin Luther King, while at Morehouse College, he inherited the social consciousness of his generation, and, like Dr. King, chose to work through the system to educate African-Americans about their true history. As such, he hopes to instill in each a sense of pride in both their heritage, and themselves, as individuals. Though he realizes that the era of slavery is a painful chapter in the nation's history, he deals with it as fact, and declines to embellish it with emotional veneer.

A poet as well as a historian, his poems have appeared in *New Negro Poets: U.S.A,* edited by eminent wordsmith Langston Hughes, and in several anthologies. His short story, *The Convert*, appeared in *Negro Digest* (later renamed *Ebony*), and his scholarly works have been translated in several languages. A speaker as well as a writer, he is sought after by schools and universities across the country, and has traveled extensively in Africa and Europe.

His other works include *What Manner Of Man: A Biography Of Martin Luther King, Jr.* (1964), for which he received the Society of Midland Authors' Literature Award, and *The Challenge Of Blackness* (1972).

Other honors he received include the Literature Award from the American Academy of Arts and Letters (1978) and the Lifetime Achievement Award from the National Association of Black Journalists (1981), as well as many honorary doctorate degrees.

Lerone Bennett, Jr. continues to play an important role in the shaping of young minds. He properly informing a people of their place on the world's stage and of their contributions that have been, for too long, distorted and diminished.

Mary McLeod
Bethune

Educator

K.B.

"He that governs well, leads the blind; but he that teaches, gives him eyes."
—South

Mary McLeod Bethune (1875-1955)
Educator

W hen Mary McLeod Bethune founded her school in 1904, it was the only African-American institution to offer education beyond elementary school in the state of Florida. As a pioneering educator, this child of former slaves dedicated her life to providing and improving educational opportunities for African-Americans.

Born in Mayesville, South Carolina, Mary was the fifteenth of seventeen children born to Samuel and Patsy McLeod, and the first of their children to be born free. For ten years, following the Thirteenth Amendment's outlaw of slavery, the McLeod family worked for their former master in order to save enough money to purchase five acres of land in Mayesville. Patsy cooked and did laundry and other chores for whites. During one of her trips to deliver laundry, the children of the white family she worked for invited Mary, who

43

often went along with her mother, into the playhouse their father had built for them. Among the dolls and other toys Mary sorted through, she found a book. When one of the other children noticed what the daughter of their laundry woman had picked up, Mary was told to put the book down because she couldn't read. At that point, Mary vowed she would one day learn to read.

In 1882, Emma Wilson, an African-American missionary sent by the Northern Presbyterian Church to start a mission school, came to the McLeod's seeking students. The family sent Mary, who stated that "Scales fell from my eyes, and light came flooding in," after hearing Emma Wilson open the first day of school with a reading of John 3:16, from the Bible. Once Mary heard her teacher read, "For God so loved the world that He gave His only Son, that whosoever believeth in Him should not perish but have everlasting life," she never again felt inferior or handicapped by her humble beginnings.

Mary graduated from Mayesville's first class of African-American students in 1886, and returned to the family's cotton field because they could not afford to further her education. In 1887, a Quaker seamstress, Mary Crissman, who gave ten percent of her earnings to help others, offered to pay the tuition for one of Emma Wilson's students to attend Scotia Seminary, a school for African-Americans in Concord, North Carolina. After being chosen, the entire community came to see Mary off. She graduated from the seminary with a Bachelor of Arts degree in 1894, and entered the Mission Training School of Moody Bible Institute in Chicago.

In 1898, she married Albertus Bethune, a former teacher, and in 1899, her son, Albert, was born. Because her husband didn't share her passion for teaching, Mary took her son and left for the resort town of Daytona Beach, Florida, seeking financial backing for the school she dreamed of starting.

The two-story building Mary chose for her school charged eleven dollars a month for rent. She put down all the money she had – one dollar and fifty cents – and rallied the support of the community to come up with the rest. When Mary opened her school in 1904, her original intent was to train teachers in the Dayton Beach, Florida area, where one-third of the population was black. Because of the area's resort status, she hoped to attract wealthy contributors for her school in the early years. One such contributor was James Gamble of Procter & Gamble. She invited him to her school. When he arrived, and found her seated on a chair beside a crate, he asked her where her school was located. Her response was, "In my mind...and in my soul."

A dynamic leader as well as educator, Mary McLeod Bethune's many awards and passion for educating all African-Americans, solidifies her place in American history.

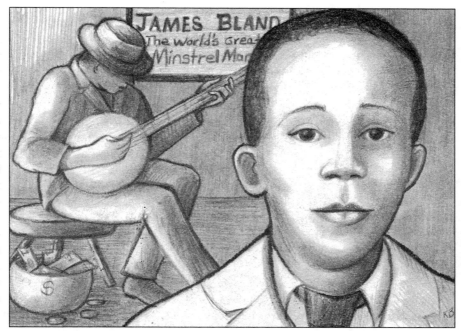

"All musical people seem to be happy; it is to them the engrossing pursuit; almost the only innocent and unpunished passion." **—Sydney Smith**

James A. Bland (1854-1911)
Composer, Musician

When James A. Bland's *Carry Me Back To Old Virginny* was adopted in 1940 by the Virginia Assembly, the state became the only one in the union whose song was written by an African-American.

Bland, who learned to play the banjo when he was just a youngster, was born in Flushing, New York. The son of a college graduate, who became the first African-American examiner for the U.S. Patent Office, and the descendent of a long line of free blacks, he was not an ex-slave as is commonly believed; he was of Indian, black and white ancestry.

Because he spent more time composing and singing than he did studying, his father sent him to college, hoping young James would forget about the banjo. The atmosphere, he no doubt thought, would focus his son's attention on a professional career. James, however, had developed an incurable love for the banjo and minstrel shows. By the time he enrolled in Howard University, he was earning money singing and playing his tunes, eventually being hired to entertain the guests of a large hotel.

When the Haverly Colored Minstrels performed in Baltimore, James joined up with them, dashing the hopes of his parents and teachers, who had hoped he would become a doctor or a lawyer. Eventually billed as "the world's greatest Minstrel Man," and "The Prince of Negro Songwriters," he went on the road, composing and performing. In 1881, his minstrel company went to England. He became so popular there that he became an independent artist, and remained there for the next twenty years, eventually becoming quite wealthy.

The most popular African-American minstrel of his time, he was also known as the most versatile and the brightest of the lot. He is reputed to have written more than seven hundred songs, though only thirty-eight were ever copyrighted.

Known to be rash and capricious, he died penniless. Though a Northerner, he wrote tender nostalgic songs about the South. His most famous compositions were *In The Evening By The Moonlight*, *Oh, Dem Golden Slippers*, and *In The Morning By The Bright Light*.

HISTORY IN A CAPSULE

Minstrel shows began on Southern slave plantations and evolved into musical, then stage minstrelsy. Their original purpose was to entertain white masters. The shows included singing, cracking Negro jokes, dancing, and playing the banjo and bones, which came from sheep and other animals. Some plantations had talented semi-professional bands that did limited traveling.

Stage minstrelsy was introduced to the public by white performers in blackface, who attempted to imitate the speech, behavior and antics of the slaves. After 1830, when black minstrels took the stage, they mimicked the white performers by blackening their faces and, in an odd reversal, imitated those who imitated them.

Black History

Before the Mayflower

by Lerone Bennett

Dr. Carleton Bryant

...ks

...oussain

by Alvin Poussain

The Complete Poems of Paul Lawrence Dunbar

E. Franklin Frazier

The Black Bourgeoisie

Carleton Bryant

Educator

Historian

KBellorte

"History is but the unrolled scroll of prophecy." **—Garfield**

Carleton Bryant (b. 1930)
Educator, Historian

W hen *Sketches in History — The African-American Experience* was first broadcast in 1980, it was the realization of a dream of Carleton Bryant, an educator and historian in the Palm Beach County School District in West Palm Beach, Florida. The first show of its kind in the area, it presented aspects of history through books, music, poetry and commentaries, by expert panelists. The show aired through 1984, with its visual parallel, *Sketches in Black*, airing in 1982.

Both shows allowed listeners and viewers additional avenues through which to learn about contributions made by historical and contemporary African-Americans. The presentations were conceptualized, written and hosted by Bryant, and included visual art, narration, and music. It focused on areas that impact history such as political, social, educational and economic issues, and sports.

47

Born to migrant workers Annie Parsons and Shelley Clinton Bryant in Bradenton, Florida, Bryant was largely raised by his grandmother instead of traveling up and down the East Coast harvesting fruits and vegetables with his parents.

Always a precocious child, he learned to read by the age of three by watching his cousins read the Sunday comics. After receiving his early education in Bradenton, and graduating as Valedictorian from Howard Academy in Ocala, Florida, Bryant attended Florida A&M, where he received his Bachelor of Science Degree and his Master of Education degree. He eventually went on to earn his Doctorate degree in Education from Florida Atlantic University in Boca Raton. He began his teaching career at Roosevelt Junior College, where he served as chairperson of his department. He followed this position up by working as the dean of boys and as an administrative assistant in various other schools. He is currently the assistant principal at Jupiter High School in West Palm Beach, Florida.

Bryant is also author of the 1972 narrative for the federally funded MOTEC-JC, a project to encourage African-American students to enroll in, and complete junior college. His other works include *With More Deliberate Speed: A Historical Study Of Six Major Issues In Secondary Education In Palm Beach County, Florida* (1972), *From A Black Perspective* (1975), and co-authored *Let's Talk So That Parents Can Understand Us*, for the Florida Reading Quarterly (1977). Also in 1977, his article *Roots Saga Spurs Renaissance For Black American Heritage* appeared in the *Palm Beach Post.*

He is a member of the National Alliance of Black School Educators, the National Society for the Study of Education, Association for the Study of Afro-American Life and History, the International Honorary History Society, Phi Alpha Theta, and several other organizations. He is also the recipient of a number of honors, including YABA (Young Afro Brothers of America) and the Historical Preservation Award.

Dr. Bryant is the prototype of the increasing movement in America toward "grassroots" empowerment, community involvement and family views.

"Once you get out there and see the sail fill up with air, it's almost a spiritual thing. Sailing gives them another view of the world." **—Isa Hamm Bryant**

Isa Hamm Bryant (b. 1942)
Black Historical & Trainer Project Director

When family friend Leone "Jazz" Trainer took Isa Bryant and other neighborhood kids out on the ocean in his sailboat, to collect oysters and dive for lobster, the experience left a lasting impression on young Isa. It taught him more than diving, and he gained more than just summer fun. It was during this trip that he developed a deep love for the sea and pride in himself.

Born in West Palm Beach, Florida, Bryant completed his early education in local schools, graduating in 1960 from Roosevelt High. He studied technical illustration in the United States Air Force and attended San Francisco State and Arizona State universities. He has also worked as an architectural and civil draftsman, photographer, graphic artist, and screen printer, and spent thirteen years as a radio broadcaster and journalist in San Francisco.

Because Bryant wanted to return some of what his merchant marine mentor and pal had given him, he instituted the Leone Trainer Sailing Project. As executive director and founder, he volunteers his time teaching inner city youths discipline and self-esteem by providing instruction in sailing and nautical history. He focuses on seamen and sailors of African ancestry, including Captain "Black Caesar" and Francisco Menendez.

The year-round project also provides on-the-water experience, which combines an overview of sailing responsibilities with the pleasures and challenges of the sea. To provide small Sunfish sailing prams and other equipment needed for the program, Bryant and supporters solicit funds from community businesses including, the Lauderdale-by-the-Sea Institute of Marine Science and other interested parties.

Bryant also heads the restoration of a historical forty-three foot wooden schooner, which provides the opportunity for youths to assist in returning the vessel to a seaworthy condition. By using the vessel as a training venue, Bryant seeks to instill a sense of accomplishment in youths and to inspire them to substitute a love of sailing in place of other negative influences in their communities.

With other African-American supporters of the project, Bryant hopes to provide a broader perspective of African-American history to youngsters – one that goes beyond slavery and captives being brought to the shores of America in chains. Florida's history, he states, is richly embroidered with black captains, spongers, fisherman – and even a few rumrunners. Though some were more rascal than hero, all were accomplished men of the sea.

In 1966, Bryant, who is of Afro-Indian descent, published *We Are Florida*, in which he included little-known facts about the impact African-Americans made on Florida, when it was still quite young. His book explores the connection between the Florida Seminoles and fugitive African-American slaves. The bond they established formed the Maroons, a group that included Seminole Indians, African-Americans and Afro-Indians.

Bryant and his associates work to expand the Florida Black Historical Research Project to preserve the contributions that African-Americans have made to Florida. As a volunteer, mentor, and role model, his life touches and impacts younger generations.

In 1997, he was profiled by the *Palm Beach Post,* one of South Florida's most widely circulated newspapers, as one of ten African-American men who make a positive impact on their community.

"The wolf also shall dwell with the lamb..." **—Isaiah 11:6, NKJV**

Ralph Johnson Bunche (1904-1971)
United Nations Official

When his outstanding negotiations as United Nations mediator in the Arab-Israeli crisis won him the Nobel Peace Prize in 1950, he became the first African-American to win the award. A brilliant scholar, he graduated Magna cum laude from the University of California and won the Tappan Prize for best doctoral dissertation in the social sciences at Harvard in 1934. He continued his studies at Northwestern University, the University of Cape Town in South Africa, and the London School of Economics.

In 1937, he became chairman of Howard University's political science department and was a specialist on information pertaining to Africa. He progressed from college professor to a troubleshooter for peace in the world during World War II, when he worked for the Office of Strategic Services, becoming, in 1944, the first African-American diplomat in the State Department. As such, he helped lay down the groundwork for the United Nations. Bunche became director of the division of trusteeships in the secretariat in 1946 and, in 1948, when Count Folke Bernadotte, to whom Bunche had served as chief aide, was assassinated, Bunche became acting mediator when a crisis arose.

In 1960, he served once more as the United Nations' special peace envoy when revolution exploded in the Congo. Bunche, who served as Undersecretary of the United States from 1955 until 1971, will always be remembered as a man of peace who had in him a gift for resolving conflicts.

HISTORY IN A CAPSULE

When Ronald Brown, who was appointed Commerce Secretary by President Bill Clinton in 1993, was first appointed Chairman of the Democratic National Committee in 1989, he became the first African-American to head a major American political party.

Born in Washington, D.C., but raised in Harlem, he attended White Plains High School, and Rhodes and Walden Preparatory Schools in New York. In 1962, he graduated from Middlebury College in Middlebury, Vermont, with a Bachelor of Arts degree in political science. After enlisting in the army, attaining the rank of captain, and serving in Germany and Korea, he returned to New York, and, in 1970, graduated from St. John's Law School.

Brown worked in the job-training center for the National Urban League, and was its deputy executive director, general counsel, and vice-president of operations through 1979. He resigned in 1980 to accept a position as chief counsel of the United States Senate Judiciary Committee, and, in 1981, became general counsel and staff coordinator for Senator Edward Kennedy.

Ronald Brown was also a trustee of the University of the District of Columbia, of Middlebury College and of the JFK School of Government at Harvard University. His promising career was tragically cut short when he was killed in a plane crash while on official business for the United States government in 1996.

Explorer

"*Courage consists, not in blindly overlooking danger, but in seeing and conquering it.*"   **—Richter**

George Bush (1791-1867)
Pioneer

A n adventurous type who loved to travel, it's no surprise that George Bush led the first small band that set out for Puget Sound.

Having gained his travel expertise while fighting with Andrew Jackson in the War of 1812, he reached the Pacific Coast in 1820 while working for Hudson's Bay Company. After reaching the western coast, Bush returned to Missouri in 1830, and, after working as a cattle rancher for 12 years, led his own family, as well as seven white families, to the Columbia River Valley, over the Old Oregon Trail. He reached Puget Sound in 1845, and, with the more than two thousand dollars he had in silver, purchased Puget Sound's first saw-and-grist-mill. French employees of the

Hudson's Bay Company helped the group survive, and the tiny colony became the first group of Americans to reside on the Sound.

As land south of the Forty-Ninth Parallel, the United States later claimed it because of the group led there by Bush. Despite his heroism in leading the band of people to the Sound, the United States government decreed he was not entitled to the land he helped settle because he was of African ancestry.

A true hero, Bush, who shared, rather than sold, his produce to help new settlers arriving on the Sound survive, eventually received clear title to his land after the first Washington legislature requested, and received, special permission entitling him to the land he had first helped settle.

HISTORY IN A CAPSULE

The submerged northern end of the three hundred and fifty-mile long Cowlitz-Puget trench, between the Cascade Range and the Coast Range, is called Puget Sound. It is a deep inlet of the eastern North Pacific, in Northwest Washington. The large western extension is Hood Canal, the southern end is the Willamette River Valley. The many deep-water harbors of the Sound, which extends one hundred miles south from Admiralty Inlet and Whidbey Island, include Port Townsend, Everett, Seattle and Tacoma. They serve as outposts for fertile farmlands along the river inlets. Once rich with salmon, Puget Sound is the southern extremity of the Inside Passage to Alaska. Among the streams that enter the Sound from the east are the Snohomish, the Duwamish Waterway and the Skagit.

Civil War
Hero

William H.
Carney

"Duty is the grandest of ideas, because it implies the idea of God, of the soul, of liberty, of responsibility, of immortality." **—LaCordaire**

William Harvey Carney (1840 - c. 1904)
Civil War Hero

After stumbling through volleys of gunfire and struggling to reach his compatriots in the 54th Massachusetts Regiment of colored troops, William Harvey Carney, who had fought to hold the flag high, cried out, "The old flag never touched the ground," as he thrust the banner into safe hands and collapsed from his wounds and loss of blood.

Born in New Bedford, Massachusetts, Carney was later immortalized along with Colonel Robert Gould Shaw, on the Saint-Gaudens monument. He was only twenty-three years old when he enlisted to fight in what was originally the Morgan Guards. The group was later absorbed into the 54th Massachusetts Regiment, the first Union regiment of free African-American soldiers, and is best remembered for its valiant assault on Fort Wagner in Charleston, South

55

Carolina, when the "intrepid colored troops," as they were called, attempted to take the stronghold, and suffered many losses. Carney, who braved Rebel bullets to rescue the flag, led a new charge when he saw that the Colors' sergeant was wounded and could no longer carry it

After serving in the regiment until 1865, he spent some time in California, before eventually returning to Massachusetts, where he became a letter carrier. He served in the position for thirty-five years before he retired and was employed at the State Capitol in Boston. Carney spent his later years speaking at special events and heading Memorial Day Parades.

In 1900, he was finally awarded the Congressional Medal of Honor, and in 1904, he delivered the address at the Shaw Monument, in the Boston Common, on Memorial Day.

HISTORY IN A CAPSULE

The first true submarine was the CSS H.L. Hunley. It was five feet high, four feet wide and about thirty feet long. An eight-man crew provided the power by turning cranks that were placed along the drive shaft. It was able to submerge, and in trial dives could stay under water for about two hours. It would then have to surface before the crew ran out of air.

The submarine towed a bomb on the end of a 200-foot rope, and could pass underneath enemy ships and move away until the bomb touched the vessels and exploded. During trial runs, it sank several times, costing the lives of its builder, Horace L. Hunley, and at least thirty-two crew members.

Confederate General Beauregard was so concerned about the safety of the vessel, that he ordered it to be operated on the surface only. The Hunley was then outfitted with a torpedo that, in February 1864, rammed the blockade USS Housatonic. It totally destroyed her stern, making it the first submarine to sink an enemy ship. The victory, however, was costly for the Rebels. Because of an undetermined mechanical problem, the Hunley and her entire crew, along with the Housatonic, perished in a watery grave.

"Rest satisfied with doing well, and leave others to talk of you as they please."
—Pythagoras

George Washington Carver (1864-1943)
Botanist

Best known for his experiments with peanuts, and the more than three hundred products he derived from them, he is also known to have developed more than one hundred products from the sweet potato, which, along with the peanut, was native to the area of Alabama where he lived and worked.

George Washington Carver was born a slave in Diamond Grove, Missouri, during the Civil War. At one point, he and his mother were kidnapped and sold in Arkansas before eventually being returned to their master. He worked his way through school after the Thirteenth Amendment outlawed slavery in the United States, earning his Bachelor of Science degree (1894), and his Master of Science degree (1896) in agriculture, from Iowa State College. While there, the school's greenhouse was placed under his charge.

The same year Carver received his Master of Science degree, Booker T. Washington persuaded him to join the Tuskegee Institute faculty. As a chemurgist and an agriculturist, Carver wanted to help the farmers of the area by showing them how to rotate their crops to keep from depleting the soil. He discovered that planting the sweet potato would act as a preventive. At the Tuskegee Institute, he conducted experiments with the peanut and sweet potato as well as crop diversification and soil conservation. He became a distinguished scientist of international renown, and also developed flour, coffee, a milk substitute, face powder, printers ink, soap, and cheese from the peanut.

In 1935, he collaborated with the Bureau of Plant Industry, in the United States Department of Agriculture, in the division of disease survey and mycology. To assure that his research would continue, he donated his life savings to the establishment of the George Washington Carver Foundation in 1938. In doing this, he also wanted to insure that young African-American scientists received the assistance they needed.

For his many contributions to his field, he was named a Fellow of the Royal Academy of England in 1916. The NAACP awarded him the Spigarn Medal in 1923, and he received the Roosevelt Medal for distinguished service to science in 1939. The Carver National Museum, near Diamond, Missouri, was the first national monument honoring an African-American. In 1977, he was enshrined in the Hall of Fame for Great Americans at the Bronx Community College in New York.

HISTORY IN A CAPSULE

Ernest E. Just was a recipient of the first Spigarn Medal in 1915. As an outstanding biologist, he contributed more than sixty scientific papers to journals, and spent twenty summers in Woods Hole, Massachusetts, at the marine biology laboratories conducting research. While professor of physiology at Howard University, he challenged traditional theories about cell life and metabolism. It was largely due to his brilliant studies in cell life that the National Research Council awarded Howard University medical graduates three fellowships.

He was chairman of the American Society of Zoologists, and was a Phi Beta Kappa Scholar.

A gifted scientist, Ernest E. Just eventually left the United States to conduct studies in Berlin, Paris, and Naples, to escape America's racial bias and restrictions.

Loretta
Claiborne
Special Olympics
Gold Medalist

"But God hath chosen the foolish things of the world to confound the wise . . . and the weak things of the world to confound the things which are mighty."
—I Corinthians 1:27, New Testament

Loretta Claiborne (b. 1953)
Distance Runner, Special Olympics International Advocate for the Handicapped

Simp. Bozo. Retard. It's hard to believe that someone who was named Special Olympics Athlete of the Quarter Century in 1988, by *Runners Magazine*, and who received an honorary Doctorate degree from Quinnipiac College in Connecticut, in 1995, could have been called all these stinging epithets, while growing up in inner city Parkway Public Homes Project.

Born in York, Pennsylvania, Loretta Claiborne was the fourth of seven children born to single mother Rita Claiborne. As a baby, she was diagnosed as legally blind, as well as mentally retarded, and did not walk until she was four years old. When she was old enough to attend school, she was placed in special education classes, where she and other children with similar disabilities were virtually isolated from the main body of students. Professional educators recommended her mother place her in an institution for the developmentally delayed — the mentally retarded. To hide the pain being called names and being isolated caused her, she learned to fight.

Loretta's honors and triumphs did not come easily. She endured several operations that significantly improved her vision, and also underwent surgeries on a foot and a knee. Although she still didn't excel in school socially or academically, her mother continued to resist professionals' recommendations that she place her daughter in Pennsylvania's Eastern State School and Hospital for the Mentally Challenged.

In the early 1970s, life began to change for Loretta. During those years, she began running along side her brother as he became a cross-country track star. This was when she realized that running was one area in which she could compete with "normal" people. Because the William Penn High School did not have a girl's track team, Loretta spearheaded a campaign to convince the administration to establish one. Although her excitement over her hard work finally paid off, it was short lived. Once the team was established, Loretta discovered that, because of her mental delay, her teammates did not want her on the squad. It ended up taking the intervention of a teacher for her to be allowed to run. Once she started running, she also started excelling. William Penn High School, where she had to fight to be allowed to run on the team she helped establish, finally recognized her in 1992 when they inducted her into their Alumni Hall of Fame.

Competing primarily in track, Loretta later became a Special Olympics athlete who also excels in ice-skating, cross-country skiing, roller skating, bowling, softball and basketball, and who has earned a fourth degree black belt in karate.

In the 1982 Boston Marathon, Loretta finished with the top one hundred women runners, and was among the top twenty-five women runners in the Pittsburgh Marathon. In 1988 she was named the Special Olympics Female Athlete of the Year by the United States Olympic committee, and, with other Special Olympians, went on to lobby the Special Olympics committee to lift the limit on distances Special Athletes could run. She won the Gold in the first Special Olympics half-marathon in 1991. That same year, Loretta won the Silver in the five thousand-meter run. She followed these successes up the following year when she was presented the Spirit of the Special Olympics Award. In 1995 she opened the Special Olympic Summer Games by introducing President Bill Clinton and Eunice Shriver, who founded the organization in 1966, and who is a Claiborne mentor. Loretta's honors didn't stop there though. In 1996, the cable sports channel ESPN, presented her with the Arthur Ashe Award for courage.

Nat King COLE

Vocalist

K Bel Monte

"Music, once admitted to the soul, becomes a sort of spirit, and never dies..."
—Bulwer

Nat "King" Cole (1919-1965)
Singer, Entertainer

I n 1955, when he became the first African-American to host his own television show, he showcased his smooth voice and distinctive style by wooing audiences with hits such as *Paper Moon, Route 66, I Love You for Sentimental Reasons, Mona Lisa, Too Young, Pretend,* and *Smile.* His following continued and grew as he put out hit after hit, becoming the first African-American to attract a large "crossover" audience of both African-Americans and whites. His first record, *Straighten Up and Fly Right* (1943), which he composed, sold over five hundred thousand copies.

Born Nat Coles, in Montgomery, Alabama, he learned to play the organ and piano in the church where his father was a minister. In 1924, his family moved to Chicago, where he formed his first band while attending Phillips

High School. Although he had a band, he often played in other small combos, including his brother Edward's, who was also a musician.

In 1936 Nat performed with the touring company Shuffle Along, and continued to work in clubs in the Los Angeles area after the show folded. In 1937, he formed the Nat King Cole trio, dropping the "s" off his last name, when his quartet's drummer went AWOL. It is mind-boggling to think that, had a customer not asked him to sing *Sweet Lorraine*, in one of the clubs he was performing in, the world might have missed out on his mellifluous voice. By complying, he made his debut as a singer, and later went on to record the song, making it a hit and an American favorite.

His music is still enjoyed today by people who appreciate his classic style and the timeless beauty of his voice.

HISTORY IN A CAPSULE

Known as the "Queen of Soul," Aretha Franklin is also the first woman to be inducted into the Rock and Roll Hall of Fame. Because she was afraid to fly, she didn't attend the 1987 induction. Instead she had her brother Cecil accept the award on her behalf.

Like Nat "King" Cole, Franklin once played the piano for the church choir. Unlike Cole, her first solo was before a church audience, and her first single, which she recorded for Chess Records, was done when she was only twelve years old.

Born in Memphis, Tennessee, in 1942, she moved to New York City in 1960 and signed with Columbia Records. Between the time her first album, *Aretha,* was released in 1961, and her contract expired in 1966, she made nine albums in different styles. After signing with Atlantic Records, she focused on rhythm and blues with a gospel piano style. In no time at all, her recordings *Respect* and *I Never Loved A Man* soared to the top of the charts, becoming soul masterpieces.

Stunt Pilot

COLEMAN

"The man who cannot wonder, who does not habitually wonder and worship, is but a pair of spectacles behind which there is no eye." **—Carlyle**

Bessie Coleman (1893-1926)
Aviator

As the antiquated World War I surplus Army plane taxied down the runway and lifted off, in preparation for a Memorial Day stunt exhibition, pilot and mechanic William D. Wills sat behind the controls, as Bessie Coleman, the nation's first African-American pilot, sat in the rear. Everything seemed fine until, at about two thousand feet, the plane went into a nosedive and ejected Bessie from her seat. Before the eyes of the horrified onlookers, Bessie, whose seatbelt had failed, and who wasn't wearing a parachute, fell to her death.

Bessie was born in Texas to an Indian father and an African-American mother. After her father deserted his family, Bessie's mother struggled to raise her along with her brother and three sisters. She and her siblings helped, and Bessie was encouraged to save as much as she could to attend school. When the time came, she enrolled at Langston Industrial College. She had to drop out, however, when her money ran out. Her next stop was Chicago, were she moved and worked for a while as a manicurist and as the manager of a chili restaurant.

Though she had to postpone her dream of a college education, she never lost her interest in reading. She became so excited reading about the strides being made in aviation, that she vowed to not only earn her pilot's license, but to establish a school so that other African-Americans could learn to fly. Unfortunately, none of the aviation schools would accept her because of her race. Out of frustration, she confronted Robert S. Abbott, the founder and editor of the *Chicago Defender*, and solicited his help. He took up her cause and became her avid supporter. On her behalf, he contacted a French flying school. Bessie learned to speak French and sailed to France, where she studied under Dutch aircraft engineer, Anthony G. Fokker, the designer of many of Germany's airplanes during World War II.

By the time she returned to the United States, she had attained her first goal of earning her license, while also becoming the first American woman to earn an international pilot's license. It was issued by the Federation Aeronautique Internationale.

In an effort to raise the capitol for her flying school, she flew breathtaking maneuvers at exhibitions and lectured around the country. Her first appearance in a United States air show was Labor Day Weekend, in 1922, at Curtiss Field, near New York City. Her manager was David I. Behnke, while her sponsor for such events continued to be newspaperman Robert S. Abbott.

Petite and attractive, she was quite a novelty. Crowds across the country were awed by the Afro-Indian, female stunt pilot, as she performed and advertised for the Firestone Rubber Company.

She was invited by the Jacksonville, Florida, Negro Welfare League to perform a benefit exhibition for their May Day celebration. On the morning of April 30, she and her mechanic, William D. Wills, prepared to make a trial run. Because the plane had been forced to make two stops while en route from Dallas, Texas, and because of engine problems, they wanted to make sure the plane was in shape. Unfortunately, fate was against them. After the plane went into a nosedive, thus killing its two passengers, a carelessly tossed cigarette ignited the wreckage. The plane exploded, and was so badly damaged that, the exact cause of the crash was never determined.

African-American aviators formed Bessie Coleman Aero Clubs, and in 1930, published a monthly newsletter in her memory. However, because of her African-American heritage, Bessie Coleman has routinely been omitted from the roll of women aviators. Her memory has only recently been revived by those who wish to ensure that the world doesn't forget.

"Leaves seem light, useless, idle, wavering, and changeable—they even dance; yet God has made them part of the oak..." —**Hunt**

William "Bill" Cosby (b. 1937)
Comedian, Actor, Businessman

Even as a child, he brought the house down. After William "Bill" Cosby's first performance, an original comedy routine he put on for his fifth grade class, his teacher thought it was so funny, he was asked to do it again. Unfortunately, as a child, he was too much into clowning around and being f unny, and not enough into being serious and studying. Because of this, Cosby, who was extremely bright, did poorly in school. After being told he would have to repeat a grade when he was a little older, Cosby pulled out of school and joined the navy instead.

Unfortunately, the navy wasn't really his cup of tea either. He soon discovered that he did not like the regimentation and taking orders that made no sense to him. However, while there, he discovered how important an education really was. Because he finally realized his opportunities would be limited if he didn't finish school, he enrolled in classes and received his General Education Development (GED) diploma, while still in the navy.

After leaving the service, he enrolled in Temple University. Because he excelled in track, he received a scholarship. To help finance the rest of his education, he became a part-time stand-up comedian, performing in clubs during his sophomore and junior years. After being so well received, and earning a steady income, he left Temple to try out his routines in New York City nightclubs. Due to his success there, he traveled to Las Vegas and Las Angeles, performing in top-rated establishments.

Next, he branched out into acting, eventually co-starring in *I Spy* (1965-1968) with Robert Culp. Cosby became the first African-American actor to be featured in a dramatic role in a television series, with a national sponsor.

His comedy routines and number one television series, *The Cosby Show* (1984-1992), often reflect the family closeness that was absent in his home when he was growing up. Born in Germantown, Pennsylvania, a north Philadelphia neighborhood, Cosby and his brothers were raised largely by their mother, because their father was frequently absent.

At his peak, Cosby won six Grammy awards for Best Comedy Album, starting in 1964 with *Bill Cosby Is A Very Funny Fellow — Right?* After *I Spy* ended in 1968, he portrayed Chet Kincaid, a high school track coach, in *The Bill Cosby Show*, and hosted two unsuccessful variety shows in 1972 and 1976. With the Saturday morning cartoon *Fat Albert and the Cosby Kids*, he found success. In 1986, he wrote his autobiography *Fatherhood*, a best-seller.

Unfortunately, even people who spread as much joy as Cosby, also experience pain. In 1997, his only son, Ennis, was the victim of a random murder. In true form, Bill Cosby continued with his life, with his wife Camille Cosby, and his four daughters, Erika, Erinn, Ensa, and Evin.

DID YOU KNOW?

♦ Bill Cosby has made more than twenty record albums.
♦ Some viewers criticized *The Cosby Show* as being an unreal portrayal of African-American life.
♦ Cosby is socially sensitive, and came out publicly to strongly oppose apartheid in South Africa.
♦ *The Cosby Show* was also number one in South Africa.
♦ He earned both a Masters and Doctorate degree from the University of Massachusetts.
♦ He and his wife gave twenty million dollars to Spelman College, a traditionally African-American women's college in Atlanta.

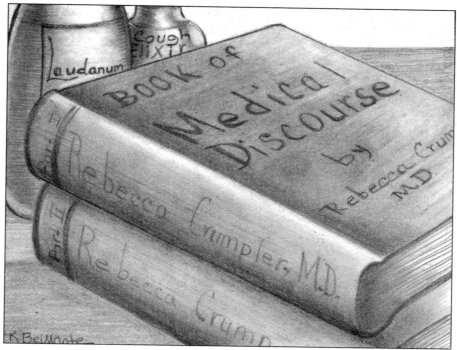

"I early conceived a liking for and sought every opportunity to be in a position to relieve the suffering of others." **—Rebecca Lee Crumpler**

Rebecca Lee Crumpler (1833-?)
Pioneering Medical Doctor

lthough a girl, Rebecca Lee Crumpler seized every opportunity to help others. All she had to do was to look to her aunt, who raised her, and who served as a doctor in her community, for a pattern to model. After performing her duties as a nurse in Massachusetts (1852-1860) so admirably, her employers also noticed the passion she had for caring for others, and suggested that she enter the New England Female Medical College in Boston.

Rebecca took their advice, and, in March of 1864, became the first black woman in the United States to earn a Doctress of Medicine Degree.

She practiced in Boston until the end of the Civil War, when she relocated her practice to Richmond, Virginia. She eventually returned to Boston, after running a successful practice and after having worked with the newly emancipated.

In 1883, she published "*A Book of Medical Discourse in Two Parts*, a manual advising women providing medical care for themselves and their children. It was based on her personal journals.

As a medical pioneer who prevailed over the severest of societal restrictions, she dedicated her life to the study and treatment of diseases affecting women and children. Her achievements created easier paths for other female physicians, both African-American and white.

HISTORY IN A CAPSULE

Elizabeth Blackwell, the first American woman physician to receive a medical degree, was the white counterpart of Rebecca Crumpler. Born in Bristol, England, she and her family moved to America in 1832. Her father, Samuel Blackwell, championed women's rights and the abolition of slavery. After many disappointments, and widespread hostility toward her in medical circles, she received her degree in Geneva in 1849.

With her sister, Dr. Emily Blackwell, and Dr. Marie Zakrzewska, she opened a medical clinic for indignant women. Dr. Zakrzewska, who was encouraged by Blackwell to become a physician, was founder of the New England Female Medical College of Boston, which allowed a quota of African-American students. This was considered a liberal policy during their time.

"Every man has a property in his own person; this nobody has a right to but himself." **—Locke**

Paul Cuffe (1758-1817)
Colonizationist

I t is a paradox that Americans of African ancestry, who hated slavery, and the violent era of Reconstruction that followed the Civil War, never gave widespread support to the concept of leaving the United States to colonize Africa. Colonial merchant Paul Cuffe was part of the minority that did. Wealthy and freeborn, he traveled to Sierra Leone, a British colony on the west coast of Africa, in 1810, to investigate it as a possible settlement for blacks who wished to escape the restrictiveness of American society. To encourage African-American emigration, he established the Friendly Society in 1811.

After the interruption caused by the War of 1812, he returned to the African nation in 1815, bringing with him eighteen adults and twenty children at his own expense. Because he thought it futile to hope that society would change, and because of the actions he took based on this belief, he won the support of spokesmen, including Richard Allen, the organizer and the first bishop of the African Methodist Episcopal Church, and James Forten, a wealthy abolitionist and inventor. In spite of the many hardships imposed on them, most African-Americans continued to oppose colonialization.

Born in New Bedford, Massachusetts, on the island of Cuttyhunk, his father, Cuffe Slocum, was an ex-slave, and his mother, Ruth Moses, a Wampanoag Indian. Young Paul's contact with area Quakers, who opposed slavery and war, no doubt influenced his feelings about bondage. Although he never experienced slavery, he grew to hate it. So opposed was he to the institution, that he had his name changed to Cuffe, since Slocum was the name of his father's former master.

Barely twenty-one years old, he ran afoul of Massachusetts law when he, his brother, and other free African-American citizens refused to pay their taxes; they used the rallying cry of the Revolutionary War, "No taxation without representation," to support their protest. After being threatened with imprisonment, and having paid the small amount he owed, he and other African-Americans appealed to the legislature. As a result of their actions, Massachusetts' African-Americans gained the privileges enjoyed by all other citizens.

Having been born on an island, Cuffe, whose interest in sailing began at an early age, became captain of his own ship, and acquired a fleet of his own. He established a successful shipping business, dealt mainly in coastal fishing and whaling, and traded with Europeans and with the Caribbean nations.

He married Alice Pequit, a Wampanoag Indian from his mother's tribe. The two of them built a school for free African-American children on their property. As an entrepreneur, a spokesman, and a philanthropist, he was held in high esteem in his community by both whites and African-Americans. He also gained a lot of respect for his generosity with his wealth; he continually used his personal finances to fight discrimination against free black citizens in the United States.

Although he was unable to continue to colonize Sierre Leone, due to his failing health, and eventual death, his dream of equality for citizens of African heritage lives on.

"The world of reality has its limits; the world of imagination is boundless... It is from their difference that all the evils arise which render us unhappy." —Rousseau

Dorothy Dandridge (1922-1965)
Actress

Along with Abbie Mitchell, Rose McClendon, and others of great talent, who were denied the opportunity to express the full range of their abilities, Dorothy Dandridge, who Ruby Dee once called one of the "tattered queens," had the beauty, talent and screen presence to become a great and successful actress.

Like other African-American pioneers, she was limited by roles that reflected Hollywood's — and society's — ideas about African-American life. Even in the title role as Carmen Jones (1954), for which she became the first African-American actress nominated for an Oscar for best actress. She played a character almost totally removed from the reality of African-American life. The movie itself, an Otto Preminger directed interpretation, by an African-American cast of Bizet's opera *Carmen*, was described by author and essayist James Baldwin as an "odd brew." It drew parallels, Baldwin stated, between an amoral gypsy and amoral African-Americans, thus perpetuating beliefs rooted in white perception rather than in fact.

Dandridge, a performer of remarkable beauty and ability, could be described as an actress before her time. She courageously played roles that challenged society's taboo on interracial relationship, and fought to make the African-American beauty an accepted fixture in Hollywood and mainstream society. She wanted to be recognized as an actress, not just an African-American actress, which restricted the range of roles offered to her.

Born in Cleveland, Ohio, she was only six years old when she and her sister, Vivian, performed as the Wonder Kids. Bright and talented, Dorothy performed acrobatics, played the violin, danced and sang. After her family moved to Los Angeles in the 1930s, she, her sister, and a friend formed the Dandridge Sisters, a singing group. They appeared at the Cotton Club in New York, and in the Marx Brothers movie, *A Day at the Races*.

After the trio disbanded, Dorothy played bit parts in movies and sang in nightclubs. Her big break came in 1953 when she co-starred as a pretty schoolmarm, with Harry Belafonte, in *Bright Road*. Because of her striking good looks, her career began to be built more on glamour roles. Since Belafonte was handsome, and a "name," she was again cast opposite him in the movies *Odds Against Tomorrow* and *Island in the Sun*. She also starred in the screen versions of *Porgy and Bess* and *Tamango*.

Unlike white actresses, many of whom were only of modest talent, and who were nurtured and groomed for stardom through long term contracts, Dorothy had no such assurances. Like other African-American actors and actresses, she often waited long periods between roles.

As she matured, her market value plummeted, and an attempted comeback in the 1960s failed. She died nearly penniless in 1965.

HISTORY IN A CAPSULE

The first African-American actress to win a Tony award was Juanita Hall (1949) for her role as Bloody Mary, in the musical *South Pacific*. Her vocal renditions of *Bali Ha'I* and *Happy Talk* became national hits.

Having studied at the Julliard School of Music, Hall made her stage debut in the chorus of *Show Boat* in 1928. In 1935, she formed the Juanita Hall Choir, and led a three hundred voice chorus at the 1939 World's Fair in New York City. Once the leading African-American star, she appeared in *House of Flowers* with Diahann Carroll in 1954.

"The brave man wants no charms to encourage him to duty, and the good man scorns all warnings that would deter him from doing it." **—Bulwer**

Benjamin Oliver Davis, Sr. (1877-1970)
United States Army Officer

When Benjamin O. Davis was promoted to the rank of brigadier general of the United States Army, by President Franklin D. Roosevelt, in 1940, he became the first African-American to attain such a rank. Even more notable, he achieved this at a time when few African-Americans were being promoted, regardless of their excellence in service.

Born and educated in Washington, D.C., he graduated from Howard University, before beginning his outstanding military career in 1898, when he entered the service as a temporary first lieutenant in the 8th Infantry, during the Spanish-American War. He finished his duties in March of 1899, and by the following June, had re-enlisted, this time as a private in the 9th Cavalry of the Regular Army. He was commissioned second lieutenant in February of 1901.

73

In 1905, after rendering outstanding service at Fort Washakie, Wyoming, and in the Philippine Islands, he was promoted to the rank of first lieutenant. He was given two other temporary positions during World War II; the first was the rank of major in 1917, followed by lieutenant colonel in 1918. After the war, during which time he served as military attaché to Monrovia, Liberia, he was returned to the rank of captain.

He was returned to the rank of lieutenant colonel on a permanent basis in 1920, and, after instructing the 372nd Infantry of the Ohio National Guard, was made full colonel in 1930. The day after he retired in 1940, he was called back to active duty, this time as a brigadier general.

He served as advisor to African-American soldiers in the European Theatre during World War II, and enforced policies related to the integration of facilities for African-American soldiers. When he retired in 1948, Davis served in Washington, D.C., as assistant to the inspector general.

A true soldier, he served his country with distinction, even in the face of racism and bigotry.

HISTORY IN A CAPSULE

On Dec. 7, 1941, when the Japanese attacked Pearl Harbor, an African-American mess attendant scored the only United States victory. Though he was not trained as a gunner, he downed four enemy planes after dragging his wounded captain to safety. For his heroism, Doris "Dorie" Miller was awarded the Navy Cross.

Miller, a Navy mess-man, first class, did not think of his own personal safety when he saw his captain lying mortally wounded. During the confusion that followed the surprise attack, when fires broke out on the U.S.S. Arizona, he seized an unmanned machine gun and fired away at the enemy planes until ordered to abandon his station. Unfortunately, the following year, he was listed as missing in action in the Pacific.

When the nineteen year old son of poor Texas sharecroppers enlisted in the Navy, he knew that he would be excluded from jobs that carried with them prestige. Though his lowly job as mess-man brought him no glory, he brought glory to his job, the Navy, and the whole of humanity by his selfless act.

K. BelMonte

"If you want to be the best...not just the black best or the Jewish best or the female best or the male best, but the best, period — you've got to work harder than anybody else." —**Sammy Davis, Jr.**

Sammy Davis, Jr. (1926-1990)
Entertainer

Having begun his career when he was only three years old, Sammy Davis, Jr., often called "The Greatest Entertainer in the World," was a polished performer by the age of five.

"Born in a suitcase" in New York City, he came from a family of entertainers. His mother was in the business, as were his father and his uncle, with whom he began his career performing with, in The Will Mastin Trio. The Trio traveled from city to city performing in vaudeville, burlesque, and cabaret shows throughout the 1930s. When they ran into situations in which the acts were unsuitable for minors, the Trio avoided running afoul with the law by billing Sammy as "The Midget." Although life was often hard for the family during these times, they always made sure that Sammy had a full stomach, even if they didn't. Their support paid off when, in 1931, Sammy made his movie debut in *Rufus Jones for President* with Ethel Waters. Soon after, he appeared in *Season's Greetings*.

75

Sammy was such a precocious performer that, even though he was little more than a toddler, he attracted the attention of the great Bill "Bojangles" Robinson, the "World's Greatest Tap Dancer." He tutored the tyke, helping him to perfect his tap dancing skills. In time, Sammy nearly rivaled his mentor, becoming one of the most sought after entertainers in the world.

In 1943, during World War II, Sammy was drafted into the United States Army and assigned to special services, which included writing, directing, and producing army camp entertainment shows. After he completed his service in 1945, he returned to the Will Mastin Trio.

Their big break came in April of 1946. During an engagement they had at Slapsie Maxie's, in Los Angeles, something clicked, and the audience loved them! Billed as the Will Mastin Trio, starring Sammy Davis, Jr., they were sensations around the country by the time Sammy's song, "Hey There," became a hit. When not playing nightclubs, they appeared on national TV.

After Will Mastin and Sammy Davis, Sr. retired in 1948, Sammy Davis, Jr. became a solo act and a household name. In 1954, he lost his left eye, and almost his life, in an auto accident. He bounced back a year later, and, undaunted, resumed his entertainment career.

In 1956, he was a hit in his first Broadway show, *Mr. Wonderful*. He followed this success by appearing in *Golden Boy*, as a boxer. The musical was based on Clifford Odets' drama, and was adapted to showcase Sammy's versatility in singing, dancing and acting. He went on to perform in movies such as *Anna Lucasta, One More Time,* and *Oceans 11.* He played Sportin' Life in the 1959 movie version of *Porgy and Bess*, and was a popular fixture in television, movies and nightclubs in the 1970s.

In 1972, Sammy incited controversy when he supported Richard Nixon, hugging him at the 1972 Republican Convention. Because most African-American voters supported the Democrats, his action raised the ire of many. Davis later renounced both Nixon and his programs.

Among his many honors, Davis appeared before the Queen of England at Victoria Palace, and was named "Personality of the Year" by the New York Press Association and "Entertainer of the Year" by *Cue* magazine. He was also presented with the Cultural Achievement Award from Israel and named "Man of the Year" by B'Nai B'Rith. Davis was chairman of the NAACP's Life Membership Committee, and in 1969 the organization awarded him the Spingarn Medal for his achievements as a great entertainer. In 1975, the National Academy of Television Arts and Sciences honored him.

Sammy was the third African-American to have his own television program, *The Sammy Davis Show.* In 1966, he published his best-selling autobiography, *"Yes, I Can."*

"The pride of the artisan in his art and its uses is pride in himself...it is in his skill and ability to make things as he wishes them to be that he rejoices."
—Hendrick Willem Van Loon

Thomas Day (c. 1700s-1861)
Cabinetmaker

When young Thomas Day was invited into a fine house to hear a melodeon, he was not mesmerized by the beauty of the music, but by the richly carved Old World antique furniture. He returned home with little memory of the music, but with a lasting impression of the furniture permanently etched into his memory.

Soon after he had his first encounter with beautiful hand-carved furniture, Day went home and carved a footstool from walnut, using a small knife. His mother was so amazed at his skill that she showed the stool to the rest of the family. They eventually decided to send the young boy to schools in Washington and Boston to develop his skills and learn the basics of cabinet making.

By 1818, he had opened his own shop on his mother's farm, and was producing the community's first mahogany furniture. He was so successful that, in 1823, he purchased a building in town and converted it into a factory. His pieces, which were designed with special emblems, making each unique to one family, brought some of the most significant citizens of the day to his shop. One of his patron's was the state's governor, who bought several sets of the highly prized furniture.

Wealthy families in the Carolinas, Georgia and Virginia completely furnished their homes with his pieces. Judges, senators, and other prominent citizens kept his furniture in their families, passing it down from one generation to another. Now scarce, Day furniture is considered a prized possession.

For many years, Day enjoyed prosperity in his business. Just before the Civil War, however, the political climate of the country changed. With all the unrest, and unsettled conditions, the demand for his furniture dropped and the price of mahogany wood increased, with shipping virtually impossible. Along with those of many white businessmen, Day's business failed.

Thomas Day used his extraordinary skills to market a highly demanded product. His talent and will to achieve brought him success and esteem, and provided an effective refute to the notion of the inferiority of his race.

"In a contest with oppression, the Almighty has no attribute which can take sides with oppressors." **—Frederick Douglass**

Frederick A. Douglass (1818-1875)
Abolitionist

Because of his beliefs, his prolific writing, and his persuasiveness as a powerful orator, Frederick Douglass' words became the fire and lightning that sparked the consciences of those who saw the enslavement of African-Americans as evil.

Born at Holme Hill Farm, near Tuckahoe Creek, Maryland, his mother was a slave and his father, a white man. Also of Native American ancestry, he escaped slavery in 1838, by borrowing a retired and free black sailor's protection papers, and traveling to Delaware. He changed his name from Frederick Augustus Washington Bailey to Douglass, to conceal his identity to slave catchers.

By the time Douglass joined the Abolitionist movement, he was the publisher of his own newspaper, *North Star*, in Rochester, New York (1845). His anti-slavery ideas, which he published in his paper, as well as his work titled, *Narrative of the Life of Frederick Douglass, an American Slave* (1845), revealed the horrors of slavery in general, as well as on the plantation where he was born. His revelations drew sympathy from both blacks and whites in the United States and Great Britain.

A personal friend of fiery abolitionist John Brown, he collected money for Brown and his raid on Harper's Ferry. Douglass, who also feared that the raid would turn sentiment against the Abolitionist movement, secretly met with "Captain Brown," in his rock-quarry hideout, and tried to dissuade his old friend from what he thought was a suicidal plan.

Instrumental in recruiting colored volunteers for the 54th and 55th Massachusetts regiments during the Civil War, Douglass was an advisor to President Abraham Lincoln, in matters related to the raising of Negro troops. So valued was his advice, that President Lincoln said to him, "...there is no man in the country whose opinion I value more than yours."

Though he was taught minimal reading and writing, by a mistress and white playmates, Douglass was self-educated, picking up "white" speech patterns through his associations. Because of his intellectual brilliance, and his courage to speak out against the injustices of slavery, Frederick Douglass was called the "spokesman for his race," and is regarded by many as one of America's greatest heroes.

DID YOU KNOW?

♦ He chose the name Douglas (but spelled it Douglass) after the Scottish Lord in the poem *Lady of the Lake.*

♦ He was assailed by his critics for not fighting with John Brown at Harper's Ferry.

♦ As well as being a businessman, he served as the elected president of the Freedmen's Bank and Trust Company (1874).

♦ Douglass' other works include *My Bondage and My Freedom* (1855), and *The Life and Times of Frederick Douglass* (1881, revised in 1893).

♦ Two of his sons served in, and returned safely home safely from, the Civil War.

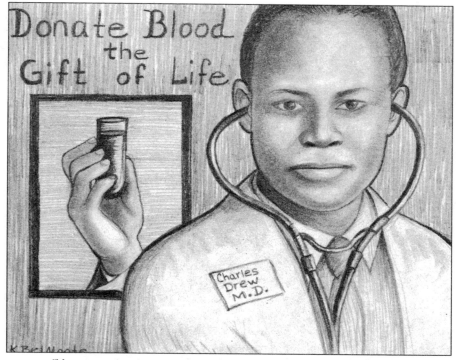

"You cannot put a great hope into a small soul." **—J.L. Jones**

Charles R. Drew (1904-1950)
Physician

Before Dr. Drew's research at Columbia University, and his discovery that blood plasma could be stored for long periods of time, transfusions were made from whole blood. This presented problems, since whole blood could not be kept for more than one week. During emergency periods, such as World War II, a ready supply was needed for soldiers wounded in battle.

During the period of 1939 through 1945, Drew was responsible for setting up many blood banks. He helped to save thousands of injured servicemen's lives during World War II, by organizing a blood-collecting program for the British government, as well as for the United States.

Born in Washington D.C., he graduated from Dunbar High School, where he excelled in sports as well as academics. His physical abilities won him an athletic scholarship to Amherst College. Because he brought so much honor to the school over a four-year period, he was awarded the Mossman Trophy.

He received his degree in medicine in 1933, from McGill University (Montreal, Quebec, Canada), where he won first prize in physiological anatomy. Drew followed this honor by being chosen to research the properties of blood plasma, at Columbia School of Medicine in New York, under a General Education Board Fellowship. Most of his research was done between 1935 and 1940.

In 1940, he published *Banked Blood: A Study in Blood Preservation*, and, in the same year, was awarded an honorary D.Sc. degree by Columbia University. In 1941, after having taught at Howard University since 1935, he became the school's professor of surgery. He also became the first director of the Red Cross program, which collected plasma for the United States' military forces, in 1941.

Drew became chief of staff at Freedmen's Hospital, which was associated with Howard University, in 1944, and, two years later, became medical director at the hospital. Having also studied surgical shock, and the problems of fluid balance in surgery, Dr. Drew remained the medical director of Freedmen's Hospital until his untimely death in an automobile accident, after falling asleep at the wheel, on his way to a professional meeting.

His pioneering efforts in studying and developing the means of storing blood plasma has had immeasurable effects on the survival of accident victims, surgical patients, and others requiring blood transfusions. Dr. Charles Drew was a giant in the field of medical research, and his contributions are a source of pride not only to African-Americans, but also to America and the world.

HISTORY IN A CAPSULE

In 1985, African-American neurosurgeon Benjamin S. Carson performed a hemispherectomy; he removed half the brain of a four year old girl who had suffered as many as one hundred fifty seizures a day. Because the other half of her brain took over all the necessary functions, the child developed normally. The year before, he had become, at age thirty-three, the youngest person in the country to be appointed director of pediatric neurosurgery at Johns Hopkins University. He led the 1987 medical team that successfully separated Siamese twins joined at the head. He gives an account of his ascent from a broken home, in which he and his mother were abandoned by his father, and his triumph over poverty, in his autobiography *Gifted Hands*.

"Heaven never helps the man who will not act." —**Sophocles**

William Edward Burghardt Du Bois
(1868-1963) Civil Rights Leader, Editor

By confronting issues through his published books, poems and articles, and through powerful oratory, W.E.B. Du Bois presented an intellectual fight against society's discrimination and disenfranchisement of African-Americans.

Du Bois, who was born in Great Barrington, Massachusetts, grew up happy in New England, until a pivotal experience altered his view of race relations. After being painfully snubbed by a newcomer, during a childhood game, he became fixated on proving himself. He graduated with honors from college preparatory school at sixteen years of age and attended Fisk University. In 1895, after two years of study in Germany, he received his Ph.D. from Harvard, and, the following year, while only twenty-four years old, wrote *Suppression of the African-American Slave Trade to the United States*, the first monograph of it's kind produced by an African-American.

An outstanding intellectual, his approach to solving the problems African-Americans experienced was more militant than that of Booker T. Washington, the most influential African-American at that time, in the United States. Du Bois produced many articles, pamphlets and books, which protested the treatment of African-Americans in the United States. In 1899, while the assistant professor of sociology at the University of Pennsylvania, he published *The Philadelphia Negro: A Social Study*, and, in 1903, published *The Souls of Black Folk*, a collection of his best-published and unpublished articles and essays. The collections, which contained works, which had appeared in *World's Work, Dial* and *Atlantic Monthly* magazines, became a classic. His next venture, *Moon Illustrated*, a literary magazine in which he invested twelve hundred dollars, his entire savings, failed after selling no more than five hundred copies.

In response to what many intellectuals and militants felt was the compromising leadership of Booker T. Washington, Du Bois founded the Niagara Movement. A series of race riots and the lack of protection of African-American citizens, by law enforcement officials, so shocked a group of white liberals, that they invited members of the movement to join them in forming a new group. The organization became the NAACP, formed February 12, 1909, on the one hundred-year anniversary of the birth of Abraham Lincoln. In 1910, after editing *Horizon* magazine, he became the editor of *The Crisis*, the official magazine for the National Association for the Advancement of Colored People (NAACP), and, in 1919, initiated the Pan Am games, to gain worldwide support for the plight of not just African-Americans, but for all oppressed people.

Other works by Du Bois include *John Brown* (1909), *Dark Water* (1920), *Black Reconstruction* (1935), a 728-page tome, and *Color and Democracy* (1945).

W.E.B. Du Bois, who at the time of his death was editor of the *Encyclopedia Africana*, dedicated his life to fighting oppression and institutionalized, as well as overt, racism. Without a doubt, he was one of the world's greatest minds.

"The literature of a people must spring from the sense of its nationality; and nationality is impossible without self-respect, and self-respect is impossible without
liberty."   —H.B. Stowe

Paul Laurence Dunbar (1872-1906)
Poet

A s the first nationally recognized African-American poet, and
as the first to use African-American dialect in his poetry, Paul
Laurence Dunbar, had a gift for translating the life he observed
around him into poetry.

The son of former slaves, he was born in Dayton, Ohio,
and, after graduating from high school, took a job as an elevator operator,
earning four dollars a week. Dunbar observed what was going on around him
while he did this job, and ended up writing it down. In 1893, he self-pub-
lished his first poetry collection, *Oak and Ivy*.

Though neither his first collection, nor *Majors and Minors*, his second
collection were best-sellers, the critics at Harper's magazine, who had seen
his work, encouraged him to become a full time writer. *Lyrics of a Lowly Life*,

published in 1896, only three years after his first collection was published, was the crowning success of his career.

Although he died at a young age, he established himself as a dominant figure in African-American poetry. Dunbar, who became known as "The Poet of the People," was known for writing his poems in the dialect that became his hallmark. He penned *Lyrics of Love and Laughter* in 1903, and in 1905, followed with *Lyrics of Sunshine and Shadow*. Unfortunately, he never witnessed the success of his enormously popular *Complete Poems*, which was published in 1913, seven years after his untimely death. The collection incorporated standard English and dialect poems, and was such a success, it still remains in print.

DID YOU KNOW?

- Dunbar began writing poetry when he was only six years old.
- When he was thirteen, he gave a public recital of his poetry.
- After his father died, he augmented his mother's income by working part-time in hotels, delivering laundry.
- Dunbar wrote the class song that was sung at his graduation, and was the only African-American in his Dayton, Ohio, graduating class.
- In addition to his poetry, he wrote four volumes of short stories, and published four novels, the most popular being *The Uncalled* and *Sport of Gods*.
- He contracted tuberculosis, developed pneumonia, and died when he was only thirty-four.

"*We do not choose our own parts in life, and have nothing to do with selecting those parts. Our simple duty is confined to playing them well.*" **—Epictetus**

Todd Duncan (b. 1903)
Opera Singer

Having played the role of Porgy, in *Porgy and Bess*, twelve hundred times in the United States, as well as abroad, Todd Duncan helped clear a path for other African-Americans interested in opera to follow.

Born in Louisville, Kentucky, he was educated at Columbia University in New York and Butler University in Indianapolis, and, in 1950, received, his L.H.D. from Valparaiso University and his Doctor of Music from Central College in Ohio. Though he appeared in operas such as *Cavelleria Rusticana* in New York, he is best remembered for his role as the crippled Porgy, in the Broadway production of *Porgy and Bess*, a role he initially won in 1935.

The same year he was first cast as Porgy, he gave a concert for President and Mrs. Roosevelt. Four years later, in 1939, he played a leading role at the

87

Drury Lane Theatre in London, in *The Sun Never Sets*. He also frequently sang with leading symphony orchestras, and regularly toured Europe, Australia, New Zealand and South America as a concert artist.

The play, *Lost is the Stars*, a Maxwell Anderson-Kurt Weill musical adaptation of Alan Paton's novel, *Cry, The Beloved Country*, slated Duncan in the lead role. And, when he sang with the New York City Opera, in 1945, as Tonio, in *Il Pagliacci*, he became the first African-American man to sing with a major opera company in the United States. He ended up being cast the same year, as Escamillo, in the opera, *Carmen*.

In 1946, he sang with the New York philharmonic orchestra, in Beethoven's *Ninth Symphony*. His honors include the Critics Award, the Medal of Honor and Merit from the president of Haiti, and the Donaldson Award for the best male performance in a musical for the year, in 1950.

Like other African-American musical greats of his era, Todd Duncan's courage in facing society's obstacles helped to make entry into opera easier for those who followed.

HISTORY IN A CAPSULE

Although internationally respected conductor Dean Dixon was a guest conductor with the Boston Symphony, the NBC Symphony Orchestra and the New York Philharmonic Orchestra, he was never offered a permanent position as a conductor. Because closed doors kept him from advancing in the United States, he left the country in 1949 to accept a position as the conductor of the Grotebarg Symphony Orchestra in Sweden. He also conducted orchestras in Germany and Israel. Like many other African-American artists before him, Dixon found that he was more readily accepted abroad, than in his homeland.

"It is art that makes life, makes interest, makes importance...and I know of no substitute whatever for the force and beauty of its process." **—Henry James**

Robert S. Duncanson (1821-1872)
Artist

He was denied entrance to art schools in Philadelphia, New York and Boston because, in Robert S. Duncanson's Day, an African-American artist was unheard of.

Born in Seneca , New York, his mother, an ex-slave from Cincinnati, who probably escaped to Canada, and his father, a Canadian of Scottish heritage, separated when Duncanson was still quite young.

He learned about poetry and literature in Canadian schools, before returning to a town outside of Cincinnati, with his mother, in 1841. Known as "Queen City of the West," Cincinnati had established art schools, that in the future, enabled Duncanson to become one of the most accomplished painters of the ante-bellum period.

As was the case with most of the artists of the Hudson River School of Landscape Painting, Duncanson was inspired by the unspoiled wilderness; panoramas became one of his favorite subjects. Having been raised in a more racially tolerant atmosphere than most ex-slaves, he found the ambience surrounding the art world to be more colorblind than outside communities. Among other artists, he found respect for his talents and an environment that accepted him as a contributor to its school.

In the spring of 1841, Kentucky slaveholders led an attack on African-Americans, beating them for four days in their homes, businesses and churches, while police ignored the riots. Duncanson joined his mother in Mount Pleasant, an Underground Railroad Station, about 15 miles north of Cincinnati. While fifteen hundred African-Americans fled to Canada, he continued to paint and exhibit in the annual Western Art Union. Because of his many contacts among the art colonies, he was able to join the Cincinnati Academy of Arts and hold his first exhibit (1842), which included *Fancy Portrait, The Miser* and *Infant Savior*. It was believed that the entries may have been copies of engravings, but they were so well done, they were listed in the exhibition catalog, along with the works of some of Cincinnati's most highly regarded artists.

White contemporaries of Duncanson's were protective of their African-American colleague. When they wrote about his works in newspapers or other publications, they never listed his race, until after his death. They apparently feared a backlash against his work, if his race was revealed. In 1848, Nicholas Longworth, a wealthy Cincinnati politician, hired Duncanson to paint a series of murals in his new mansion. He completed them in the span of two years and became the nation's first African-American muralist.

Unfortunately, Duncanson, who was largely self-taught, and who had become quite successful, died in a mental institution in 1872. His symptoms pointed toward a brain tumor, but in a time before the development of neurosurgery, his condition was diagnosed as a mental breakdown.

Katherine Dunham

"Tropical Revue"

Dancer-Choreographer

"It was in me to dance and I had to do it to be satisfied...there is a purifying process in dancing..." **—Katherine Dunham**

Katherine Dunham (b. 1909)
Dancer, Choreographer

T hough she felt compelled to dance, when she received a Rosenwald Fellowship for a year, in 1935, it was to study anthropology. Because she wanted to learn native folklore, with a focus on the social custom aspect of dance, she traveled to the West Indies, where she gathered first-hand information on Haitian dance, while she lived and danced among the people. With that experience as her base, she eventually formed a dance company, which went on to tour the United States as well as Europe.

Having been born in Chicago, Illinois, she was raised in the suburb of Glen Ellyn. Although her first love had always been dance, her parents had hoped that she would become a teacher. After her mother died, when she was very young, Dunham and her brother were taken to live with an aunt, while their father worked as a traveling salesman. Another relative challenged the

the aunt, and won custody of the two children, after going to court with her case. After their father remarried, he regained custody. The family then moved to Joliet, Illinois. While attending Joliet High School, she excelled in athletics and was a member of the dance club, Terpsichorean. She also played the piano, was president of the girl's athletic club, and played on the girls basketball team. Upon graduating, she entered Joliet Junior College, where she continued her academic as well as dance studies. When she was admitted into the University of Chicago, she helped to finance her education by working as a librarian's assistant, and giving dance lessons.

In addition to modern dance, she also studied ballet. With a member of the Chicago Civic Opera Company, she established the Chicago Negro School of Ballet. In 1931, her troupe performed at the Chicago Beaux Arts Ball, and, in 1934, she played the lead at the Chicago Civic Opera Theatre, in *La Guiablesse*, which was based on Martinique folklore.

Although she received her Bachelor of Arts degree from the University of Chicago, she became so involved in her company's *Tropical Revue* production (1943), she put off completing the work for her Master's degree. She later completed the requirements at the University of Chicago. She earned her Doctorate degree at Northwestern University, while at the same time restructuring modern dance by injecting components of Caribbean and African cultures. In the 1940s and 1950s, she traveled the world, performing with her troupe.

Dunham also appeared as a dancer in the movies *Cabin in the Sky* (1940), and *Stormy Weather* (1943). In addition, she was a guest artist with the San Francisco Symphony Orchestra (1943), and the Los Angeles Symphony Orchestra (1945). She choreographed *Windy City, Pardon My Sarong*, and *Ida*, at the Metropolitan Opera House. A writer as well as dancer, choreographer, and anthropologist, she penned her autobiography, *A Touch of Innocence*, in 1959, as well as articles for various magazines.

DID YOU KNOW?

♦ She founded the Katherine Dunham Center for the Performing Arts, which promotes socialization through the arts, in the late 1960s, at Southern Illinois University.
♦ She received the Kennedy Center Award in 1983, and, the Scripps American Dance Festival Award in 1986.
♦ Her studies also include African-based ritual dance in Jamaica, Martinique and Trinidad.

"There are but three classes of men, the retrograde, the stationary, and the progressive." **—Lavater**

Lee Elder (b. 1934)
Golfer

L ike most African-American golfers, Lee Elder began playing while employed as a caddie, because a segregated society prevented him from playing on the best courses, thus hindering him from developing his full potential.

Born in Dallas, Texas, Robert Lee Elder developed an interest in golf when he began working as a caddy, when he was only fifteen years old. After his father died during World War II, Lee, as he came to be known, and his mother, traveled to Los Angeles, where he met Ted Rhodes. Rhodes was an accomplished African-American golfer who took it on himself to mentor the youngster, allowing him to travel with him while Elder honed his golfing skills.

Later Lee was drafted into the United States Army, and was made captain of the golf team at Fort Lewis, Washington. After his discharged from the military in 1960, he taught golf and began his career as a member of the black United Golf Team (UGA). Although he won eighteen out of twenty-one tournaments at the beginning of his career, the UGA did not afford him the kind of competition that would help him become a world-class professional golfer.

In 1962, when the color line became relaxed in most United States institutions, Elder was able to attend the Professional Golfers Association (PGA) School, to earn the credentials required to play on the PGA tour. In 1967, he became the first African-American to qualify for membership in the PGA, and in 1968 finished a close second to Jack Nicklaus, in the American Golf Classic, in Akron, Ohio.

Elder became the first African-American to play in the South African Professional Golf Association tournament in 1971, and, in the same year, won the Nigerian Open. In 1974, he qualified to compete in the Masters Tournament, when he won the Monsanto Open in Pensacola, Florida, and the Houston Open in 1976. He also took home six thousand dollars when he won the Westchester Classic in 1978, was the first African-American to make the Ryder Cup team, and the first African-American to top a million dollars in prize money. Other wins include the 1984 Seniors PGA Tour of Suntree Classic; the Hilton Head Invitational; the Coca-Cola Grand Slam, Japan, 1984; the Jamaica PGA Championship, Kingston, also in 1984; and the 1985 Citizens Bank Seniors.

He established the Lee Elder Scholarship Foundation and the Lee Elder Celebrity Pro-Am Golf Classic, is founder of the Lee Elder Summer Youth Golf Development Program, and is director of Lee Elder Enterprises, Inc.

Elder also serves on the Goodwill Industries Advisory Board and is a member of the NAACP. His many honors include Lee Elder Day, declared on May 3, in Washington, D.C., and having been given the keys to the cities of Washington, D.C. (1974), and Pensacola, Florida (1975). Additionally, he received the Charles Bartlett Award from the Golf Writers of America in 1977, and was inducted into the Washington Hall of Stars in 1979.

DID YOU KNOW?

- ◆ Golf and tennis have historically been white elitist sports.
- ◆ Some segregated golf associations sponsored caddy tournaments to provide competition for African-American caddies.
- ◆ George F. Grant, a black dentist, patented the wooden golf tee in 1899, so players no longer had to balance balls on mounds of earth.

"Those who attain to any excellence commonly spend life in some one single pursuit, for excellence is not often gained upon easier terms." **—Johnson**

Ralph Ellison (1914-1994)
Essayist, Novelist

O ne of the few novelists whose reputation remained established on the publication of only a single novel, Ralph Ellison, who is said to have been a perfectionist, spent years writing *The Invisible Man*. It was worth the wait though; upon its publication in 1952, it touched the collective conscience of America and was given the National Book Award for fiction.

Ellison, who did not start out with the intention of becoming a writer, was initially interested in sculpture, and actually studied music at Tuskegee Institute for three years. T.S. Elliot's poetry, and his friendship with Richard Wright, awakened in him the desire to write.

A giant, if not one of the most prolific writers of the social protest era, Ellison studied for a time in Italy under a 1955 award from the American Academy of Arts and Letters. His works following this period include his second publication *Shadow and Act* (1964), a collection of essays. From 1970 through 1980, he was an Albert Schweitzer Professor of Humanities at New York University, and, in 1986, published *Going to the Territory*, another collection of speeches and essays.

He was awarded honorary Doctor of Letters degrees by Harvard University (1974), and Wesleyan University (1980). His other awards and honors include his election to the National Institute of Arts and Letters, and to the American Academy of Arts and Letters. He was also the recipient of the Medal of Freedom, from President Nixon (1969); the winner of the Langston Hughes Medallion, given by the City College of the City University of New York (1984); and the recipient of the National Medal of Arts, awarded by President Ronald Reagan.

In 1976, he was the subject of a profile in *New Yorker* magazine, and Oklahoma City, Oklahoma, named its library after him, while Brown University held a Ralph Ellison Festival in 1979. In 1980, two authors, Michael S. Harper and John Wright, edited *A Ralph Ellison Festival, The Carleton Miscellany,* which contained three of his essays.

Born in Oklahoma City, Oklahoma, Ellison moved to New York in the late 1930s, following his stay at Tuskegee Institute. During his career, he taught at Bard College, Rutgers University and the University of Chicago.

Although Ellison never completed his second novel, several literary journals published excerpts from what was to be his second magnum opus, thereby giving the world one last peek into the mind of one of the great writers of our time.

DID YOU KNOW?

♦ Ellison wrote *The Invisible Man* with the aid of a Rosenwald Scholarship.

♦ *The Invisible Man* was termed "the most distinguished single work," published in the United States since 1945, in a 1965 poll.

♦ *The Invisible Man* explored the many ways in which African-Americans are alienated in a predominantly white, hostile society.

"The world cannot do without great men, but great men are very troublesome to the world." **—Goethe**

Medgar Evers (1925-1963)
Civil Rights Activist

His assassination in 1963 made him one of the Civil Rights Movement's first martyrs. Although his death, by all other definitions was senseless, as well as tragic, it served as an impetus for President John F. Kennedy to seek congressional support of a comprehensive civil rights bill.

A former soldier in the United States, Evers, who graduated from Alcorn A&M College in 1952, was born in Decatur, Mississippi, one of America's most segregated states. Always aware of the danger he and his family faced, as he stood firm in his belief of justice for all citizens. Medgar Evers, saw first hand the deplorable living conditions of destitute, desperately poor, African-American families, during his travels around the Mississippi countryside, as an insurance salesman. This experience acted as a catalyst, moving him to become part of the struggle to improve the living conditions of African-American people.

He joined the National Association for the Advancement of Colored People (NAACP) and was outspoken in his demands for equal rights for all citizens, regardless of race. In 1954, Evers, who advocated boycotting as a means of obtaining equal rights from businessmen who practiced discrimination in the hiring and treatment of African-Americans, was appointed Mississippi's first field secretary of the NAACP.

Evers was a voter's rights supporter, and a vocal proponent of Brown v. The Board of Education of Topeka, which challenged the legality of segregated public schools. Uncompromising in his demands, he became a symbol of African-American resistance to generations-old Southern traditions, a concept foreign to old-South whites, with their entrenched codes of racial ethics.

Although his fiery speeches and fearless confrontations of Mississippi's policies of discrimination generated personal threats, he bravely continued his attack on the state's unfair system. Sadly, as he was returning home from a civil rights meeting, on June 13, 1963, he was shot in the back by a sniper, as he stepped out of his car and onto his driveway. He died from his wounds as his wife and children looked on.

His untimely death, though tragic, served to focus the attention of America on the injustices perpetrated by state governments not only in Mississippi, but all of the United States. Evers' assassination also generated righteous anger that was so consuming, it replaced the fear that had paralyzed Southern African-Americans for generations. Channeling their rage into positive action for change, African-American protesters marched en masse against the senseless slaying. After the assassination of President John F. Kennedy, the sympathy following the assassination — this time that of a head of state, created a political climate ripe for the passage of the 1964 Civil Rights bill, which was finally signed into law by President Lyndon Baines Johnson.

Because of the danger he knowingly faced in his fight for civil rights, Medgar Evers made the ultimate sacrifice, his own life, to improve the quality of life for his children, and for generations of children to follow.

"Music moves us, and we know not why..." **—L.E. Landon**

Ella Fitzgerald (1918-1996)
Jazz Singer

lthough she was orphaned at a very young age, and attended a Yonkers, New York school for orphans, at the age of fifteen, she tried her luck in an Apollo Theater amateur contest, in New York City. She so impressed Chick Webb, a popular bandleader who happened to be in the audience, that he immediately hired her to sing with his band.

Under his mentorship, Ella's untrained talent was polished to perfection. By 1938, she achieved worldwide renown for her syncopated version of the familiar nursery rhyme, *A Tisket-A-Tasket*.

When Chick Webb died in 1939, Ella inherited his band. By 1942, however, she began a solo act, recording such memorable tunes as *Hard Hearted Hannah*, *He's My Guy*, and *Love You Madly*. She eventually became known as the "Queen of Scatting," which was a vocal imitation of instrumental music.

At the height of her popularity, Ella, also known as the "First Lady of Song," toured all over the United States, as well as Europe and Japan. She recorded for Decca Records from 1936 to 1955, and later for Verve and Pablo, and was a featured artist at Ronnie Scott's in London, and Las Vegas's Caesar's Palace and Sahara Hotel.

She performed with more than forty symphony orchestras, and appeared in the movie *Pete Kelly's Blues* (1955), as well as quite a few television specials, including the All-Star Swing Festival in 1972. During her stellar career, she also recorded scores of memorable songs and albums, including *Mack the Knife*; *Ella in Berlin* (1960); *A Perfect Match*, with Count Basie (1979); and *The Intimate Ella* (1990). In 1993, she celebrated her seventy-fifth birthday by releasing the two retrospectives, *First Lady of Song* and *75th Birthday Celebration.*

Her many honors include winning twelve Grammy awards, as well as being named the number one female singer in 1968 by the 16th Jazz Critics Poll. She also received the National Medal of the Arts in 1987, and, in 1990, received the Commander of Arts and Letters, in Paris, France.

Having been born in Newport News, Virginia, and growing up in an orphanage, while being educated in affiliated schools, Ella Fitzgerald was not only talented, but also courageous. Her talent show gamble not only launched a successful career, it introduced the rare talent of one of the world's most popular jazz singers.

DID YOU KNOW?

♦ "Grammy" is derived from the word "gramophone." The award is presented to artists for outstanding achievement in phonograph recording. It is a gold-plated replica of a record, and is given annually by the National Academy of Recording Arts and Sciences.

"Opposition inflames the enthusiast, never converts him." —*Schiller*

Curtis Charles "Curt" Flood
(1938-1996) Baseball Player, Activist

In 1922, the United States Congress granted baseball the right to bargain outside the field of the federal anti-trust laws, through its "reserve clause," which stated a player is property of the club that owns him, unless that club trades him to another or releases him outright.

When brilliant St. Louis Cardinals center fielder Curt Flood was traded after the 1969 season, he refused to go to the Philadelphia Phillies, because he felt that baseball was at variance with other employers in society, which allowed employees the right to bargain freely. He wrote to Commissioner Bowie Kuhn and stated his objection to the reserve clause, and subsequently filed a lawsuit against the National League. The clause, he pointed out, violated the right of employees to consider multiple employers in an open market. Because many other players were in agreement with Flood's position, the Major League Players Association unanimously supported his suit.

Flood lost in the lower courts, and the United States Supreme Court ruled that baseball was not interstate commerce; its special exemption from anti-trust laws was legal. By the time the Supreme Court ruled on his case, Flood had retired from baseball. He had sat out the 1970 season, and was sent in absentia to the Washington Senators. Although he later signed with the team, he played only ten games.

Born in Houston, Texas, Flood's parents were both hospital workers, who held several jobs in order to support the family. When they moved to Oakland, California, he excelled in baseball at Oakland Technical and McClymonds High School. After graduating in 1956, he signed with the Cincinnati Reds. In 1958, he was traded to the St. Louis Cardinals, and, as one of baseball's star defensive center fielders, he won seven consecutive Golden Glove awards. He played for the Cardinals for twelve seasons, with a batting average of .293. His brilliant performances helped the Cardinals win the 1964 and 1967 National League pennants, as well as the World Series for those two years.

After spending his first year out of baseball managing his bar on the Spanish island of Majorca, he returned to Oakland in 1976, to become a radio commentator for the Oakland Athletics, as well as Oakland's Little League commissioner.

Also a talented portrait painter, he moved to Los Angeles, where he worked as an artist, participated in fantasy baseball camps, and played in exhibition games. In 1970, he published his autobiography, *The Way It Is*.

Though his lawsuit challenging the National League's reserve clause met with defeat, it helped to institute changes in salary arbitration and free agency work.

HISTORY IN A CAPSULE

In 1872, when John W. "Bud" Fowler joined a white New Castle, Pennsylvania team, he became the first African-American salaried player in baseball. Though he was a star second baseman, he was able to play other positions. Following his departure from professional baseball, Fowler, who had played for mainly white teams in the United States, for twenty-five years, organized the African-American team, the All-American Black Tourists, who played in top hats.

"Where slavery is, there liberty cannot be; and where liberty is, there slavery cannot be." **—Sumner**

James Forten (1766-1842)
Inventor, Abolitionist

S aid to be the first militant civil rights champion for African-Americans, James Forten, a man of great wealth, was born a free Negro in Pennsylvania, a descendent of several generations of free African-Americans.

An equalitarian capitalist, as well as an abolitionist, he went to work at the age of ten, after receiving some education in Quaker schools. When he was fifteen years old, he entered the navy to serve in the War of Independence, working as a powder boy on a Continental Army ship. Unfortunately, the vessel was captured. Forten spent seven months in a British prison.

While in the navy, he also developed an instrument for handling sails. When he returned to the United States, after being held captive by the British, he went to work for sailmaker Robert Bridges, who sold the company to Forten when he retired. As a result of using his skills, Forten managed to operate a thriving business, which, as a result, led him to become the wealthiest African-American in Philadelphia. A man of integrity, he used his money to support equal rights for African-Americans and women, and to promote peace and temperance.

Forten also fought the policy of deportation, which the American Colonization Society advocated, and wanted full recognition as a citizen and as a man. So passionate were his beliefs, he was instrumental in spearheading a meeting at the African Methodist Episcopal Church in Philadelphia, to denounce the plans of the colonizationists in 1817.

In 1830, he was one of the organizers of the Convention of Free Colored People, whose goal was to bring focus to, and oppose the issue of African-Americans being sent back to Africa. They believed that, as members of old American stock, they were eligible for citizenship.

Rumored to have also been responsible for convincing William Lloyd Garrison and Theodore Dwight Weld of the equality of the races, James Forten believed that the ultimate survival of all African-Americans depended on abolishing slavery. He believed that all races deserved to enjoy the rights America promised her citizens.

HISTORY IN A CAPSULE

Though he is most famous for helping Frederick Douglass escape from slavery, David Ruggles was also a self-educated and multi-talented man of many interests. A minister and conductor on the Underground Railroad, he also served as Secretary of the Committee of Vigilance of New York, in 1835.

As one of the first African-Americans to have escaped slavery, he is reputed to have helped more than six hundred slaves escape to the North and into Canada. A militant anti-slavery advocate, Ruggles also used the quarterly magazine he established, *The Mirror of Liberty*, which was the first magazine edited by an African-American, to publicize the plight of the African-American.

Like James Forten, he disagreed with the "Back to Africa" beliefs of the Colonization Society. With other Northern African-Americans, he helped to raise funds, arrange transportation, and provide shelter for fugitive slaves, as well as help organize the network of the Underground Railroad.

E. Franklin Frazier

The Rise of the Middle Class

Black Bourgeoisie

Sociologist

K. Belmonte

"When a man argues for victory and not for truth, he is sure of just one ally — that is the devil." **—G. MacDonald**

Edward Franklin Frazier (1894-1962)
Sociologist

As one of the most eminent and widely outspoken African-American scholars, he created quite a controversy when his book *Black Bourgeoisie: The Rise of a New Middle Class*, was published. Largely blaming the influence of educator Booker T. Washington, E. Franklin Frazier wrote about the collective feelings of inferiority, frustration, and insecurity of middle-class African-Americans. They were derived, he believed, from the make-believe world of "Negro Business," and the myth of "Negro Society." In spite of the stir it caused, Frazier received the MacIver Award from the American Sociological Association, of which he was president.

Born in Baltimore, Maryland, he recognized the value of a college degree, through the love of education his father, who had never had the opportunity to obtain an education, instilled in him. In 1916, he earned his Bachelor's degree, with honors, from Harvard University, and accepted a position as a mathematics instructor at the Tuskegee Institute in Alabama. He received his Master's degree in sociology in 1920, from Clark University in Massachusetts, and, from 1920 to 1921, was a research fellow at the New York School of Social Work. From 1921 to 1922, he traveled to Denmark, as a Scandinavian Foundation Fellow, to study their high schools.

Frazier also taught African-American studies and sociology at Morehouse College in Atlanta from 1922 to 1924, and directed the Atlanta School of Social Work from 1922 to 1927. From 1931 to 1936, after receiving his Ph.D. from the University of Chicago, where he was a research assistant in the department of sociology, he was a professor at Fisk University. He received a Guggenheim Foundation Fellowship in 1940, and completed an independent research project on culture and race, in the West Indies, in 1949. In addition to all this, he also lectured extensively in Europe.

Though his writings, which include *Negro Youth at the Crossroads*, *The Negro in the United States*, *The Negro Family in the United States*, and *The Negro Church,* sometimes created controversy, he was a highly respected sociologist, writer, and scholar.

HISTORY IN A CAPSULE

As a contemporary of Edward Franklin Frazier, and also an educator and sociologist, Charles Johnson Spurgeon was a recognized scholar in social science. Even before he was named president of Fisk University, he had published research on aspects of African-American life.

Born in Briston, Virginia, in 1893, he attended the University of Chicago, and Virginia Union University. He was also awarded honorary degrees from Harvard, Howard and Columbia Universities.

Having eventually been chosen by the White House, to be a consultant on problems facing American youth, he also directed investigations and research for the Chicago Urban League from 1917 to 1919, and investigated patterns of Negro migration for the Carnegie Foundation in 1918. In addition, Spurgeon served on the committee of Race Relations, in Chicago, from 1923 to 1929.

"...I asked, 'where is the black man's government? Where is his king and his kingdom?' ...I could not find them, and then I declared, 'I will help make them.'"
—*Marcus M. Garvey*

Marcus M. Garvey (1887-1940)
Colonizationist

 aving discovered early that he had the power to persuade and to influence people, he used this ability to persuade the black people on his native land of Jamaica, and later in the United States, to return to Africa. Because he believed that returning to Africa was the only option he had, if he was going to live with dignity, he became the best-known advocate of the "back-to-Africa" movement.

Born in St. Ann's, on the northern coast of Jamaica, Marcus Moziah Garvey was the youngest of eleven children. At the age of fourteen, he went to work as an apprentice in a printing shop, and, at age seventeen, had learned his trade well enough to go work for an uncle in Kingston, Jamaica's capitol. Bright and ambitious, he moved up rapidly, and became a foreman in the company. It was during this time that he discovered his gift of oratory, and began to participate regularly in popular street debates. Both a foreman and a master printer in Jamaica, by the time he was twenty, he was the only foreman to join the workers when the printers union went on strike in 1907. Although most of the workers were eventually rehired, Garvey was blacklisted.

After discovering that, in Jamaica, whites and mulattos were the most affluent, and had the best jobs and positions of power, he realized that blacks needed to organize and communicate. It was at this time that he began publishing the periodicals *Garvey's Watchman* and *Our Own*.

He traveled to Costa Rica, and throughout Central and South America during the next few years, and, in 1912, spent time in London. It was there that he met others like him. By associating with the many students in the area, he learned about Africa, and, after reading *Up From Slavery*, it was there, that he became enamored with Booker T. Washington.

Garvey settled on the idea of "uniting all Negro peoples of the world... to establish a country and government absolutely their own." In 1914, he returned to Jamaica, and quickly organized the Universal Negro Improvement and Conservation Association and African Communities League. With Garvey as president and traveling commissioner, the organization had its own staff and constitution. When whites discovered the organization's plan for industrial education of blacks, they, as well as the governor, a Catholic bishop, and the mayor of Kingston, offered support. This plan drew its inspiration from Booker T. Washington's Tuskegee Institute.

Because Washington died before Garvey had the chance to visit him in America, and seek his help in raising funds for his school, Garvey did not arrive in America until 1916. After first visiting Harlem, Garvey traveled to a number of other states to propose his idea. In 1917, he finally had the chance to address the people of Harlem, to organize the Liberty League.

Preaching the purity of the African race, Garvey had six million dues-paying members in his league by 1923. Because of this support, he was able to organize the Black Star Steamship Line to transport African-Americans back to Africa. Unfortunately, his dream began to fall apart, as each ship he purchased met with disaster and most of his backers lost their money. Garvey, who was convicted of mail fraud in 1923, refused to allow a lawyer to defend him. Although he was sent to Atlanta Federal Penitentiary, his sentence was commuted in 1927, at which time he left the United States.

Although he often met with failure, Marcus Garvey shook hands with success by instilling in African-Americans the feeling of self-worth and by giving them a sense of the history which connected them with their African origins.

"Open wide your mouth for the speechless...and plead the cause of the poor and needy." **—Proverbs 31: 8-9 NKJV**

Willie Edward Gary (b. 1947)
Attorney-at-Law

ollowing the rap of the gavel, the verdict was announced, "Judgment is for the plaintiff, for five hundred million dollars." The year was 1995. The prosecuting attorney was Willie Edward Gray, or as he came to be known, "Willie, the Giant Killer."

The son of sharecroppers, Gary was born in Eastman, Georgia on July 12, 1947, to Turner and Mary Gary. Because his mother had complications following his birth, and because they were too poor to pay the bills, the Gary's had to sell their two-hundred-acre farm. The following year, Turner Gary moved to Florida with his wife and seven children.

Over the years, a total of eleven children were born to the Garys, each traveling with their parents to Georgia and the Carolinas, to harvest sugar cane and beans. For Willie, the hardest part of this life was missing school. Because, as a migrant child, he was only allowed to attend for half a day, young Willie yearned for more. He knew that education was his way out of the lifestyle he currently had. Because he was an All-State football player, he looked forward to an athletic scholarship that would make it possible for him to attend college. Unfortunately, he failed to make the team at Bethune-Cookman College and was instructed to vacate the campus. After swallowing his disappointment and returning home, his former coach and mentor told him to, "Just show up and take your chances at Shaw University." Two days later, he was on a Greyhound bus, headed for Raleigh, North Carolina.

Despite his optimism, history repeated itself; there was no room on the Shaw team for Gary either. Penniless, with only a cardboard suitcase and a few clothes, Gary had no place else to go. He slept in the lobby of one of the dormitories, making a couch his bed, borrowing blankets to keep warm. Not able to even afford something to eat, his meals came from the leftovers of other students.

Finally, though, he received the break he needed. Due to an injured player, on Shaw's team, who had to be replaced, Gary was given another chance. Because he made sure he put all he had into his performance, he was finally awarded an athletic scholarship to Shaw University.

While still a student, he married his childhood sweetheart Gloria Royal and witnessed the birth of the first of his four sons. He went on to graduate from Shaw with a Bachelor's degree in business administration. After earning his L.L.D. degree from North Carolina Central University, he moved back to Florida. In 1975, he was admitted to the Florida Bar, and became the first African-American to open a law firm in Martin County, Florida. In one year, through consistent delivery of excellent services, Gary's firm added on an associate, two secretaries, and a second office in Fort Pierce, Florida.

Considered one of the nations best trial lawyers, Gary now has a firm with eighteen attorneys, as well as a professional staff of eighty, and serves as general counsel to former presidential candidate and Rainbow Coalition founder Reverend Jesse Jackson.

Gary's honors include Turner Broadcasting System's Golden Trumpet Award and the NAACP Image Award Key of Life. In addition, he has appeared on the *Oprah Winfrey Show*, and Robin Leach's *Lifestyles of the Rich and Famous*. Gary was also featured on *CBS Evening News*.

Stories about Gary have appeared in the *National Law Journal*, *Ebony* magazine, *The New York Times*, the *Orlando Sentinel*, *Black Enterprise*, and *The Boston Globe*.

Willie Edward Gary demonstrates that through courage, tenacity and faith, not even the sky is the limit.

"To manage a business successfully requires as much courage as that possessed by the soldier who goes to war. Business courage is the more natural because all the benefits which the public has in material wealth come from it."

—*Charles F. Abbott*

Berry Gordy, Jr. (b. 1929)
Music Executive

s a child, he won a talent contest singing his own song, *Berry's Boogie*. He was once a boxer. His sparring partner was the great soul singer Jackie Wilson, but his mother decried his giving up high school to become a professional prize fighter. He is a U.S. Army veteran (1951 - 1953), who returned from military service to work in the family's construction and printing businesses. And always, he carried within him the love of music.

He opened *Jazz*, a record store in Detroit in 1953, but the business failed in two years because of the stiff competition from rhythm and blues. Berry Gordy then went to work on a Ford Motor Company assembly line. In his spare time, he wrote and published songs, including *Money, That's What I Want*, and Jackie Wilson hits including, *Lonely Teardrops* (1958) and *I'll Be Satisfied* (1959).

He recorded *Get A Job*, the first record of Smokey Robinson and the Miracles (1958). Gordy became less satisfied, however, with leasing his recordings to larger companies, since they often took over distribution also. The answer was to form his own company. Under the suggestion of Robinson, Gordy borrowed eight hundred dollars and founded both Gordy Records and Tamla Records, which would later carry the Motown label. Gordy would go on to build Motown Industries, which would include a record, motion picture and publishing division.

With his own company, he began releasing popular tunes including *Way Over There* (1959), and *Shop Around* (1961). As his business grew, Gordy began hiring family and friends. He attracted new talents including Marvin Gaye, Mary Wells, Stevie Wonder and Diana Ross. He hired a songwriting team from his headquarters at Detroit's Grand Boulevard, and formed the management and publishing companies that would become part of Motown. For ten years, it would dominate the soul music market.

Gordy developed a strong interest in film and television in the mid-1960s and began spending more and more time in Los Angeles. Discontent arose in his ranks, as writers, producers and performers complained about the way he handled their finances and how he had misled them. He was quite wealthy by then, and eventually moved Motown to Los Angeles, where he produced *Lady Sings The Blues* (1973); *Mahogany* (1975); and *The Wiz* (1978). None were very profitable. But by 1983, Motown had become the country's most successful African-American owned business. Gordy allowed MCA to distribute Motown's records in 1984, and in 1988, he sold it for six million dollars. He maintained control of Gordy Industries, which includes the music publishing, television and film subsidiaries. In 1986, *Forbes* estimated his financial worth at more than 180 million dollars. He had become one of America's wealthiest businessmen. By the late 1980s through the 1990s, Gordy's business interests expanded to include ownership and training of racehorses, and sports management.

It has been said that he is responsible for selling soul music to the white population, and in doing so, created a vast multi-racial youth audience. In 1988, he was inducted into the Rock and Roll Hall of Fame.

HISTORY IN A CAPSULE

The oldest African-American business in America is the C.H. James and Company Fresh Fruit and Vegetable distributors. It began in West Virginia in 1883, when Charles H. James sold trinkets, vegetables and fruit door to door. It is now an 18 million-dollar-a-year food wholesaler, headed by Charles H. James III, James' great-grandson.

Earl Graves
Publisher
Businessman

BLACK ENTERPRISE Magazine

"America is the greatest country in the free world. Our best history is in front of us if we are willing to accept the reality that African-Americans must share in its bounty." **—Earl G. Graves**

Earl G. Graves (b. 1935)
CEO, Earl G. Graves Ltd.

His company has been listed consistently in the top one hundred most successful African-American businesses in America, and in 1972, the President of the United States named Earl Gilbert Graves one of the ten most outstanding minority businessmen in the country.

Born in Brooklyn, New York, to Winifred and Earl Godwin Graves, he attended the public primary and secondary schools of the area. He earned his bachelor's degree in economics from Morgan State College (Baltimore, Maryland) in 1958. He was a ROTC graduate, attended Airborne and Ranger School, and finished his Army career as a Captain. He was a member of the 19th Special Forces Group of the Green Berets, and received the U.S. Army Commendation Award.

He once worked as a natcotics agent with the Justice Department, and sold real estate in the Bedford Stuyvesant area of Brooklyn. He was Administrative Assistant to Robert F. Kennedy from 1965 to 1968. After the Senator's assassination, Graves formed his own management consultant firm. His clients included major multi-national companies.

In 1969, with a grant from the Ford Foundation, he studied black-owned businesses in the Caribbean. It was during this period that the idea for a magazine for black American professionals, executives, policy makers and entrepreneurs was born.

He launched *Black Enterprise* in 1970, with a one hundred fifty thousand dollar loan from Chase Manhattan Bank. The monthly glossy magazine had an initial subscriber list of one hundred thousand. By providing his initial subscribers with timely articles, tips on running a successful enterprise and interviews with successful black bosses, his readership has expanded to 3.1 million. His subscriptions number three hundred thousand. Yearly sales are now over twenty-four million dollars and are increasing steadily.

One of the magazine's most popular features is the *BE 100,*which ranks the top black-owned businesses in America. Premiering in 1973, it became the standard by which African-American businesses are judged successful. Other favorite features include the *Twenty-five Best Places for Blacks to Work, The Top Twenty-five African-Americans on Wall St.*, and the *Forty Most Powerful Black Executives.*

Though best known as the publisher of Black Enterprise, Graves is also chairman and Chief Executive Officer of Pepsi-Cola of Washington, D.C., L.F., the largest minority-controlled Pepsi-Cola franchise in the United States. The sixty million dollar franchise, acquired in July, 1990, stretches over four hundred square miles, that includes Washington, D.C. and Prince George's County, Maryland.

Earl Graves is also director of Aetna Life and Casualty Company, AMR Corporation of American Airlines, Chrysler Corporation, Federated Department Stores, Inc., and Rohm and Haas Corporation.

As a staunch advocate of higher education and equal opportunity, he established BE Unlimited, which is responsible for the Entrepreneurial Conference and the BE/Pepsi Golf and Tennis Challenge. He plans to develop new businesses to expand early entrepreneurial training for youngsters ages five through eighteen. He recently made a one million dollar pledge toward the advancement of business education at Morgan State University.

Graves has received many business and professional citations, 37 honorary degrees, and was inducted into the National Black College Hall of Fame. He is a Poynter Fellow, has lectured at Yale University, and is a sought after speaker. Earl Graves is also the author of *How To Succeed in Business Without Being White* (April 1997).

"Whoever shuts his ears to the cry of the poor will also cry himself and not be heard." —**Proverbs 21:13, Old Testament, NKJV**

Addie L. Greene (b. 1943)
Government Official

As the first African-American elected to represent Palm Beach County in the Florida House of Representatives, Addie L. Greene became the voice of the powerless. Her first bill to become law was the Farmworkers-Right-to-Know. This gave all migrants the right to know which pesticides were being used in the fields in which they worked.

In 1995 Greene accompanied Florida's governor, Lawton Chiles, on a historic mission to Johannesburg, South Africa, to sign a sister-state agreement. This marked the first formal state-to-state relationship a South African province has established with an American state since President Nelson Mandela's inauguration.

Greene was born in Birmingham, Alabama. She received her Bachelor of Science degree from Stillman College in Tuscaloosa, Alabama, in 1961, and her

Master of Education degree from Florida Agricultural and Mechanical University (Tallahassee, Florida) in 1963. She began her career in politics when she became the first African-American female to serve on the Council of Mangonia Park. She later became vice-mayor, and in 1990, was elected mayor. In 1992, Greene was, again, the first African-American woman elected to represent Palm Beach County in the Florida House of Representatives. During her first term, she was elected secretary of the Florida Conference of Black Elected Officials and is presently in her third term. As a member of the Florida House of Representatives, Greene has served as Chairman of Employee and Management Relations, is a member of Aging and Human Services, Agriculture and Consumer Services, Higher Education, Community Affairs, and Corrections.

She is active in many organizations, including the Florida Conference of Black State Legislators, Enterprise Florida, the NAACP, the Urban League, Big Brothers/Big Sisters, and the Conference of Women Legislators.

Several publications list her biography, including *Who's Who in Education in the South and Southeast* and *Who's Who in American Politics.*

Other memberships include Alpha Kappa Alpha Sorority, the Business and Professional Women of Palm Beach County and the Palm Beach County Minority Consortium. She also serves on the Haitian American Democratic Association, Inc. She is an active member of Mount Olive Baptist Church.

DID YOU KNOW?

♦ Greene has taught in several Palm Beach County schools.
♦ She is also a communications instructor at Palm Beach Community College.
♦ Greene was a JM Family Enterprises Minority Achievement Awards nominee.
♦ She was the first African-American to be selected Teacher of the Year at Pahokee High School.

"...when you start talking about family, about lineage and ancestry, you are talking about every person on earth."   —*Alex Haley*

Alex Haley (1921-1992)
Journalist, Lecturer, Historical Novelist

His first book was his first best-seller. *The Authobiography of Malcolm X*, published in 1965, sold over five million copies. But it was the historical novel, *Roots: The Saga of an American Family* that is best described as a phenomenon. Though more copies of *Malcom X* were sold, the *Roots* television series, aired in eight segments, attracted an estimated one hundred thirty million viewers. It ranks among the most watched events in history. According to *Time* magazine, some African-American leaders referred to *Roots* as "the most important civil rights event since the march on Selma."

Newsweek stated, "Instead of writing a scholarly monograph of little social impact, Haley has written a blockbuster...that will reach millions of people and alter the way we see ourselves."

A combination of history and fiction, Haley used factual narrative, but created the characters' dialogue and feelings, and some of the events in their lives. To truly empathize with his ancestor, Kunta Kinte, who was kidnaped, brought to the United States, and sold into slavery, Haley slept on board in the hold of a ship bound for America from Liberia, clad only in his underwear.

Both *Malcom X*, coauthored with Malcolm, and *Roots*, published in 1976, have become required reading in many schools and universities.

Haley initiated the interview feature in *Playboy* magazine in 1962, and it was his dialogue with Malcolm X, that led to the writing of his autobiography.

He was born in Ithaca, New York, to Professor Simon Alexander Haley, and teacher Bertha George Haley, but grew up in Henning, Tennessee. His career in school was lackluster, and he spent only two years at Elizabeth City Teacher's College before dropping out to volunteer to serve in the Coast Guard. He spent his leisure time writing letters, reading, and composing adventure stories. He served from 1939 through 1959. While there, he served as Chief Journalist, a position that was created for him.

Upon reentering civilian life, he tried making a living as a freelance writer, and endured many rejections before becoming an established author. He wrote articles for magazines such as *Reader's Digest, Atlantic, New York Times* and *Harper's*.

Inspired by vivid stories of his ancestors, he spent twelve years exploring libraries, repositories, and archives to establish the existence and origin of Kunta Kinte. His research led him to the Gambia in Africa, where a griot — an oral historian — recited the circumstances of the disappearance of Kunta Kinte over two hundred years ago.

As a celebrated author, Haley served as script consultant for *Roots, Roots: The Next Generation*, and *Palmerstown, U.S.A.* He was a founding member of the Black Academy of Arts and Letters, and was founder and president of the Kinte Foundation, whose purpose was to establish the first African-American genealogical library in Washington, D.C.

His many awards include special citations for *Roots* from the National Book Award and Pulitzer Prize committees in 1977, the NAACP's Sprigarn Medal, also in 1977, and a nomination to the Black Filmmakers Hall of Fame in 1981 for producing *Palmerstown, U.S.A.* He also became the first person in the history of any race to be awarded an honorary degree from the Coast Guard Academy.

Many credited Haley's unparalleled success with *Roots* to its appeal to the oldest institution on earth — that of family.

George Cleveland Hall - Physician

"The actions of men are like the index of a book; they point out what is most remarkable in them." **—David Thomas**

George Cleveland Hall (1864-1930)
Physician, Educator

He was the total package: diagnostician, surgeon, educator, suave politician. He was one of the founders of Chicago's Provident Hospital, and helped to build a continuing education program so black surgeons could have a place, and the opportunity to increase their skills in an age, when they were largely excluded from mainstream medical facilities. The institution served physicians nationwide. He also established regional programs to accommodate Southern doctors, who could not afford to travel to Chicago, to attend the clinics.

Dr. George Cleveland Hall used his persuasive ability and political savvy to raise three million dollars to build a new, modern hospital with the help of Julius Rosenwald and other benefactors.

He spent most of his career at Provident Hospital, serving, at different times, as chief of staff, surgeon, assistant in gynecology, chairman of the medical advisory board, and as a member of the board of trustees.

His undisputed leadership came after a clash of egos, when eminent surgeon Dr. Daniel Hale Williams returned from a stay at Freedman's hospital to find that Hall had taken over the leadership of Provident. The feud became public and personal, with Dr. Williams finally resigning from the institution he had co-founded.

Dr. Hall, with his brilliant professional and social skills, expanded the services of Provident to include clinics in Tennessee, Alabama, Georgia, Virginia, and Missouri, and helped to institute infirmaries throughout larger Southern cities.

He was also sensitive to the political climate of the times, and was active in the National Association for the Advancement of Colored People. He was responsible for bringing the Urban League to Chicago, and was director and treasurer of the Frederick Douglass Center. He was one of the founders of the Association for the Study of Negro Life and History, along with Dr. Carter G. Woodson, who instituted Negro History Week (which later became Black History Month).

Born in Ypsilanti, Michigan, his family moved to Chicago where he completed high school. He earned his Bachelor's degree from Lincoln University in Pennsylvania and received his M.D. degree from Bennett Medical College in Chicago (1888), with a specialty in surgery. He practiced in Chicago for a while, and later teamed with heart surgeon Dr. Daniel Hale Williams. Hall was chief surgeon, and Williams performed heart surgery.

After their conflict resulted in Williams' resignation from Provident, Hall remained active in the hospital as well as in other civic and political pursuits. As a member of the library board of Chicago, he advocated African-American needs and interests.

He also supported other institutions, including Fisk University, Tuskegee Institute, and Meharry Medical College. He helped to obtain a half-million dollar endowment for Lincoln University. Many outstanding citizens, including Governor Lowden of Illinois, and Booker T. Washington, the famous educator, solicited his opinions on civil, political, and education issues.

Dr. George Cleveland Hall, a man of great intelligence, with many skills and interests, supported, without hesitation, other individuals and institutions that sought to better the lives of African-Americans.

"All my life, I've been sick and tired. Now I'm sick and tired of being sick and tired." —**Fannie Lou Hamer**

Fannie Lou Hamer (1917-1975)
Civil Rights Activist

Because she passed a test on the Constitution that was designed to keep African-Americans from voting in Mississippi, she and her husband lost their jobs, and were forced to leave town. Wherever they went, however, harassment followed them. Sixteen shots were fired into their home by night riders in 1962, but Fannie Lou Hamer, unintimidated, stepped up her voter registration activities.

In 1963, she and fellow Student Nonviolent Coordinating Committee (SNCC) members were arrested upon returning from a committee workshop in Montgomery County, Mississippi. She was beaten severely by a state patrolman.

Still undeterred, she became a candidate for Congress in the Second Congressional District of Mississippi. Figures show that only 4 percent of blacks from a fifty-nine percent African-American majority were registered to vote in

1960. The discriminatory practices of the state frightened most of the prospective voters away from the Mississippi voting booths. Even though Fannie Lou Hamer no doubt knew that her campaign was futile, it did accomplish a victory — it mobilized African-Americans to action.

It was during this time that she became an instrumental figure in organizing the Mississippi Freedom Democratic Party. They were defeated at the 1964 Democratic Convention in a struggle to represent the state, but at the 1968 convention in Chicago, the violent tactics employed in the state of Mississippi, to exclude blacks came to light. Only the Freedom Democrats were seated.

Because of Hamer's courage and her refusal to be intimidated, the South's institutionalized racism was dealt a death blow in the State of Mississippi.

Though she faced violence and the threat of death for many years as she labored to bring the right to vote to African-Americans, her courage was not given national recognition before the 1968 Democratic Convention.

She spent the remainder of her life working to improve economic opportunities for Mississippi blacks. She founded and operated a garment factory and the Freedom Farm Cooperative.

The youngest of twenty children born to poor parents in Montgomery, Mississippi, Fannie Lou experienced the sting of segregation at an early age, and because of the many obligations to her family, never completed her education. Though she was unlettered, she possessed keen insight into the human psyche.

She and her husband, Parry Hamer, adopted two girls and lived an uneventful life until her attempt to register to vote in 1962. A courageous woman of great inner strength, her life was cut short by cancer at age fifty-eight.

". . . I aimed to use all that is characteristic of the Negro from Africa to Alabama."
—W.C. Handy, on composing "St. Louis Blues"

William Christopher (W.C.) Handy
(1873-1958) Musician

He won the title of "Father of the Blues" after writing *Mr. Crump* for a Memphis politician — a composition that caused dancing in the streets. It was a new kind of syncopated music that began a tone on an unaccented beat, and held it into an accented one. The tune was retitled *Memphis Blues.*

His initial venture into publishing and marketing *Memphis Blues* met with unscrupulous dealers who cheated him out of proceeds from his work. As a result, he established the Pace and Handy Music Company in 1913, and published *St. Louis Blues* the following year.

Born in Florence, Alabama, the son of a minister, W.C. Handy, as he came to be known, learned the elements of music in chuch and the public schools. While in junior high, he began arranging parts in the church chorus. By the age of

123

eighteen, he left home and went to Chicago, then St. Louis. To earn money for food and other necessities, he worked at odd jobs, and played his trumpet. It was in 1896 that Mahara's Minstrels hired him as bandmaster. He traveled the United States, Mexico, Cuba and Canada.

After serving as a music teacher for a short while, he decided that Memphis was where he could make the greatest impact with his music, and where his chances of success were better. There he created and renamed *Mr. Crump,* and published his *St. Louis Blues.*

By 1918, his new music form was in demand and he relocated his publishing company to New York. World War I came and went, and jazz became the craze. His fame soared, and by 1928, he found himself directing "History of Music," a concert held at Carnegie Hall. He employed African-American artists to reenact the historical development of black music from slavery to the then present.

He wrote both sacred and secular music. Tragically, he lost his eyesight, but continued his production of music. In 1931, the city of Memphis honored him by naming a park for him, and established the two hundred thousand dollar W.C. Hardy Theater in 1947.

DID YOU KNOW?

- ◆ His grandfather was also a clergyman.
- ◆ He received his early education at home.
- ◆ Handy once worked in the iron mines.
- ◆ He helped form the National Association of Negro Musicians and the National Association of American Composers & Conductors.
- ◆ He established the W.C. Handy Foundation for blind people of color.
- ◆ Other famous compositions include *Harlem Blues* and *Beale Street Blues.*

HISTORY IN A CAPSULE:

Musical research suggests that the roots of the blues are African, based on repeated refrain patterns, the falsetto break in the vocal style, and the expressive pitch inflections or blue notes. Early historians place it in the rural South, in the Mississippi Delta region, where W.C. Handy reported hearing it for the first time in 1895. It influenced all styles of jazz, contemporary, rock and popular music.

"There is only one virtue, pugnacity; only one vice, pacifism. That is the essential condition of war." **—Shaw**

Lemuel Haynes (1753-1833)
Minister, Minuteman

He was as much an activist as a minister, and apparently saw no contradiction between the two vocations. His interest in the ministry was no doubt whetted by Deacon David Rose, in whose home he lived after being deserted by his mother.

Because it was the custom that esteemed pastors read their sermons on the evening before the delivery, Haynes was familiar with biblical principles from his youth. And inasmuch as the deacon was nearly blind, it became Lemuel's duty to read Rose's sermons. One evening, he surprised the family by reading an unusual text. The deacon enjoyed it so much, he inquired who the author was. Lemuel admitted that he had written it.

Because of the depth of the sermon, the family felt that he was called to minister. At the outbreak of the Revolutionary War, however, Haynes joined the revolutionaries.

In 1774, he served as a minuteman. After the Battle of Lexington, he enlisted as a regular soldier. It was after his duty in the Continental Army that he seriously devoted his time to studying for the ministry. He also learned Latin and Greek.

In 1780, he was licensed to preach, ordained shortly afterward, and pastored the Congregational Church of Middle Granville.

Born of a black father and a white mother, in West Hartford, Connecticut, he attended the district's schools. His early training in the Christian religion received full realization as he progressed as minister from the Middle Granville to a Torrington, Connecticut church, where he was rejected because of his black ancestry. In time, however, the congregation accepted him.

He was eventually called on by the Vermont and Connecticut Missionary Societies to conduct revivals, and was prominent in the church's "Great Awakening."

Haynes lost the support of many of his members because he denigrated New Englanders who supported states' rights. The controversy was of such magnitude that Haynes resigned, and accepted a Congregational pastorship in New York.

Lemuel Haynes overcame racism and desertion by his mother and focused on his patriotic and pastoral duties. He dedicated his life to the positions to which he felt he called.

HISTORY IN A CAPSULE:

Said to be ready for service in a minute's notice, the minutemen were created in Massachusetts in 1774 by an act of the provincial congress. They were most active in Boston and surrounding areas before the actual commencing of the United States War of Independence. Minutemen fought in the opening actions in defense of the Americans against the British, at Lexington and Concord, in 1775. Shortly after, they were absorbed into the newly formed Eight Months Army. Upon the recommendation of the Continental Congress the same year, minutemen regiments were formed in other colonies.

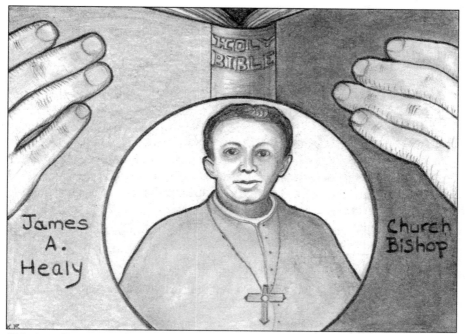

James
A.
Healy

Church
Bishop

"It is too often seen, that the wiser men are about the things of this world, the less wise they are about the things of the next." **—Gibson**

James Augustine Healy (1830-1900)
Catholic Bishop

Toward the end of James Augustine Healy's life, he was assistant to the papal throne, a position that ranks just below that of cardinal in the Catholic hierarchy.

In 1875, he was consecrated Bishop of Portland, Maine, and was the first American of African descent to become a bishop in the Roman Catholic Church.

The son of a slave mother and a white planter, he was born in Macon, Georgia. Healy was educated in Burlington, New York, at the Franklin Park Quaker School and also attended school in New Jersey. He continued his education at Holy Cross College in Worcester, Massachusetts. He graduated with highest honors in 1849.

By then, both of Healy's parents were dead, and his father's wealthy friends provided the financial means and the encouragement for him to continue studying at the Sulpician Seminary in Montreal, Canada. Three years later, he enrolled in a corresponding institution in Paris, France.

After being ordained to the priesthood at Notre Dame Cathedral in Paris in 1854, he returned to the United States and worked for eleven years as a bishop's secretary and as chancellor of the diocese in Boston. In 1866, he became pastor of St. James Catholic Church located in a Boston neighborhood with a heavily Irish constituency. They were initially reluctant to accept him. After an outbreak of influenza, tuberculosis and typhoid, however, he administered the sacraments to the victims at the risk of his own life. The Irish parishioners then fully accepted him after witnessing the faithful execution of his duties as priest.

As chancellor of the diocese, he assisted Bishop John Fitzpatrick of Boston, took charge of official correspondence, the account books and other required duties. Well-prepared by his experience, he was elevated to bishop by Pope Pius IX in 1875. For twenty-five years, Healy presided over the diocese of New Hampshire and Maine. During his tenure, eighteen parochial schools, sixty-eight missions and fifty new churches were established.

Healy was made assistant to the papal throne in 1900 by Pope Leo XIII. Two months later, he died.

His brother, Patrick Francis Healy, S.J., Ph.D., was the only president of African descent in the history of Georgetown University in Washington, D.C., and the first American of African descent to earn a Ph.D.

DID YOU KNOW?

♦ Healy's father, an Irish immigrant, challenged Georgia's law and married Healy's mother, who was a slave.
♦ Because of his work with needy youngsters, he was known as "the children's bishop."
♦ Healy's work with the poor was brought to the attention of Pope Pius IX prior to his being elevated to bishop.

"A coward flees backwards, away from new things. A man of courage flees forward, in the midst of new things." **—Jacques Maritain**

Josiah Henson (1789-1883)
Abolitionist

His master mistook Josiah Henson's "Uncle Tom" affectation for submissiveness and acceptance of slavery as his lot in life. He came to trust him and made Henson an overseer. He allowed him to transport a group of fellow slaves to a relative in Kentucky. After working there for three years, he tried to purchase his own freedom but was badly cheated. To make matters worse, Henson heard that he was to be sold to another owner in New Orleans. He took his wife and two children and made a daring escape into Ohio, but the Fugitive Slave Law of 1850 made his existence as a free man perilous. He then fled to Canada where he worked to free other slaves.

To make clear to the Canadians the brutality of slavery, Henson showed them his scars, and how he had been maimed while in Maryland.

His virulent hatred for slavery was instilled in him at an early age when he saw his father mutilated because he came to the aid of his wife, who was being badly beaten by an overseer. Both of his parents were subsequently sold, and Josiah was left without either parent. He was unable to obtain an education as a child, but was taught to read and write by one of his sons.

He was forty years old when he escaped by the Underground Railroad. He co-founded the British-American Manual Labor Institute while in Canada, and also worked fervently as an abolitionist. He became an Underground Railroad agent, and in fourteen days, freed thirty Kentucky slaves. On another occasion, he freed one hundred eighteen. To play it safe, he took a roundabout route to Kentucky, which carried him through New York, Pennsylvania and Ohio. The arduous journey paid off in the freeing of others in bondage.

Henson was born in Maryland, and witnessed and endured slavery at its worst. The horrors he experienced made such an impression on him that he returned to the South several times at risk of his own life and freedom, to help other slaves to escape. He and other emancipators entered the South at great risk, and took great care not to arouse suspicion.

As an Underground Railroad agent, Josiah Henson was among the most courageous figures of the pre-Civil War era. But for all of his daring and close brushes with danger, he lived to be ninety-four years of age.

HISTORY IN A CAPSULE

Though information on Saul Matthews is scarce, this Virginia Army spy was granted his freedom in 1792 because, in the words of Colonel Josiah Parker, he deserved the acclaim of his country for his bravery.

Matthews did not support the British as did some other slaves, who hoped that doing so would gain them their freedom. He offered his services to Virginia in a time when Cornwallis controlled Portsmouth (Virginia). Colonel Josiah Parker, who commanded the four area counties, was ordered by his superiors to determine the position of British troops, and their movement on the James River.

Parker had full confidence in Saul Matthews, and sent him to gather information essential to the survival and victory of the Virginia Army. He penetrated the British lines, and gathered the necessary data. Matthews later led a raiding party in which the Virginia army captured many British prisoners. Cornwallis became so agitated that he moved his troops to another position. Because an African-American risked his life and safety to gather necessary information for American soldiers, a British officer in command of a superior army rerouted his troops.

Matthew A. Henson

Explorer

KBelMonte

"It is a profound mistake to think that everything has been discovered; as well as think the horizon the boundary of the world."   **—Lemierre**

Matthew Alexander Henson
(1866-1955) Explorer

When the Eskimos saw his brown skin, they thought Matthew Henson to be akin to them. He became an expert in handling dog sleds and equipment during his many expeditions with Admiral Robert E. Peary to the polar region. As an associate, he accompanied Peary on his expedition to the North Pole in 1891. Born in Charles County, Maryland, he attended the N Street School for six years. He became an orphan at the age of 8 and was reared by an uncle in Washington, D.C. Possessing the heart of an adventurer, he sailed to China as a cabin boy when he was 13 years old and later made trips to the South Pacific Islands, Africa, Asia and Europe.

He met Peary in 1888, and the civil engineer of the United States Navy allowed Henson to accompany him to Nicaragua. He also became the League Island Navy yard messenger. As his trusted friend and helper, Henson accompanied Peary to the Arctic on expeditions in 1900, 1902 and 1905. In 1908, they traveled inland for 100 miles from Disko Bay, across the Greenland ice sheet. During their expeditions, they studied an isolated tribe of Eskimos (Arctic Highlander) that assisted them greatly. Once they determined the precise point of the North Pole, they reached the spot in March of 1909, with four Eskimos. By then, Peary was unable to continue on foot. Accounts differ, with some citing snowblindness, frozen toes and illness as reasons Henson went ahead and planted the United States flag on the exact spot that they had determined. Thus, Henson became the first man to set foot on the North Pole.

Though Dr. Frederick A. Cook claimed to have reached the Pole in 1908, ahead of Peary and Henson, his claim is generally discredited. Though Peary and Henson were both hailed as having discovered the North Pole together, Henson was generally left out of historical accounts.

After his days of exploring were over, he spent the next 30 years working as a clerk in a New York Federal Customs House. It was not until 1945 that he was awarded a silver medal, which was a duplicate of the one given to Admiral Peary.

Through the tenacious effort of a Harvard University professor of history, his body was moved to Arlington National Cemetery and interred next to Admiral Peary's. He had been previously buried in a shared grave in New York.

Before his death in 1955, Henson was honored for his contributions by Presidents Truman and Eisenhower.

DID YOU KNOW?

♦ Henson mastered the Eskimo language during his many trips to the Arctic.

♦ Peary chose Henson as one of a team of six, in his third attempt to reach the North Pole.

♦ In 1912, Henson published his account of the expedition in *A Negro Explorer at the North Pole*.

♦ He was also an accomplished seaman.

♦ While Admiral Peary received many awards and honors, Henson was largely ignored.

♦ He was reburied at Arlington National Cemetery with full military honors.

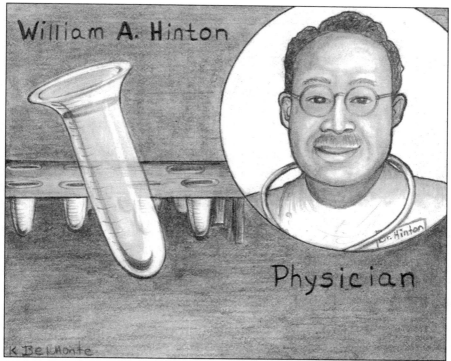

William A. Hinton

Physician

K Belmonte

"Human learning, with the blessing of God upon it, introduces us to divine wisdom, and while we study the works of nature, the God of nature will manifest Himself to us." —**George Horne**

William Augustus Hinton (1883-1959)
Physician, Educator

is book, *Syphilis and Its Treatment*, published in 1936, became a universally recognized medical reference work. As a bacteriologist and serologist, he developed the sensitive Hinton test for syphilis and dedicated his life to the study and cure of venereal diseases. He was co-developer of the Davies-Hinton tests of blood and spinal fluids.

Born in Chicago, Illinois, he graduated from Harvard University, where he received his B.S. degree in 1905, and his M.D. degree, with honors, in 1912. He was appointed as director of the Boston Dispensary's laboratory department in 1915 and served as its chief for 38 years. Also in 1915, he was appointed director of the Wassermann Laboratory of the Massachusetts Department of Public Health and was simultaneously assigned as instructor of preventive medicine and hygiene at Harvard. He was instructor in bacteriology and immunology (1921 - 1946) and was later promoted to clinical professor.

He served as special consultant to the Massachusetts School for Crippled Children and for the United States Public Health Service. He was a member of the American Medical Association, the American Association for the Advancement of Science and the American Society of Clinical Pathology.

Dr. Hinton did much to challenge the belief that contracting syphilis was largely due to race. He believed it to be related to socio-economic conditions and largely the result of ignorance and poverty. He was held in such high esteem that his book on the treatment of syphilis was well respected in both the United States and Europe. *Lancet*, the highly regarded British medical journal, hailed it as a great contribution to the study and treatment of the disease.

From many classes of volunteers, he established a technician's school at the Boston Dispensary and graduated 432 students over a twenty-year period. Each graduate received immediate employment in the country's laboratories and hospitals.

In 1940, Hinton lost a leg in an automobile accident, but did not allow his misfortune to interfere with his continuing achievements.

He was also a skilled carpenter and gardener. In the early years of marriage, he and his wife had little money and bought a "handyman's special" house. Dr. Hinton added rooms, a porch and a garage, and landscaped it with beautiful trees and flowers. His home became known for its beauty and charm.

In spite of his many achievements, he declined the Sprigarn Medal that was presented to him during the late 1930s, feeling that he had not accomplished enough for such an honor.

HISTORY IN A CAPSULE

The first African-American male to earn a medical degree was James McCune Smith, who graduated from the University of Glasgow (Scotland) in 1837. His father was an affluent merchant, and Smith was an ardent abolitionist. He opened a practice in New York City.

"It is not possible to found a lasting power upon injustice, perjury, and treachery."
—Demosthenes

William Meredith Holland, Sr. (nda)
Attorney, Civil Rights Advocate

T he administrative complex of the Palm Beach County (Florida) School System is modern and imposing. In 1997, it was renamed the Fulton-Holland Educational Complex, for a former superintendent and a once-bitter foe, William M. Holland Sr., a slightly built, soft-spoken attorney whose demeanor has been known to lull his adversaries into a false sense of security.

In August, 1956, his son, William Holland, Jr., was denied entry into a Palm Beach County school because of his race. Attorney Holland challenged the discriminatory practice and prevailed. As a result, the county, with one of the largest school districts in the nation, was required to desegregate and to admit all children regardless of race. It was also required to integrate its teaching and administrative staffs.

The first integration came in 1961, with the county's junior college and high schools. The desegregation of elementary schools followed in 1962, and by 1972 Palm Beach County achieved a unitary school system.

Other Civil Rights and Constitutional law victories include the integration of, and nondiscriminatory transportation to and from, Palm Beach International Airport as well as the integration of municipal swimming pools, golf courses, playgrounds, parks, cemeteries, libraries, and other public facilities. Holland also played major roles in opening employment for minorities in Palm Beach County municipal companies and department stores, and in the desegregation of the facilities of Florida's Turnpike and county beaches. He worked to achieve fair housing and was an Attorney at Case establishing "Totten Trusts" in Florida.

Born in Live Oak, Florida, his father, Isaac Holland, was a caretaker and labor contractor and his mother, Annie, was a housewife and maid. He attended elementary and high school in Orlando, Florida, where he grew up, and later graduated from Jones High School. He earned his Bachelor of Arts degree from Florida A&M, and also attended Boston University, where he earned his Doctor of Juris degree.

He was admitted to practice in Florida in 1951, to the United States District and the United States Court of Appeals in 1952, and to the United States Supreme Court in 1956. Holland was a Municipal Judge in Riviera Beach, Florida from 1972 to 1977.

His affiliations include the Florida Bar, American Bar Association, Civil Rights and Responsibilities Committee of the American Bar Association, Palm Beach County Bar Association and the American Judicata Society. He is a past member of the Board of Directors of Florida Rural Legal Services Inc., and director of the Florida Municipal Judges Association.

A veteran of World War II, he served in the European and Asiatic Theaters. He has traveled extensively through North, Central and South America, Europe, Asia and Africa.

His honors include the National Business League and Phi Delta Kappa service awards, the Human Resources Award of the American Bicentennial Year, the Florida Alumni Association Award, the Hadassah Myrtle Wreath Award for Outstanding Contributions to Civil Rights, the Distinguished Award of the State of Florida, Phi Beta Sigma Fraternity Social Action Award, the Urban League's Martin Luther King Award, and the NAACP Community Service and Equal Justice Award. He was a torchbearer for the 1997 Olympics, and received the 1997 Sigma Gamma Rho Sorority Distinguished Community Service Award in Law.

He is listed in *Who's Who in the South and Southwest, The Dictionary of International Biographies of Community Leaders of America, Who's Who Among Black Americans, The National Social Directory, Two Thousand Men of Achievement, Who's Who in American Law* and *Who's Who of Intellectuals.*

"The one exclusive sign of a thorough knowledge is the power of teaching."

—Aristotle

John Hope (1864-1936)
Educator

John Hope, along with W.E.B. Du Bois, considered Booker T. Washington's leadership of the Negro as compromising and designed to keep African-Americans out of the professions, thus assuring that they would be a permanent under-class.

He was an active NAACP supporter, a member and official in the Association for the Study of Negro Life and History, and served on the Commission on Interracial Cooperation, and the Georgia State Council of Work Among Negro Boys.

Hope was also founder-president of Atlanta's University System. He conceptualized its creation out of concern about the numerous schools in the Atlanta area that operated as separate entities. Du Bois voiced his idea to amalgamate the schools in *The Voice of the Negro* as early as 1904.

His dream was to bring together the Gammon Theological Seminary, Spelman, Clark, Morehouse and Morris Brown Universities. It was partially realized in

1929 when Spelman, Atlanta University and Morehouse became members of the system, each sharing facilities, while maintaining their own administrations.

Atlanta University was the center of graduate study, while Morehouse and Spelman dedicated their efforts to preparing undergraduates with excellence in training. Morris Brown and Clark Universities later joined the system.

John Hope was educated at Worcester Academy, in Massachusetts. He distinguished himself by becoming editor of the student monthly, *The Academy*. In 1886, he graduated with honors. He attended Brown University, again graduating with honors in 1894, and earning his M.A. from the institution in 1907. In 1919, he became a member of Phi Beta Kappa, an honor fraternity.

In a distinguished career, he taught at Roger Williams University, Nashville, Tennessee, and Atlanta Baptist College (Morehouse) where he taught Greek and Latin. He later became one of the first African-Americans to head a black college after the Civil War.

His legacy is the still-thriving kinship of educational institutions originally designed to provide excellence in education for persons of African descent.

DID YOU KNOW?

♦ Morehouse College was referred to as "the Black Harvard."
♦ John Hope received the Sprigarn Medal, posthumously, in 1936 for his contributions to African-Americans.

HISTORY IN A CAPSULE

When Alexander Lucius Twilight received his degree from Middlebury College in 1823, he became the first African-American in the United States to graduate from college. The school later named a building in his honor. He was born in 1795, and was an indentured servant who worked on a farm. He became a minister, teacher and school principal of Brownington Academy, the county's secondary school. He was elected to the Vermont State Legislature in 1836, making him the first African-American state legislator.

He organized surgical demonstrations, developed a continuing education program for Negro doctors, and also served as chief surgeon at the hospital. He supported Meharry Medical College, as well as many other education institutions.

"We love music for the buried hopes, the garnered memories, the tender feelings it can summon at a touch." **—L.E. Landon**

Lena Horne (b. 1917)
Singer

I n 1934, at age sixteen, Lena Calhoun Horne left high school to perform in the Cotton Club in Harlem, for twenty-five dollars per week, to help support her desperately poor family. In an attmept to watch over her pretty daughter, and keep everyone around her "honest," Lena's mother sat in her dressing room while Lena danced in the chorus.

She was born in the Bedford Stuyvesant section of Brooklyn, New York, to Teddy Horne, a numbers banker, and Edna Scottron Horne, an aspiring actress working with the Lafayette Stock Players. Because neither of her parents managed their finances well, they ended up moving in with Teddy's parents, during which time, Lena was born.

Soon after her parents divorced, when she was three, Lena was sent to live with Teddy's mother, Cora Calhoun Horne, while her mother resumed her acting career. An authoritative woman, Cora had registered her granddaughter as a member of the NAACP when she was only two years old.

After developing health problems, Edna returned to New York in 1924, and resumed her care of Lena. In 1933, a friend of Edna's, who worked at the all-white Cotton Club arranged an audition for, then sixteen years old, Lena. Because she was a lovely girl with the light complexion, long straight hair, and tall slim build the promoters liked, she was immediately hired for twenty-five dollars a week. Wisely, she put part of her earnings toward voice and music lessons.

In 1934, Lena was hired by Lawrence Schwab to make her Broadway debut in the unsuccessful *Dance With Your Gods*. She left the Cotton Club and increased her stature among African-Americans when she joined Noble Sissle's Society Orchestra (Philadelphia, 1935).

Over her mother's opposition, she married Louis Jones. During their marriage, which only lasted four years, her two children Gail and Teddy were born. After starring in *Blackbirds*, in 1939, she left Pittsburgh, Jones and her children, and returned to New York. Her career finally took off when she landed a spot with Charlie Barnet's band, becoming the first African-American woman to sing with an all-white orchestra. Having reestablished herself, Lena returned to Pittsburgh for her children. Unfortunately, she was only allowed to take Gail with her; she and Jones shared custody of Teddy.

As her career blossomed, Lena moved to Los Angeles to sing at the prestigious Trocadero and Mocambo nightclubs, where she was spotted by a talent scout for MGM movie studio and offered a contract for two hundred dollars a week. Her first film, *The Duke is Tops*, was made in 1938, before she moved West. She starred in *Cabin in the Sky* and *Stormy Weather* in 1943. Interestingly enough, Lena was given singing roles in "white" movies which didn't relate to the plot, so that she could be cut out when the shows ran in the South. Other early shows include Broadway Rhythm, *Ziegfield Follies*, and *Till The Clouds Roll By*.

She was cast in a dramatic role in 1969, when she appeared with Richard Widmark in *Death of A Gunfighter*. As her movie career ebbed, Lena was featured in Broadway musicals such as *Jamaica*. She continued to record songs, and, in 1981, won a Tony award for *Lena Horne: The Lady and her Music*.

DID YOU KNOW?

♦ Along with Lena Horne, *Stormy Weather* co-starred dancers Katherine Dunham and Bill "Bojangles" Robinson, as well as Cab Calloway, Fats Waller and the Nicholas Brothers.

♦ The revue *Blackbirds* closed after only nine performances.

♦ While travelling with her mother, at age six, she made her acting debut in the play *Madam X*.

"Words are both better and worse than thoughts . . . they give them power for good or evil." —**Tryon Edwards**

James Langston Hughes (1904-1967)
Author

nown as "The Poet Laureate of the Negro Race," Langston Hughes wrote his first short story while still a high school student. His first book of poetry, *The Weary Blues*, published in 1926, brought him recognition in the literary world. A writer of poetry, short stories, novels, biographies, essays, plays and children's books, he was one of the twentieth century's most prolific writers.

Though born in Joplin, Missouri, he graduated from Central High School in Cleveland, Ohio in 1920. He attended Columbia University for a year, and then Lincoln University in Pennsylvania. He left school, and traveled to Africa, China, Europe and Siberia. As he did, he wrote, observed, collected and embodied his experiences in his writings.

He held a variety of odd jobs. While a busboy in a hotel in Washington, D.C., he left some of his poems by the plate of the renowned poet, Vachel Lindsey. He was impressed with Hughes' work, and read them to the audience.

In 1925, he won his first award for poetry. After graduating from Lincoln University in 1929, he published his first novel, *Not Without Laughter.* It was marketed worldwide, and was translated into four languages. His works, which dealt with universal themes, have been translated into more than twenty-five different languages.

In 1950, a play titled *Mullatto* was adapted into *The Barrier*, an opera. The play was written in 1934. He supplied lyrics and libretto for *Troubled Land* in 1949. In 1954, he collaborated with Greer Johnson and Charles Sebree, African-Americans, on *Mrs. Patterson.* In 1957, *Simply Heavenly*, based on Jesse B. Simple, a popular character, made it to Broadway. His *Tambourines to Glory* was directed by Vinette Carroll in 1963.

In his long career, his works of poetry include: *Weary Blues, Dear Lovely Death, Fine Clothes to the Jew, Ask Your Mama,* and *One Way Ticket.* He also authored books, including *The Big Sea, Not Without Laughter, Fields of Wonder, Simple Speaks His Mind, The First Book of Negroes, Famous American Negroes, The First Book of Jazz, I Wonder and I Wander,* and *The Best of Simple.*

Among his many awards and honors are the Witter Bynner prize for excellence in poetry (1926), the Anisfield-Wolfe award (1959), Guggenheim and Rosenwald fellowships, and the Sprigarn Medal (1960).

One of the most sophisticated and esteemed writers of the Harlem Renaissance, Langston Hughes drove faculties and students to re-examine themselves and include curricula that instilled racial pride.

DID YOU KNOW?

♦ Langston Hughes was also a lecturer.
♦ That he was visiting professor at Atlanta University.
♦ He was poet-in-residence at the Laboratory School of the University of Chicago.
♦ He helped to develop young writers and college students.

"Others are affected by what I am and say and do. And these others have also these spheres of influence. So that a single act of mine may spread in widening circles through a nation of humanity." **—Channing**

Frederick S. Humphries (nda)
Educator, Chemist

rederick S. Humphries, a former chemistry professor, proved that he also had the right formula for a successful institution of higher learning. When he was appointed eighth president of Florida A&M University (FAMU) in 1985, he brought new tools and ideas designed to impact the national perception of Historically Black Colleges and Universities (HBCUs). In little more than a decade, he has reestablished FAMU as one of the nation's premier institutions of higher learning. A major goal early in his administration was to challenge Harvard University, the Ivy League giant, in attracting the most National Achievement Scholars (NAS), and America's most academically talented African-American students. During the 1992-1993 school term, Humphries achieved his goal when FAMU enrolled seventy-three NAS students, with Harvard trailing significantly with only forty-nine of the nation's top black students.

Humphries also initiated the Graduate Feeder Program, an innovative approach that increases the number of minorities attending school and the Life-Gets-Better scholarship for academically talented students, which is also a creative recruitment tool. Both initiatives have earned statewide and national recognition.

Under his leadership, FAMU received nearly twenty million dollars in federal and state research monies, nearly tripling the amount at the beginning of his tenure. He also increased a University endowment program from less than five million to over twenty-five million dollars — the largest endowment by a public HBCU in the nation.

He volunteers time to the National Academy of Science, the Planning Committee of the United Negro College Fund Pre-Medical Program, and the Apalachicola Bay Area Resource Planning and Management Committee. Humphries is also a member of the Commission on the Future of the South, the White House Science and Technology Advisory Committee and the Nissan Advisory Committee for HBCUs.

He established the Warner-Lambert (College of Pharmacy and Pharmaceutical Sciences), Garth Reeves (Journalism, Media and Graphic Arts), Anheuser-Busch and Centennial (School of Business and Industry) Eminent Scholar Chairs. Under Humphries' leadership, FAMU recently received a grant from the Department of Defense to establish a Center for Translation Services, which is the only one of its kind in the State University System.

He began his professional career as a commissioned officer in the United States Army (1957-1959). From 1967 to 1968 he was a chemistry professor at FAMU, and joined the staff of the Institute for Services to Education in 1968. He was director of its Innovative Institutional Research Consortium, Summer Conferences, Thirteen-College Curriculum Program, Three-Universities Graduate Programs in the Humanities, and the Knoxville College Study of Science Capability of Black Colleges.

His many honors include the Drum Major for Justice Award in Education (1992), the Distinguished Alumnus Award, University of Pittsburgh (1986), and the FAMU Centennial Medallion (1987). He also received a Certificate of Appreciation, from the Governor of Tennessee, for outstanding service to the state (1982).

Dr. Humphries graduated from Wallace M. Quinn High School in Apalachicola, Florida, earned his B.S. degree at FAMU (Magna Cum Laude, 1957) and his Ph.D. in chemistry from the University of Pittsburgh (1964). A dedicated and dynamic leader, he continues to provide opportunities and services that promote excellence in education for tomorrow's leaders.

"How empty learning, how vain is art, but as it mends the life and guides the heart." — *Young*

Zora Neale Hurston (1903-1960)
Anthropologist, Novelist

 Her characters were three-dimensional, whether in fiction or non-fiction. They were real. They were human. And they lived off the main highway of life, down the dusty lanes and paths that led to scattered flurries of churches, and small frame houses of the unlettered.

Hurston lived and wrote with a passion, impulsiveness, and candor that eventually ostracized her from many of her own people. Though she was one of the more prolific and gifted writers of the Harlem Renaissance, her falling from favor with the black intelligentsia impacted on the popularity of her work. She died penniless in a Fort Pierce nursing home, never to celebrate the rebirth of her work or participate in the Zora Neale Hurston Festival of the Arts and Humanities.

In her first book, *Mules and Men*, she portrays humble blacks in their own cultural matrix. Another anthropological study, *Tell My Horse,* was about a Haitian black. Segregation, carrying with it all the racial hatred, and economic woes that the system spawned, were all explored in 1937's *Their Eyes Were Watching God.* Though it is considered her finest work, black literary contemporaries roundly criticized it because she chose to portray her characters as overcomers who could enjoy their lives, rather than as victims.

Born in Eatonville, Florida, she attended Howard University. It was there that Hurston began writing. She published her first short story in 1921. When she moved to New York in 1925, she found herself amid some of the Harlem Renaissance's most talented and prolific writers.

Earning little money, though she won her share of literary prizes, she worked as novelist Fannie Hurst's secretary, and later earned a scholarship to Barnard College. While there, she studied anthropology under Dr. Frank Boas. When the Association for the Study of Negro Life and History wanted to make a special study of an African-American community in Plateau, Alabama, Dr. Boas recommended Hurston. She was to gather materials about the generations that followed the last slaves to be brought to the United States in 1859. Her article *Cudjo's Own Story of the Last African Slave,* was written for the *Journal of Negro History* in 1927.

In writing her autobiography, *Dust Tracks on a Dirt Road,* in 1943, she again refused to portray herself as a victim. Black critics accused her of pandering to whites. Novelist Richard Wright accused her of reinforcing the minstrel stereotype.

She also alienated black progressives by decrying integration. She believed that black children could learn just as well while sitting next to another black. Yale University, she believed, was no better than Howard. She dubbed black intellectuals the "niggerati," and because her stance endeared her to white racists, she was further ostracized.

Seraph on the Suwannee, published in 1948, was her last novel, and did not receive positive reviews from either her supporters or her critics. By 1950, she was reduced to working as a maid. She also wrote a column for a black weekly newspaper, *The Fort Pierce Chronicle*, and did some substitute teaching. She suffered a stroke in October, 1959, and died three months later. In 1973, novelist Alice Walker paid for a marker for her grave, and wrote an article in *Ms.* magazine, which once more focused attention on her work.

Not only did all of her books eventually come back into print, in January, 1997, the eighth Zora Neale Hurston festival was held. A gifted writer who chose to portray the humble and the marginal of society, her politics and abrasive candor alienated her from those whose acceptance she needed but refused to solicit. She chose, instead, to write with passion, humor, and abandon, stories filtered through her own experience.

"Good thoughts, though God accept them, yet toward men are little better than good dreams except they be put into action." **—Bacon**

Jesse Louis Jackson (b. 1941)
Politician

I t was "Super Tuesday," March 8, 1984. When the votes were tallied, Alabama, Georgia, Louisiana, Mississippi, and Virginia — all Southern States — had given their support to Jesse Jackson in the Democratic Primary. In addition, he won the Michigan Democratic caucus on March 26, becoming the first African-American presidential candidate to win an industrial state. He had received ninety-two percent of the African-American vote and twenty percent of the white vote.

Born in Greenville, South Carolina, to Helen Burns and Noah Robinson, who never married, Jesse was eventually adopted by his stepfather, Charles Jackson. An accomplished athlete from Sterling High School, he decided to attend the University of Illinois at Champaign, on a football scholarship.

After enrolling, he discovered that, regardless of their skills, African-Americans were denied the opportunity to play the position of quarterback. After also noticing that he was subtly excluded from social events, he decided to leave for

Greensboro, North Carolina, where he enrolled at North Carolina A&T.

During this time, he became active in the civil rights struggle, acting as the front for the Greensboro sit-ins. He would enter a restaurant and ask to be served. When refused, African-American students would picket the establishment. In 1963, he helped organize the Chicago Freedom Movement, to challenge Northern racism, and, during his senior year, worked for the Congress of Racial Equality (CORE), as director of Southeastern operations.

Jackson graduated from A&T in 1964, with a degree in sociology, and, married Jacqueline Brown, whom he had met during his participation in civil rights activities. Although he had dreams of entering law school, he chose instead to become an ordained minister, enrolling in the Chicago Theological Seminary in 1974. After becoming a minister, he left the seminary in 1965 to work on the staff of the Southern Christian Leadership Conference (SCLC), led by a young pastor named Martin Luther King, Jr. Because Jesse's leadership skills so impressed King, he was appointed by King to head Operation Breadbasket, in 1966.

Jackson soon became a regular member of the King entourage and was present in 1968 when King was assassinated in Memphis, Tennessee. His relationship with the SCLC, however, cooled after King's death, as his tendency to initiate actions — actions King had admired and encouraged — came under fire. The SCLC also criticized his leadership of Operation Breadbasket. In 1971, he was suspended for sixty days by Ralph Abernathy, who headed the SCLC after King's death. Jesse's transgression was that he organized a Black Expo fair without the SCLC's endorsement. Jackson left the organization the same year and organized People United to Save Humanity, also known as Operation PUSH.

In 1972, Jackson was a keynote speaker at a Black Power convention, where he urged African-Americans to form a separate African-American political party.

Regarded, by some, as the one who most nearly fills the leadership void left following Dr. King's assassination, Jackson took his leadership abilities one step further when he ran for president of the United States.

DID YOU KNOW?

♦ Jackson earned a sharp rebuke from the Jewish sector by referring to New York as Hymietown, and for his association with the controversial Nation of Islam leader Louis Farrakhan.

♦ He negotiated with Syrian President Hafez al-Assad, to obtain the freedom of African-American pilot Robert Goodman.

♦ Many African-American leaders supported Walter Mondale because they felt Jackson's presidential candidacy would divide the party.

Nell
C.
Jackson

Olympic Gold Medalist, Track Coach

K.B.

"Great designs are not accomplished without enthusiasm . . . It is the inspiration of everything great." **—Bovee**

Nell Cecilia Jackson (1929-1988)
Olympic Track Star, Coach

Not every child prodigy plays the piano or solves complex mathematical problems. A few, like Nell Cecilia Jackson, compete in track and field at the university level while barely into their teens. Born in Athens, Georgia, to a dentist father and a mother who worked at the Veterans Administration Hospital, Nell always excelled in sports, and it became her life. By the time she was fourteen, she was participating in a special Tuskegee Institute Track and Field Club for outstanding high school and college female athletes.

In 1948, she was an All-American sprinter on the United States Olympic team. She won the silver medal in the two hundred meter run, at the first Pan-American games in Buenos Aires, Argentina, in 1951, and won the gold on the four hundred meter relay team. She set an American record of 24.2 in the two hundred meter relay, in 1949, that stood for six years.

Jackson became the first black female head coach of the United States women's Olympic track and field team in Melbourne, Australia, in 1956. She coached the 1972 Olympic team in Munich, Germany, and in 1980, was one of only five Americans chosen to attend the International Olympic Academy in Olympia, Greece. She also coached the United States women's track team in 1987, when they competed in the Pan-American games.

Jackson directed many clinics and workshops all over the country, and was on the board of directors of the United States Olympic Committee. She served on the National Collegiate Athletic Association Committee, the National Association for Girls and Women in Sports (NAGWS), and the American Alliance for Health, Physical Education, Recreation and Dance. She was also secretary of The Athletic Congress (TAC).

Jackson received the Alumni Merit Award from the University of Iowa, and the Outstanding Alumni Award from Tuskegee University.

In 1977, she was inducted into the Black Athletes Hall of Fame, and in 1989, into the National Track and Field Hall of Fame. In 1989, after her death from influenza, she was inducted posthumously into The Athletic Congress Hall of Fame, and received the Robert Giegengack Award for contributions and exceptional leadership in track and field.

Nell Cecilia Jackson earned her Bachelor's degree in 1951 from Tuskegee Institute, her Master's degree in 1953 from Springfield College, and in 1962, her Ph.D. from the University of Iowa. She was a coach and teacher of physical education at Tuskegee Institute, the University of Illinois, Illinois State University and Michigan State University, where she was also the women's athletic director. She was professor and athletic director at the State University of New York, at Binghampton, when she died.

Jackson was the author of *Track and Field for Girls and Women* (1968), and a number of other related articles, published in books and periodicals.

She was both an athlete and educator, totally dedicated to womens and girls sports, and established a standard of excellence for the many lives she touched.

"The things that hurt us the most can become the fuel that propels us toward our destiny." **—Bishop T.D. Jakes**

Bishop Thomas D. Jakes (b. 1957)
Evangelist

He has been called the "Black Billy Graham with the potential impact of a Martin Luther King," as he wields the word of God like a flaming sword. He has become one of the most sought-after preachers in the world. He attracts "cross-over" audiences of over forty thousand people that include all races. He appeals to his congregations with sermons about a God who gives hope to a lost generation.

He believes that female pastors are making a significant contribution to the church, but disdains the concept of a "black" church. He does, however, credit the "black" church community with taking the initiative in promoting racial harmony, and in establishing a high profile in the black community, where, traditionally, church has been the focal point.

Though he was raised a Baptist, T.D. Jakes received his greatest awakening in a storefront Apostolic church. Soon after, he became a traveling minister who was so nervous, he hid his shaking hands behind his back, as he preached to small congregations. He labored for twenty years before his crusades began drawing the big crowds. He believes that his great appeal stems from a ministry which supports the expanding roles of women in the church, ministering to those who are "broken" and hurting, and attacking the national sin of racism. At the same time, he preaches a personal God who cares.

Born in Charleston, West Virginia, he was the youngest of Earnest Sr. and Odith Jakes' three children. Early in his life, his parents instilled self-confidence in him, and the belief that there was nothing that he could not accomplish. His father introduced the work ethic, with a successful janitorial service in a small black community. His mother, a classroom teacher, taught him to read before he entered school. After graduating from high school, he enrolled in West Virginia State College, but earned both his Bachelor's and Master's degrees from Friends University. He also attended Center Business College.

He started preaching full-time at Greater Temple of Faith Congregation, and began *The Master's Plan,* a local radio ministry, around 1982. In 1983 he created *Back to the Bible,* a study later named *The Bible Conference.* His powerful 1992 *Woman Thou Art Loosed: Songs of Healing and Deliverance* message was adapted, in 1993, into the best-selling book of the same title. In the same year, he launched *The Manpower Conference* series (a counterpart to *Woman*), and began *Get Ready With T.D. Jakes,* a weekly television broadcast on Trinity Broadcasting Network (TBN), and Black Entertainment Television (BET). He established T.D. Jake Ministries, a nonprofit organization, to produce his conferences, television ministries and books.

In 1996, he moved his family and staff to Dallas, Texas, and established The Potter's House, "where broken vessels are repaired and restored." *Get Ready* became a nationally syndicate series, and he began writing for Ministries Today.

He has paid off a three million dollar home mortgage from the sale of his books, and sees no contradiction between honest financial gain and preaching the word of God. Other publications include *Daddy Loves His Girls, Help! I'm Raising My Child Alone,* and *Water in the Wilderness.*

His honors include the Gospel Heritage Award for Ministry (Gospel Today magazine), the Gospel Music Association's Dove Seal (for *Woman Thou Art Loosed*), and received the Key to the City of Dallas for Raven's Refuge, the homeless shelter of The Potter's House

He is married to Serita Jakes, who is also a minister. They have five children.

Caterina Jarboro

"How wonderful is the human voice! It is indeed the organ of the soul . . ."
—Longfellow

Caterina Jarboro (1903- ?)
Opera Singer

She was the first woman of African Heritage to sing in an all-white opera company in the United States, when she sang with the Chicago Opera Company in the Hippodrome, in New York City, in 1933. In a time when black artists were expected to sing spirituals, play the buffoon, or perform in minstrel-type roles, Jarboro electrified the opera world with her sensational rendering in *Aida*. She was so successful in the role that, two days later, there was a demand for a repeat performance. She had already sung the role in Milan, Italy, at the Puccini Theater, in 1930.

The manager of the Chicago Opera Company was so encouraged by the success of Caterina that, in the same year, he signed her for a twenty week season of grand opera. She played *Selika* in Meyerbeer's *L'Africaine*. Both as a singer and as an actress, she won the acclaim of the foremost critics of the day.

Born Caterine Yarborough, in Wilmington, North Carolina, she received her early education at the Gregory Normal School, and the Catholic schools of the city. When she was thirteen years old, she went to live with an aunt in Brooklyn, New York, to study music. Funds for her education were not plentiful, so she earned money to study in Europe by performing in musical productions such as *Running Wild* and *Shuffle Along*. While in Europe, she studied under singing masters in Milan and Paris.

After spending six years in Europe, she returned to America, and created sensations by appearing in opera houses. Unfortunately, her victory was short-lived. White America opera lovers expected to see an Italian performer. The demand for her dwindled quickly when the opera-goers learned that Jarboro was an African- American.

She continued to make tours, however, and at one time performed before an audience of six thousand, in 1935, at the Chicago Opera Company. Even so, the New York Metropolitan Opera Association would not accept her membership in the newly formed grand opera company.

Jarboro eventually returned to Europe and never again performed with an American opera company. After her limited success in America, it was not until 1945 that another African-American opera singer, Todd Duncan, appeared at the New York City Center, in the role of Tonio in *Pagliacci*.

Though she never won total acceptance in the United States as an opera singer, Caterina Jarboro's efforts to tear down the walls which prevented black artists from performing with opera companies in the United States, paved the way for aspiring artists who followed.

DID YOU KNOW ?

- ◆ The black church has historically been the aid of the African-American singer.
- ◆ Church organizations sponsored concerts which helped to develop many African-American singers.
- ◆ One of the earliest opera singers was Elizabeth Taylor Greenfield, who was brought to Philadelphia at one year of age, and reared by a Quaker lady.

"Wonder, connected with a principle of rational curiosity, is the source of all knowledge and discovery . . ." **—Horsley**

Mae Carol Jemison (b. 1956)
Astronaut, Physician

hen the space shuttle Endeavor thundered off the launching pad on September 12, 1992, Dr. Mae Carol Jemison, the first African-American woman to travel in space, was on board. Her job was the stuff of science fiction. In a laboratory that orbited the earth for eight days, she tested the effects of weightlessness on people and animals, studied animal growth and reproduction in space and developed new methods for making semiconductors and other technological materials.

Jemison was selected by the National Aeronautics and Space Administration (NASA) in 1987. She was one of fifteen chosen from a field of nearly two thousand candidates. She completed a one-year program of training and evaluation in 1988. Because of her qualifications, she became mission specialist on space shuttle crews. In addition to conducting experiments, she was responsible for ensuring that the computer software was in perfect condition and working order, and preparing thermal protection systems and launch payloads.

She was born in Decatur, Alabama, to Charlie and Dorothy Jemison and was the youngest of three children. The family moved to Chicago when she was very young. She graduated from the city's Morgan Park High School, and was awarded a National Achievement Scholarship. She entered Stanford University at the age of sixteen, and graduated with a B.S. degree in chemical engineering (1977), and a B.A. in African and Afro-American Studies. Jemison earned her M.D. degree at Cornell University Medical School in 1981. She traveled to rural Kenya and Cuba, and completed a medical clerkship at a Cambodian refugee camp in Thailand. In 1982, she completed her internship at the University of Southern California at Los Angeles Medical Center.

Dr. Jemison currently teaches Environmental Studies at Dartmouth College, and directs the college's Jemison Institute for Advancing Technology in developing countries. The institute was established to assess, implement and identify advanced technologies for use in less industrialized countries.

She hosts and is technical consultant to *World of Wonder,* on the Discovery Channel. She established the Jemison Group, Inc., based in Houston, Texas, to research, develop and implement advanced technologies for the individual and the developing world.

In 1992, the Detroit Public School System established the Mae C. Jemison Academy, an alternative public school, in recognition of her advocacy of science and technology, and for other outstanding achievements.

She received the Essence Award (1988), Gamma Sigma Gamma Woman of the Year (1989), an Honorary Doctorate of Science from Lincoln College, Pennsylvania (1991) and was selected as one of *McCall's* Ten Outstanding Women for the 90s (1991). She also received the Johnson Publication's Black Achievement Trailblazers Award (1992), and was elected to the National Medical Association Hall of Fame (1993). Jemison's memberships include the Association for the Advancement of Science, Association of Space Explorers, Board of Directors of Houston's UNICEF, the Keystone Center, and the National Research Council Space Station Review Committee. She resigned from NASA in 1993.

DID YOU KNOW?

- NASA was established in 1958 to plan and conduct a program of space exploration for the United States.
- Mae Jemison's parents encouraged her childhood interest in astronomy and other sciences.
- She is trained in dance and choreography.

"Perfect freedom is reserved for the man who lives by his own work, and in his work does what he wants to do." —**R.G. Collingwood**

John H. Johnson (b. 1918)
Publisher, Entrepeneur

I n 1942, he borrowed five hundred dollars on his mother's furniture, to launch what was to become the most successful black publication in history. Beginning as a small magazine, *Negro Digest* lauded the accomplishments of African-Americans. The profits were very small, and were reinvested into John H. Johnson's fledgling company.

When he expanded the magazine to become *Ebony*, the most widely circulated black-oriented magazine in history, he approached white advertisers to orient them to the concept of aiming their products toward an African-American market. Though the magazine was an instant hit with blacks, it was a hard-sell to advertisers, who had seen the demise of thirty similar ventures.

Johnson argued that African-Americans spent a greater percentage of their incomes on goods and services than did whites. Eager to establish a lucrative market in a previously unknown area, advertisers began to pitch their products on the glossy pages of *Ebony*, and, by 1970, the magazine had attracted approximately one and a quarter million readers.

Tan Confessions, a women's magazine, debuted in 1950, and, in 1951, *Jet*, a news weekly, was added. It went on to take the honors as the highest circulated black weekly. *Negro Digest* was renamed *Black World* in 1970, after being revived in 1961. *Hue* and *Ebony Man* were added to the list of Johnson Publications.

The success of *Ebony* magazine spawned other opportunities for African-Americans which had not existed before; white industries found it feasible to use black models to advertise their products. Black models, whose beauty and success encourage other women of color, who wish to pursue careers in the lucrative business, are featured annually in the popular *Ebony Fashion Show*.

In 1961, historian Lerone Bennett's *Before the Mayflower* ushered in Johnson Publication's venture into the book publishing business.

Born in Arkansas City, Arkansas, Johnson graduated with honors from DuSable High School, and furthered his education at Northwestern University and the University of Chicago.

Other Johnson businesses include Fashion Fair Cosmetics, Supreme Beauty, and the *American Black Achievement Awards* television program, which debuted in 1978.

Johnson has received many honors and awards. He was inducted into the Illinois Business Hall of Fame in 1989, received the Excel award from the International Association of Business Communicators, was inducted into the National Sales Hall of Fame, and received the Founders Award from the National Conference of Christians and Jews (NCCJ). In 1990, he was inducted into the Chicago Journalism Hall of Fame, and in 1996 was awarded the highest civilian honor given in the United States, the Presidential Medal of Freedom.

He holds honorary Doctorate degrees from thirty colleges and universities, including Chicago State University, Malcolm X College, Shaw University and the University of Southern California. Johnson is a trustee of the Art Institute of Chicago and the United Negro College Fund, and is director of the National Conference of Christians and Jews.

His initial investment of five hundred dollars, along with faith and an entrepreneurial spirit, have yielded great profits for Johnson and for all African-Americans.

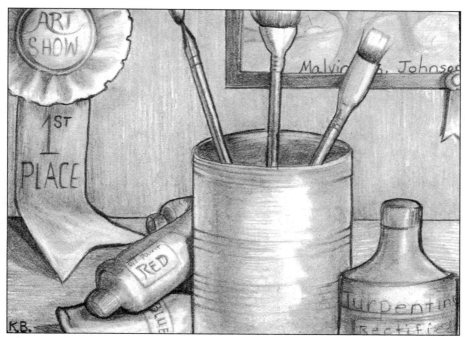

"Illusion on a ground of truth, that is the secret of the fine arts."

—Joubert

Malvin Gray Johnson (1896-1934)
Artist

His original Southern landscapes, including *Convict Labor, Brothers* and *Red Road,* placed him in the high echelons of artistic achievement, though his promise of much greater works were halted by his untimely death.

He painted in a number of styles, experimenting with impressionism and cubism, and finally, black folk art. Rendered in vivid hues, and depicting rustic types, he chose the difficult medium of water color to produce many works which reflected his mastery of style and technique.

Johnson also worked in oil colors. He won the Otto Kahn Special Prize in 1928 for *Swing Low, Sweet Chariot.* In it, his subjects (slaves), exhausted after their labor, travel to the river's edge to plead to God for their freedom. Though the painting was not technically perfect, the judges appreciated what it attempted to portray.

Born in Greenboro, North Carolina, he studied at the National Academy of Design in New York City, where, during the Great Depression, he worked on a Federal Arts Project. While influenced by other movements, he was original and inventive in his creations.

He held exhibitions at the Library of Congress, the Smithsonian Institution, Howard University, the Texas Centennial Exposition in Dallas, the Salon of Americas, and the Harmon Foundation, in New York City.

His works are in the Harmon Collection, Oakland (California) Museum, the Smithsonian Institute, the Howard University Gallery of Arts, the Whitney Museum of American Art, New York City, and other collections.

A prolific artist, he produced many works in his short life, including *All Day Meeting, Backyard, The Bakers, Climbing up the Mountain, Elks, Head of a Child,* and *Jenkin's Band.*

His death was said to have left a permanent void in the artistic world.

HISTORY IN A CAPSULE

Malvin Gray Johnson experimented with many styles. One was Cubism, whose chief creators were Pablo Picasso and George Braque, in Paris between 1907 and 1914. The style utilized flat, two-dimensional surfaces. Rejecting traditional techniques such as modeling, chiaroscuro, and perspective, forms were fragmented, with several sides viewed simultaneously. Cubists achieved perspectives by using warm colors to advance, and cool colors to recede.

Though Picasso and Braque are considered the creators of Cubism, it was embraced and further advanced by painters including Robert Delaunay, Marcel Duchamp, and Juan Gris. It is chiefly a form of painting, but the style is also extended to architecture and sculpture.

"My faith in the Constitution is whole, it is complete, it is total . . ."

—Barbara Jordan

Barbara Jordan (1936-1996)
Congresswoman

With perfect diction, the first African-American woman to serve in the Texas Senate and the first black elected to Congress from the South, since Reconstruction, expressed her faith in the promise of the American dream. The Texas Democrat was elected to the House of Representatives and served from 1973 to 1979. In 1976, she performed another first; she delivered the keynote speech at the Democratic party's national convention.

America first glimpsed her greatness during the hearings to consider impeaching President Richard M. Nixon in 1974. It was on this occasion that she shared her faith in the Constitution of the United States, as a member of the House Judiciary Committee.

A brilliant constitutional lawmaker, she was a member of the Texas Senate for six years before serving in the U.S. Congress, and during her final year in the senate, her peers held her in such esteem, they chose her as president pro tempore.

Jordan supported legislation which combated environmental problems, and banned discrimination. She sponsored Texas' first minimum wage law, to aid those not covered by standards, as established by the federal government.

It was at Texas Southern University that she became part of a debating team which made short work of opponents, from such prestigious schools as Harvard and Baylor. She graduated from TSU as an honor student (1956), and earned her law degree from Boston University (1959). She won a seat in the Texas Senate in 1966, after two unsuccessful runs for state office.

Her accomplishments and the power of her presence so impressed President Lyndon B. Johnson, he invited her to take an advance look at his 1967 civil rights message. Johnson did not forget her efforts and helped to raise money for her successful 1972 bid for the United States House of Representatives.

Though there was some talk of her being the running mate for Jimmy Carter, she chose instead to join the faculty of the Lyndon B. Johnson School of Public Affairs, at the University of Texas. When she was awarded the Presidential Medal of Freedom in 1994, President Clinton referred to her as "the most outspoken moral voice of the American political system."

In 1971, she worked to get Texas its first black congressional district and was a champion of the poor and disenfranchised. Known for her riveting baritone voice, and precise diction, she commanded respect and attention. She chose her words carefully and crafted them to convey her ideas.

She dealt with overt racism and condescension when she first came to the Texas Senate, overcoming its effects with the armor of her wit, intelligence, skill as a debater and great dignity. Before long, even her worst detractors gave homage to her conscientious work, dedication to her job and her ability to cut deals.

Although Barbara Jordan was stricken with multiple sclerosis, and her brilliant potential cut short by her death from viral pneumonia, her legacy of excellence will continue to serve as the standard for those who follow in her footsteps.

DID YOU KNOW?

♦ When Jordan won her seat in 1972, she defeated Representative Paul Merritt to represent the 18th Congressional District of Texas.

♦ In 1990, she was elected to the National Women's Hall of Fame in Seneca Falls, New York.

♦ Her induction ceremony coincided with the seventeenth anniversary of the Nineteenth Amendment, granting women the right to vote.

Michael Jordan

Basketball Player

"*Great men undertake great things because they are great; fools, because they think them easy.*" **—Vauvenargues**

Michael Jordan (b. 1963)
Basketball Player

He has been called the greatest player ever to pick up a basketball. In 1987, he scored 3,041 points, the most ever for a guard in NBA history. In 1982, at age nineteen, he made the basket that took the University of North Carolina to victory over Georgetown, winning the school's first NCAA men's basketball championship in twenty-five years. *Sporting News* named him Player of the Year for the next two seasons. He was captain of the United States men's basketball team, at the 1984 Olympic Games in Los Angeles, and led his teammates to a gold medal.

Michael Jordan left college after his junior year and was third pick in the 1984 draft, chosen by the hapless Chicago Bulls. The team's performance experienced an immediate turn-around, as the 6'6" guard led the team in scoring, assists and rebounding, with Jordan being selected as Rookie of the Year. Because of a broken foot, he sat out most of his second season, but scored sixty-three points in a playoff game with the Boston Celtics. Though his team lost, Jordan's individual performance was one of the greatest in post-season history.

Born in Brooklyn, New York, he was the fourth of James and Deloris Jordan's five children. He grew up in the rural North Carolina towns of Wallace and Wilmington. His skills lay dormant for a while, and his Lancy High School varsity basketball team released him during his sophomore year. Major college programs gave him only lukewarm attention.

During his 1987-88 season with the Bulls, however, he became the first player ever to win Defensive Player and Most Valuable Player of the Year in the same season.

He is also the most successful product spokesman in the history of team sports. He endorses the Air Jordan athletic shoes for the Nike® Shoe Company, Quaker Oats®, Gatorade® and Wheaties® cereal. It is estimated that he earned sixteen million dollars in product endorsements alone, in 1992. He continues to be one of the business world's most sought-after pitchmen for their products. He also became a pop idol by appearing in commercials with movie producer Spike Lee.

After winning Most Valuable Player three times between 1988 and 1992, he retired in 1993. He cited a number of reasons, including his despair over the murder of his father, his most avid fan. He played baseball for the Chicago White Sox organization in 1994, but left after one year to resume his basketball career with the Chicago Bulls.

For all of his success, he is not without his detractors. He has been accused of being a one-man show, has been criticized for incurring sizable gambling debts and for refusing to wear the uniform of a competing sponsor during the 1992 Olympic Games. He remains, however, one of the nation's most popular personalities, and one of young America's favorite icons.

HISTORY IN A CAPSULE

In 1966, Bill Russell became the first African-American head coach of a major league team, when he accepted the position with the Boston Celtics. Like Michael Jordan, he was not an outstanding player in high school and improved greatly during his college years. Entering the University of San Francisco, in 1952, on a basketball scholarship, Russell progressed to team captain during his junior and senior years.

Like Jordan, he sparked an Olympic basketball team (1956) to a gold medal. He led the Boston Celtics to eleven championships.

"The winner is he who gives himself to his work, body and soul."

—Charles Buxton

Percy L. Julian (1898-1975)
Research Chemist

His grandfather, a former slave, lost his right hand. It was punishment for learning to read. Percy Julian inherited this thirst for knowledge, and his brilliant mind was nurtured through opportunities provided at a number of prestigious universities.

He owned over one hundred chemical patents. Many of them were developed from the soybean. Included is the synthetic female hormone progesterone. It is prescribed for pregnant women who are in danger of miscarriage. He created synthetic physostigmine to treat the eye disease glaucoma. During 1939-1945, the years of World War II, his fire-fighting solution saved many lives. Julian also developed a cost-effective method of manufacturing cortisone, which is used in treating certain muscle diseases and arthritis, and a new process for paints.

He became a millionaire businessman and scientist, having established Julian Laboratories, Incorporated, in 1953, with branches in Chicago, Guatemala and Mexico City. He sold the company in 1964, and became president of Julian Associates, Inc., manufacturing products made from soybean compounds.

Born in Montgomery, Alabama, he was the son of a railway mail clerk. Because of his inventive mind, he earned a grant from the General Education Board. He also received financial help from a wealthy classmate, during his early struggle to obtain his education. At one point, he worked as a waiter and slept in the attic of a fraternity house, while earning his way through college.

He graduated with a B.A. degree from DePaul University (1920); he won a fellowship to Harvard in 1922, where he earned his Master's degree in 1923, and in 1931, received his Ph.D. from the University of Vienna (Austria).

He was a chemistry instructor at Fisk University (Nashville, Tennessee) from 1920-1925, and taught at West Virginia State. He was also chemistry professor at Howard University (1927), and established its chemistry building. He was a Research Fellow at DePaul University from 1932 to 1936. Because the board of trustees was reluctant to appoint a black to the faculty, he accepted a research position at the Wisconsin Institute of Paper Chemistry. He was also the Glidden Company of Chicago's director of research, on soya products, from 1936 to 1953.

"Citius. Altius. Fortius." **—Olympic Motto**

Jackie Joyner-Kersee (b. 1962)
Heptathlon Olympian

Running faster, jumping higher, and using her strength to throw farther in the Olympic heptathlon is what made Jackie Joyner-Kersee the greatest female athlete in the world. She first dazzled the world when she competed in the 1988 Olympics in Seoul, Korea, and broke the world record twice when she won gold medals in the heptathlon and the long jump. In the 1992 Games, she also won two Olympic medals in multi-event competitions. Joyner-Kersee was the first woman ever to be named Woman of the Year by *Sporting News*. The magazine once bestowed the honor only on the Man of the Year. In 1989, she was named Female Athlete of the Year by the Associated Press.

Jacqueline Joyner, named for First Lady Jacqueline Kennedy, was born in East St. Louis, Illinois. Her grandmother, who insisted upon the name, predicted that "some day this girl will be the first lady of something." A bright scholar as well as consummate athlete, she graduated in the top ten percent of her high school class in 1980. Because of her academic and athletic excellence, the University of California at Los Angeles recruited her for scholarships in pentathlon and basketball. Though she chose basketball, she also trained in track events, that included the long jump. Assistant track coach, Bob Kersee recognized her potential as a world class athlete, and after tallying her points in heptathlon events, discovered that she was a mere four hundred points behind Jane Frederick, the nation's then-reigning heptathlete. He placed Jackie in an intensive training program, and by 1984, she was setting records. In Moscow, at the 1986 Goodwill Games, she became the first American woman since Babe Didrikson, fifty years before, to set world records in multi-event competitions.

In 1986, Bob Kersee and Jackie were married, and he continued as her coach for events including the 1987 Olympic Festival held in Houston, Texas, the Seoul Olympics, and the 1996 Olympics held in Atlanta, Georgia.

HISTORY IN A CAPSULE

During the Summer Olympic Games in London, in 1948, Alice Coachman leaped 5 feet 6-1/4 inches to set a new world record in the high jump. She became the first African-American woman to win an Olympic gold medal. She began competing in track events when she was thirteen years old, and won a number of AAU championships. She held titles in the 50 yard dash, 100 yard dash, and the 440 yard relay.

Coachman was born in Albany, Georgia. She earned her Bachelor's degree from Albany State College, where she held a dozen national titles in the high jump.

"Old music is like an old friend in this world of constant change."
—Everett A. Kershaw

Everett A. Kershaw (1917-1985)
Educator, Promoter, Radio Personality

He was a teacher. He was a promoter. He was a teacher who promoted what he taught. By day, the classroom was his venue, by night, the recording studio.

Setbacks and refusals were commonplace in his quest to become the first African-American deejay in Tallahassee, Florida. He was once told by a station manager that "Cleaning is all you can do here, and that job is already filled." On another occasion, he was advised that sponsors would cancel if he were hired.

Ten years of such treatment did not dampen his passion to be on radio. When manager Frank Hazelton finally hired him on WTNT, *Kuzzin's Kabaret* debuted in the summer of 1953. It was the first show of its kind, and Kershaw was Tallahassee's first African-American deejay. Though it was somewhat of an experiment, WTNT Dynamite in Dixie, became a fixture of the 1950s and 1960s.

Known for his elegant manner and smooth voice, Kershaw promised Hazelton the best and delivered the best. As a result of having broken the color taboo in radio, however, he and his family received threats of violence.

Though the path to radio was beset with thorns and brambles, his career as a promoter was almost a cinch. He was the first African-American in the area to work with national promoters such as Ralph Weinberg. Largely through Kershaw's efforts, the black community had the opportunity to see and hear such gospel greats as Sister Rosetta Tharpe, The Travelers, The Original Blind Boys of Mississippi, and Reverend C.L. Franklin, whose daughter Aretha, was then a teenager tagging after her father on his tours.

Because public facilities were segregated, these barn-burners took place in the gymnasium or the auditorium of Lincoln High School.

Kershaw was one of the early promoters of jazz greats Nat and Julian "Cannonball" Adderley. He brought in top entertainers including Duke Ellington, Lionel Hampton, Count Basie, Arthur Prysock and Woody Herman.

He was the first black editor of *Capital City Chatter*, a 1950s news insert in the *Tallahassee Democrat,* for the African-American Community. Later, he was the first reporter and editor of Tallahassee's *Black Page*.

Along with a cousin, he opened Kuzzin's Drive Inn, a diner that largely targeted college students, and was sole owner of Kuzzin's Music Box, a store that specialized in African-American music.

Born in Key West, Florida, his father was a medical doctor, his mother a classroom teacher. He graduated from Florida A&M College, as did both of his parents. In 1941, he served in the Army in World War II. He began his teaching career in Walkulla County, taught at Lincoln High School, and was principal of Bond Junior High School. He spent his last sixteen teaching years at Rickard High School as department head for work experience.

Wherever he taught, he borrowed his experiences in entertainment to pique and to keep the interest of students in danger of dropping out. He used rhymes and "raps," making them up as he went along. He mixed wisdom and wit to teach self-pride, along with encouraging and promoting students' skills and talents. Always, he stressed the importance of good manners. He called radio his "challenge," and promoting and teaching, his loves. His greatest pleasures, however, were his children and grand-children.

Exemplifying all of the heroic educators of the "old school," Kershaw parented as he taught. For his many contributions to education, a scholarship was established in his memory. Among the contributors were Mayor Hurley Rudd, once part-owner of the station, and Frank Hazelton, who hired Kershaw at WTNT. To commemorate his contributions to African-Americans in radio, a *Classic Showcase* honors him each August. Carl McBride, whom Kershaw mentored, instituted the tribute, and now hosts the show on WAMF.

Coretta King

Human Rights Activist

"The two great movers of the human mind are the desire of good, and the fear of evil." **—Johnson**

Coretta Scott King (b. 1927)
Human Rights Leader

Her name was in the headlines, but often appeared on lists of the most admired.

She was the first woman to preach at a statutory service in St. Paul's Cathedral in London, and the first woman to deliver the Class Day address at Harvard University. In a poll conducted by the *World Almanac* in 1977, she was chosen as one of the twenty-five most influential women in the world.

Coretta Scott King was the stoic beauty who abandoned her dream of a career as a concert singer and pianist. Instead, she chose to support the dream of her husband, Dr. Martin Luther King, Jr., of confronting and eventually eradicating the deeply ingrained evil of racism.

Born in Marion, Alabama, her parents believed that each person is born to a purpose and plan in life. Early in her childhood, they taught her that to accomplish is to enrich one's life.

Though her dream of being a concert performer was re-routed, her talents were used in the Freedom Concerts sponsored by the Southern Christian Leadership Conference (SCLC), in which she worked along with her husband. She also used narratives and poetry with her musical selections, which chronicled the history of the Civil Rights movement. Funds raised at these concerts were used for SCLC activities.

A year after the assassination of Dr. King, in 1968, she founded the Martin Luther King, Jr. Center for Nonviolent Social Change. Based in Atlanta, Georgia, the purpose of the memorial is to ensure that the study of the philosophy of nonviolent resistance, in dealing with economic and political injustices, continues throughout the world. It is a coalition of organizations which advocates women's rights, civil rights, and employment issues.

She has been awarded the Wateler Peace Prize, the International Viareggio Award, and The Women of Conscience Award.

In 1977, she was appointed as a public delegate to the session of the United Nations General Assembly by President Jimmy Carter. In the same year, she was named commissioner of International Women's Year, and was chairperson of the Full Employment Action Council, to promote the passing of the Humphrey-Hawkins Bill.

She worked to develop a nexus with Third World countries and lends her voice to causes affecting oppressed minorities. She was a sponsor for the Sane Nuclear Policy Committee, was a delegate to the White House Conference on Children and Youth, and performed many concerts throughout the United States and India. She is a member of the Margaret Sanger Memorial Foundation and was co-chairperson of Clergy and Laymen Concerned About Vietnam. She is also a member of the National Council of Negro Women, the NAACP, an honorary member of Alpha Kappa Alpha Sorority, the Links, and the Women's International League for Peace and Freedom.

In 1969, she authored *My Life With Martin Luther King, Jr.*, which became a best-seller. She also contributes articles to magazines and other periodicals. From 1990 to 1994 she was a syndicated newspaper columnist for the *New York Times*.

Though her grace and elegance are disarming, she has proven to be a tough leader, who has weathered many tragedies while maintaining her vision of a society, where all citizens receive equitable treatment under the law, and where all people dwell in peace.

"I have a Dream... !"

Martin Luther King, Jr. Civil Rights Leader

"...any religion which professes to be concerned about the souls of men and is not concerned about the social and economic conditions that scar the soul is a spiritually moribund religion." —**Martin Luther King, Jr.**

Martin Luther King, Jr. (1929-1968)
Civil Rights Leader, Orator

He was the David that assailed the last great vestige of slavery; the Goliath of racial segregation. Through the organizing of peaceful protests, he challenged the Deep South's — and the nation's — most cherished tradition, the separation of whites and blacks in nearly every area of society.

King sprang into the headlines in 1955 when he led the Montgomery bus boycott, after seamstress Rosa Parks was arrested for refusing to give up her seat for a white passenger. His philosophy of nonviolence was first influenced by Thoreau's *Essay on Civil Disobedience*, which was his first intellectual experience with nonviolent resistance. He later studied the peaceful protest tactics of Mohandas Mahatma Gandhi.

The success of the Montgomery experiment led to similar protests all over the country. Largely led by students, sit-ins, swim-ins and eat-ins were organized and carried out to end the practice of racial segregation of public facilities. With a group of Atlanta pastors, Dr. King organized the Southern Christian Leadership Conference (SCLC) in 1959. Its mission was to carry nationwide the message of the nonviolent struggle for equality, for people of African ancestry, and to confront the evils of racism in America.

His *I Have a Dream* speech, the summation of the hopes of African-Americans, was delivered with unparalleled power at the 1963 March on Washington. The largest civil rights demonstration ever, it attracted two hundred fifty thousand attendees — sixty thousand of them white — with millions more watching worldwide by television. In January, 1964, *Time* magazine honored him as their Man of the Year, and in December, 1964, he was awarded the Nobel Peace Prize.

In 1965, he led the fifty mile march from Selma to the state capital in Montgomery, to protest the denial of voting rights to African-Americans which eventually attracted thirty-two hundred participants. The success of the march influenced the passage of the Voters Rights Act.

Born in Atlanta, Georgia, he was the son of a pastor, and was educated at Morehouse College (Atlanta, 1948) and the Crozer Theological Seminary in Chester, Pennsylvania, where he graduated a straight-A student (1951) with a Bachelor of Divinity degree. He earned his Ph.D. from Boston University (1955) and his D.D. degree from the University of Chicago. In 1954, he became ordained pastor of the Dexter Avenue Baptist Church in Montgomery, Alabama.

He organized voter registration drives, while his stirring speeches drew the attention of the world to the virulent hatred in the South. He also exposed de facto segregation in Northern cities such as Chicago (1966), where he was stoned for his message of nonviolence. In 1967, he announced the Poor People's Campaign to focus on employment and other concerns of people of all races.

He was assassinated in Memphis, Tennessee, on April 4, 1968, where he had gone to support a sanitation worker's strike. On April 11, President Lyndon B. Johnson signed into law the Fair Housing Act, which prohibited discrimination in the sale and renting of houses and apartments on the basis of race.

DID YOU KNOW?

♦ In 1957, he became the second black to be featured on the cover of *Time* magazine. The first was Emperor Haile Selassie of Ethiopia.
♦ The first person arrested for refusing to give up a seat on a Montgomery bus was Claudette Colvin, a fifteen year old schoolgirl.
♦ He was the youngest man ever to be awarded the Nobel Peace Prize.

Theodore
K.
Lawless

Dermatologist

"We ought not to judge of men's merits by their qualifications, but by the use they make of them." —Charron

Theodore K. Lawless (1892-1971)
Dermatologist, Philanthropist

He was one of the world's leading skin specialists. In a time when physicians of African ancestry were largely excluded from mainstream American medicine, were limited in their opportunities to advance and largely isolated professionally, he had an international roster of clients. It cut across racial, social, and regional lines. Because of the demand for his services, he saw an average of one hundred patients a day. Though he specialized in both common and rare skin diseases, including the treatment of leprosy, as a medical scientist, he also contributed significant medical literature in the treatment of syphilis.

Born in Thibodeaux, Louisiana, he received his B.A. (1914) and D.Sc. (1915) degrees before receiving additional training in France, Austria, and Switzerland. He also attended Talladega (Alabama) College and earned his M.D. (1919) and M.S. (1920) degrees from Northwestern University School of Medicine (Evanston,

Illinois). From 1920 to 1921, he was a fellow of dermatology and syphilology at Massachusetts General Hospital in Boston, Massachusetts, at Saint Louis Hospital in Paris, France, and at Kaiser Joseph Hospital in Vienna Austria. He studied dermatology at Harvard Pathological Institute and at Freiburg, Germany between 1922 and 1923.

From 1924 to 1941, he conducted research and taught dermatology at Northwestern University. He was also a senior attending physician at Chicago's Provident Hospital.

As a philanthropist, he gave generously of his considerable earnings. The dermatology clinic of Israel's Beilinson Hospital Center bears his name in honor of his assistance in raising five hundred thousand dollars for the building of the facility. In 1956, he gave seven hundred thousand dollars for an apartment building for New Orleans' Dillard University. The school named a chapel in his honor.

Theodore Lawless worked in the center of the African-American community in Chicago. He received the Harmon Award in 1929, and in 1954, the NAACP awarded him the Sprigarn Medal.

HISTORY IN A CAPSULE

Solomon C. Fuller, psychiatrist and neuropathologist, came to the United States, from Liberia, when he was seventeen years of age. He realized his lifelong desire to become a physician when he earned his M.D. degree, from Boston University, in 1897. Because of his scholarship, he was appointed to teach pathology, psychiatry, and neurology at Boston University Medical School. He held the position for thirty years. He completed his internship at Massachusetts' Westborough State Hospital, and two years later, was appointed pathologist. He edited the *Westborough State Hospital Papers* in 1913, which was a publication for scientific exploration into mental disorders.

He maintained a medical practice in Framingham, Massachusetts, from his home office. He also practiced in Boston. The son of a Liberian government official and coffee planter, he contributed widely to medical knowledge in his speciality. Toward the end of his life, he became totally blind, but maintained his mental sharpness and his interest in the field.

"The object of art is to crystallize emotion into thought, and then fix it in form."
—Delsarte

Jacob Lawrence (b. 1917)
Artist

When Jacob Lawrence was hospitalized for physical and emotional exhaustion in 1950, he turned a minus into a plus: once he was again able to work, he created a series of paintings about the experience. *Occupational Therapy, Sedation, Psychiatric Therapy* and *Depression* all depict some phase of hospital life.

Born in Atlantic City, New Jersey, he is considered by many to be the best-known contemporary African American artist. His family moved to New York in 1931. He began drawing and painting when he was a child. He studied under Charles Alston at Utopia House, and at the Harlem Art Workshop. He paints mostly in tempera, and his paintings are noted for their brilliant colors and narrative quality. He creates many of his paintings on historical subjects which he researches in order to render accurately.

177

His simple outlines and complicated groupings of figures combine with mood to depict canvases of power and substance. Some of his historical subjects include Frederick Douglass, Harriet Tubman, and the mass migration of blacks from the South to the North during the World War I era, and their ultimate decline into the abject conditions of life in the slums.

Lawrence joined the United States Coast Guard during World War II, and true to his work pattern, created a series of paintings on wartime activities. The group now hangs in the United States Coast Guard archives for its depiction of the role the branch played during the war. After the war, he was awarded a Guggenheim Fellowship which assisted him in completing another series of war paintings.

He was awarded second prize in 1940 at the Art of the American Negro exhibition. He has exhibited at the Harlem Art Center (New York, 1936 to 1939), the Ford Foundation retrospective, the Whitney Museum of American Art, and the Museum of Modern Art (New York).

In 1970, Lawrence became the first artist to receive the NAACP Sprigarn Medal. His work is represented in the Harmon Foundation (New York), the Museum of Modern Art, and the Virginia Museum of Fine Arts, as well as other galleries.

He illustrated a children's book, *Harriet and the Promised Land,* in 1968, and in 1972, was named department head at the University of Washington.

DID YOU KNOW?

♦ A war series, developed under a Guggenheim Fellowship after World War II, is believed by some to be Jacob Lawrence's best work.

♦ His *Harlem* series was reproduced and published in *Vogue* magazine, and received nationwide attention.

♦ The life of Toussaint L'Ouverture, the Haitian patriot, so interested Lawrence, that he researched his life in the Schomberg Collection on Negro history.

♦ He has developed as many as sixty paintings on a single subject.

"O snap the fife and still the drums and show the monster as she is."
—Richard Le Gallienne

Lewis Sheridan Leary (1835-1859)
Anti-Slavery Fighter With John Brown

 passionate and daring man, Lewis Sheridan Leary always believed that slavery was evil. He also believed that no slave should be subjected to inhumane treatment. His courage landed him in trouble early in his life; he once intervened and beat a white man who was beating a slave. Such actions were almost unthinkable, and an almost sure death sentence. His act caused so much turmoil he was forced to flee for his life across the Cape Fear River, at night, to Oberlin, Ohio.

Though Leary was born of free parents in Fayetteville, North Carolina, he always despised slavery. During his childhood, he was tutored privately at home. He also attended the school for free colored people in Fayetteville, and was a skilled musician who played several instruments.

His father taught him the trade of designing and decorating saddles. When he fled to Ohio, he was able to use those skills to support himself.

Though he lived as a free man in Ohio, he was still troubled by the existence of slavery. During trips to Cleveland, he met and befriended a group of abolitionists who were John Brown sympathizers. Like Brown, they believed that the only way to rid the nation of the scourge of slavery was through violent confrontation. By the time he actually met Brown, young and impressionable Leary was more than ready to follow this bigger-than-life emancipator.

When John Brown called for volunteers into his army, to raid the Federal arsenal at Harpers Ferry, Virginia, an eager Leary and his cousin, John A. Copeland, joined. The tide of battle, however, did not favor the freedom fighters. When Leary saw that the fight was futile, he tried to retreat across the Shenandoah River. In the ensuing pursuit, he was killed. His cousin was captured along with John Brown and his soldiers. Like their commander-in-chief, Copeland and the others were hanged.

Lewis Sheridan Leary strongly believed in freedom for all men and the right of each person to live with dignity. He and the other Harpers Ferry martyrs gave their lives for those beliefs.

HISTORY IN A CAPSULE

He was one of the most enigmatic figures of the pre-Civil War white abolitionists. Born in Torrington, Connecticut, in 1800, fiery John Brown so hated slavery that he planned the risky raid on the Federal arsenal at Harpers Ferry, Virginia, in 1859.

Obsessed with freeing black slaves, he followed five of his sons to Kansas Territory in 1855, to help abolitionist forces there. He settled in Osawatomie, with a wagonload of guns and other ammunition, to train area anti-slavery guerrillas. He led a night raid on pro-slavery forces, and killed five whites.

Brown later established a stronghold in the Maryland and Virginia mountains, and was elected commander-in-chief of his band of followers. With his armed and disciplined army of sixteen whites and five blacks, he set up headquarters in a rented farmhouse near Harpers Ferry, and on the night of October 16, 1859, he and his followers captured the arsenal, and took approximately sixty hostages. They managed to hold off the militia the following day and night, until the United States Marines broke through and overpowered them. Brown was wounded in the battle while ten of his followers — including two of his sons — were killed. He was tried for treason against the State, leading a slave insurrection, and murder. Brown was convicted and hanged.

"It is but a base, ignoble mind that mounts no higher than a bird can soar."
—Shakespeare

Carl Lewis (b. 1961)
Olympic Track and Field Athlete

He has been known to speak his mind, and to complain about the lack of compensation for athletes in amateur sports. And, the business-like demeanor he assumes is often interpreted as aloofness or arrogance. Though he is not a "media darling," his solid record speaks for itself. In the 1984 Summer Olympic Games held in Los Angeles, California, he won gold medals in the 100 and 200-meter dashes, and the long jump and the 4 x 100 meter relay. His achievement was compared to that of the great Jesse Owens.

He was born in Birmingham, Alabama, and raised in Willingboro, New Jersey. He comes from a family in which both parents were athletes, and who founded and coached the Willingboro Track Club. His sister and brother were athletes as well, and in Carl's early years, they out did his performance on the track field. It was not until high school that he began to exhibit his extraordinary abilities in the long jump, and the amazing speed that was to dominate track and field during the 1980s and early 1990s.

Lewis attended the University of Houston, and became the first athlete of the twentieth century to win both the 100-meter dash and the long jump, in consecutive championships. During the 1988 Games, he won the gold in the 100-meter dash, after first-place finisher, Canadian Ben Johnson, tested positive for the use of a performance-enhancing drug.

In 1991, at the age of thirty, he set the world record at 9.86 seconds in the 100-meter dash. In 1992, during the Summer Games in Barcelona, he won his eighth career gold medal by winning the long jump again, and his ninth by anchoring the 4 x 100 United States relay team. In the same year, however, as he became "the grand old man" of track and field, and his competitors became younger and tougher, he failed to qualify in the sport in which he had excelled for a decade — the 100-meter dash.

When he was at his peak, his excellence as an athlete struck fear in the hearts of all who competed with him. History will record him as one of the greatest track and field athletes of all time.

HISTORY IN A CAPSULE

George Poage, a quarter-miler and hurdler, finished third in the 400-meter hurdles, in the 1904 Olympic Games, held in St. Louis, Missouri. He became the first African-American to win an Olympic medal. While a student at the University of Wisconsin, he set a record for the low hurdles and the 440-yard dash.

When he won the gold in the 1924 Olympics, in the long jump, for a distance of 24 feet and 5 1/8 inches, William DeHart Hubbard of Cincinnati, Ohio, became the first African-American to win an individual event. A University of Michigan student, he set records in a number of track and field events.

"In all ranks of life the human heart yearns for the beautiful . . ." —**Stowe**

Mary Edmonia Lewis (c. 1845-1890)
Sculptor

C alled "Wildfire"in her youth, she was of Chippewa Indian and African-American ancestry. With racial oppression a recurring subject in her sculpture, she was the first American sculptor of African ancestry to be internationally recognized for her work.

Born of an African-American father, who was a gentleman's servant, and a Chippewa mother, who was known for the beautiful designs she embroidered, on the moccasins she made and sold, Edmonia wandered with the tribe. She also made moccasins and baskets, which she sold in cities, as they traveled.

She attended grade school near Albany, New York, at the insistence of Sunrise, her older brother. She described herself as difficult to manage in school. By the time she was ready for college, her brother paid for her trip by stagecoach to Oberlin College in Ohio. It was there that she changed her name to Mary Edmonia

183

Lewis. Her college preparatory courses included lessons in watercolor and drawing. Between 1860 and 1863, she enrolled in a college level liberal arts program.

It was also at Oberlin where she began making drawings of people and objects. She lived with abolitionist and women's rights advocate John Keep. Though she was well-liked in the liberal community of Oberlin, she was accused of attempted murder after two of her white friends became violently ill from a drink of hot mulled wine she had given them. Though no evidence was found to support such a serious charge, she was dragged from home and beaten so badly, she was required to use crutches to appear in court. Her case was dismissed, and the experience tempted her to return to life with the Chippewa.

But she recovered her courage, and with a letter of introduction from abolitionist publisher William Lloyd Garrison, traveled to Boston. Neoclassical sculptor Edward Brackett encouraged her work, and gave her advice. With minimum instructions, she made a medallion of the Civil War insurrectionist, John Brown.

Having seen Colonel Robert Gould Shaw, as he led the 54th Massachusetts Regiment of black soldiers, she made a bust of him, and sold each of one hundred copies made. With her earnings, she left for Rome, the international center of sculpture.

Anna Quincy Waterston, daughter of a Harvard president, supported Lewis and raised the funds to purchase her first piece of marble while in Rome. There, she did her own carving, unlike other sculptors who hired carvers. Once she overcame her fear of being accused of having others do her work, she allowed artisans to do the carving for her.

Works such as *The Freed Woman and Her Child* depicted her social consciousness, and were inspired by the Emancipation Proclamation.

Forever Free, showing a muscular freed slave and a kneeling woman with her hands clasped in prayer, was acquired by Howard University in Washington, D.C. Though the execution is flawed, it succeeds in what it attempts to portray. The two figures were an ambitious undertaking that neoclassical sculptors of more experience and maturity than Lewis, hesitated to attempt.

Her finest rendering is said to be the biblical figure Hagar, the Egyptian maidservant of Abraham, who, after bearing him a son, was cast out by Sarah, his wife. The symbolism of Hagar's crinkly hair and despair depict the feeling of alienation that women of color experience in America.

The first major sculptor in the United States, Edmonia Lewis created from a context of overt racism inherent in the time in which she lived. She used her mixed ethnic background and her perception of a racially polarized society as a matrix for her works. After many years of being recognized by African-Americans, her sculptures have finally received mainstream attention in the United States in the National Museum of American Art.

"There is a strength of quiet endurance as significant of courage as the most daring feats of prowess." **—Tuckerman**

Joe Louis (1914-1981)
Prize Fighter

he television age had not yet arrived. So they came by car. They crammed into buses. Some came by train. The affluent flew in by plane. America was angry, and blacks especially, wanted vengeance against German Max Schmeling. He had bragged about Aryan superiority in his defeat of the African-American champion Joe Louis, in the twelfth round of their first bout in 1935. It was payback time.

The bell sounded for the first round. Louis left his corner. He flew to the attack. An explosion of blows that even the ring-siders couldn't count, sent Schmeling to the canvas three times; two minutes and four seconds into the first round, it was all over. Harlem danced. African-Americans had their hero back, and he had done more than just win. He had punctuated Jesse Owens' Olympic victory when he made myth of the belief in Aryan superiority, before a world audience, during the 1936 Olympic Games.

185

Born Joseph Louis Barrow in Lafayette, Alabama, his family moved to Detroit, Michigan when he was ten years old. They had hoped for an opportunity to earn higher wages, but life was hard, even in the North. Young Joe dropped out of school and went to work in River Rouge at the Ford plant. It was heavy work, and he grew strong and muscular because of it. In his spare time, he street-boxed with boys in the neighborhood, and became good at it.

When amateur Thurston McKinney asked Joe to be his sparring partner, the boy demonstrated his remarkable strength and skill by knocking McKinney out. He later went on to win the 1934 Golden Gloves title and became the light-heavy-weight champion. In the same year, he fought his first professional fight. By 1937, after thirty-six professional bouts, he won the heavyweight championship, by defeating James J. Braddock. Known as "The Brown Bomber," he held the title from 1937 to 1949, having defended it more than twenty-five times.

An earlier fight includes a bout against Italian hero Primo Carnera (1935), who weighed more than two hundred sixty pounds and stood six feet five inches tall. The political matrix of the fight was Emperor Haile Selassie of Ethiopia's war with Italy and the propaganda that emanated. A victory over Carnera would boost the esteem of African-Americans all over the world. Louis did not disappoint. The referee halted the fight in the sixth round after Carnera was knocked down three times.

Four victories and one year after the fight with Carnera, he had his first fight with Max Schmeling. The German defeated Louis in the twelfth round, knocking the champion out. African-Americans, in grief over this humiliating defeat, in a time when they had few heroes, were understandably elated when he followed the defeat with seven victories, winning with knockouts over his opponents. His win over Braddock, on June 22, 1937, set the stage for the mania which preceded the rematch with Max Schmeling. A crowd of seventy thousand, one thousand of them Germans who had come to America to view the fight, massed into Yankee Stadium for one of the most famous fights in boxing history.

DID YOU KNOW?

- ◆ As an amateur, he won fifty-four of fifty-eight boxing matches.
- ◆ In his professional career, he won sixty-eight of seventy-one bouts, fifty-four of them by knockouts.
- ◆ Two of his losses occurred when he was past his prime fighting years, at the end of his career.
- ◆ He published his autobiography, *My Life Story,* in 1947.

"If we neglect our own interest, we deserve the calamities which come upon us."
—*John Conybeare*

Mary Eliza Mahoney (1845-1926)
Pioneer in Nursing

n 1879, the New England Hospital for Women and Children in Boston, Massachusetts, was considered liberal; it's charter stipulated that one Jewish and one black student be included in each class. It was the first institution in America to offer a regular nursing program.

Mary Eliza Mahoney was thirty-three years old when she registered in the hospital to begin the sixteen-month course. Described as "a bundle of energy," who weighed scarcely ninety pounds, she performed the cleaning, scrubbing, ironing and washing duties included in student nurses' sixteen-hour-a-day, seven day-a-week requirements. One of forty students, only she and two white women passed the rigorous test. When diplomas were handed out on August 1, 1879, Mary Mahoney became the nation's first African-American graduate nurse.

187

Like most new nurses, Mahoney's first job was as a private nurse. It was only after WWII that hospitals would provide positions for most white nurses, with black nurses having to advocate longer for equal opportunities.

She became a member of the Nurses Associated Alumnae of the United States and Canada, which was organized in 1896, and later became the American Nurses' Association (ANA). By 1900, the organization still accepted few African-American nurses, because of the requirement that graduates first become members of the state nursing associations. Southern organizations, of course, refused to admit black women. In response to being excluded from the ANA, black nurses organized their own union.

In 1908, the National Association of Colored Graduate Nurses (NACGN) was founded, and Mary Mahoney delivered the welcoming address at its first convention, in Boston, in 1909. The NACGN awarded her a lifetime membership and elected her national chaplain, which made Mahoney responsible for inducting new officers.

Still active in 1911, she was made supervisor of the Kings Park, Long Island, Howard Orphan Asylum for black children.

The NACGN established the Mary Mahoney Medal in 1936, to honor distinguished service by African-American nurses. When the NACGN merged with the ANA in 1949, the new organization preserved the Mary Mahoney Award.

For her pioneering efforts in the field of nursing, she was named to nursing's Hall of Fame in 1976.

HISTORY IN A CAPSULE

Dr. Marie Zakzewska, head of the New England Hospital for Women and Children in Boston, was a militant advocate of both women's rights, and equal rights for African-Americans. A pioneering physician, she was born in Berlin, Germany. She emigrated to the United States around 1853, where she met Dr. Elizabeth Blackwell, who persuaded her to learn English, and to enroll in medical school. She received her M.D. from Cleveland Medical College (the medical department of West Reserve College), in 1856. She became resident physician of the New York Infirmary for Women and Children, the country's first hospital staffed by women, in 1857, and in 1859, became professor of obstetrics and diseases of women and children, at the New England Female Medical College. By 1899, only six African-American nurses had graduated from the institution, the first being Mary Eliza Mahoney.

"Negroes must earn their way to higher achievement. They can't get it by throwing rocks, preaching anarchy or making demands that go beyond reason."
—Thurgood Marshall

Thurgood Marshall (1908-1993)
United States Supreme Court Justice

 hen he was appointed to the Supreme Court by President Lyndon Baines Johnson in 1967, he became the first American of African descent to receive such an honor. He became known as "Mr. Civil Rights," and the man who compelled society to grant African-Americans the rights already guaranteed to all citizens by the Constitution of the United States.

Marshall did not condone violent confrontation as a way of winning equal rights. He chose instead to make the courtroom his battleground. Throughout the 1930s, 1940s and 1950s, he won landmark victories for the cause of justice for people of color. It was from 1940 through 1961 that the civil rights giant made his greatest contributions to black Americans. He won twenty-nine out of thirty-two cases that he argued before the Supreme Court. The most famous, Brown v. Topeka Board of Education, was the pivotal case which resulted in the desegregation of the nation's schools. He made the Fourteenth Amendment a reality.

Though he is best known for his courtroom victories fought on behalf of civil rights, he was also in private practice in Baltimore, from 1933 to 1938, and served as part-time assistant to Charles H. Houston, special counsel to the NAACP from 1936 to 1938. He succeeded Houston in 1938 and served until 1962. President John F. Kennedy then appointed him as judge of the United States District Court for the Second Judicial Circuit of New York. He served from 1962 to 1965.

Marshall was a key figure in the new strategy of attacking the policies of segregation rather than merely insisting on equality. By winning the Sweatt v. Painter case, Marshall made it possible for blacks to enter the University of Texas law school (1950). The Smith v. Allwright victory (1944) allowed blacks to vote in Texas primaries. Morgan v. Virginia (1946) made it illegal to segregate interstate passengers in Virginia, and Shelly v. Kraemer (1948) declared restrictive housing covenants unconstitutional. Marshall believed that the answer to inequities lay in the Constitution, thus his love for Constitutional law.

Born in Baltimore, he was named "Thoroughgood," but by the time he reached the second grade, he shortened it to Thurgood, because, in his words, he "got tired of spelling all that out." He received his education in the Maryland public schools, and had memorized the Constitution of the United States by the time he graduated from high school.

He went on to graduate with honors from Lincoln University in Pennsylvania, but was refused when he applied for admission to the Law Department of Maryland University. He was accepted at Howard University Law School, and graduated with highest honors in 1933. He went into private practice in Baltimore, and returned to do battle against the University of Maryland Law School. He savored his victory when the case of Murry v. Pearson won African-Americans the right to study at the university.

So dedicated was Marshall to the cause of civil rights, that when he was offered the position of Solicitor General by President Johnson, he accepted it, even though it paid a lower salary. Because he would be the people's advocate and would argue the cases of the government before the Supreme Court, Marshall felt that the sacrifice was worth it. He retired in 1991.

DID YOU KNOW?

♦ Thurgood Marshall was known as the most outstanding constitutional lawyer in the United States.
♦ His father was a country club head waiter, and his mother a teacher.
♦ In 1946, he was given the NAACP Sprigarn Medal.
♦ Originally, he wanted to be a dentist.

"Monuments are the grappling-irons that bind one generation to another."

—Joubert

Joanne M. Martin (nda)
Elmer P. Martin (b. 1946)
Founders, Great Blacks in Wax Museum

ach year during the month of February, more than two thousand students file off school buses to visit Malcolm X, Dr. Martin Luther King, Jr., Frederick Douglass, and other historical and contemporary African-Americans displayed in the context of their time. The impact of the visual experience lends an air of authenticity to the people they read about during Black History Month.

What began as a traveling show in 1983, is now the nation's first black wax museum. Housed in what was once an old fire station, the Great Blacks in Wax museum stretches over three thousand feet.

Founders Elmer and Joanne Martin hold Ph.D. degrees and are each educators who searched for a way to make African-American history an enticing subject. Their idea originated when they watched the rapt attention children paid to mannequins in a Florida wax museum.

Beginning with only four figures that they transported in their van and displayed at churches, malls and schools, they now have more than one hundred twenty, each clad in the costume of its era.

The museum, occupying the second largest block in Baltimore, Maryland, attracted more than 103,000 visitors in 1995, and has brought in admirers from as far away as Europe and Africa.

Elmer Martin was born in Kansas City, Missouri, to Harriet and Elmer P. Martin, Sr., and was reared by grandparents Alberta and Emanuel Cason in Glasgow, Missouri. He graduated from Glasgow High School in 1964, and received his B.A. degree in sociology from Lincoln University (Jefferson City, Missouri) in 1968. He earned his Ph.D. in Social Welfare from Case Western Reserve University (Cleveland, Ohio) in 1975. As a part-time professor, he taught at both Morehouse College (Atlanta, Georgia) and Case Western. He also taught social work at Grambling (Louisiana) State College, and is presently a tenured full professor of social work at Morgan State University (Baltimore), where he has taught for twenty years.

Joanne Mitchell Martin was born in Yulee, Florida, and receive her Bachelor of Arts degree in French from Florida A&M University (Tallahassee, Florida). She earned her Master's in reading from Case Western Reserve, and her Ph.D. in educational psychology from Coppin State College (Baltimore), where she coordinated the Learning Skills Center from 1985 to 1992, when she became the center's director.

Elmer and Joanne Martin had no initial background in museums, and therefore spent five years educating themselves. They used money they had saved to buy a house, to purchase their first wax figures. As the nation's first and only museum of its kind to focus on black history and culture, it attracted the attention of State Senator Clarence Blount, who sponsored a bill providing it with a one hundred thousand dollar grant. The City of Baltimore provided another one hundred thousand dollars to renovate the old firehouse, and Elmer and Joanne raised an additional five hundred thousand dollars through grants, loans and donations.

The Martins have been guests on major television networks, including *NBC* and *CNN*, have been interviewed by the *New York Times, Wallstreet Journal,* and the *Washington Post,* and have been profiled in *Essence, Black Enterprise* and *Jet* magazines.

They have also co-authored the three books *Social Work and the Black Experience, The Helping Tradition in the Black Family and Community,* and the *Black Extended Family.*

Current plans are to expand the museum, and to help provide alternatives for troubled youths.

"Ideas are cosmopolitan. They have the liberty of the world."   **—H.W. Beecher**

Jan Matzeliger (1852-1889)
Inventor

Had he lived, Jan Matzeliger would have become one of the world's wealthiest men. His death at age thirty-seven, however, negated his chance of realizing the tremendous profit his creation of a shoe-lasting machine eventually generated.

The invention of this immigrant of African ancestry, who spoke little English, earned Lynn, Massachusetts the title of "shoe capital of the world." When he was ten years old, Jan was employed in the government machine works of Paramaribo, Dutch Guiana, where he was born. He was the son of a mother of African heritage, and a Dutch engineer. He immigrated to the United States as a sailor when he was eighteen years old, and eventually settled in Lynn, Massachusetts.

Matzeliger designed the devise when, as a shoe factory employee, he noticed that machines could cut, tack and sew, but not last a shoe. This resulted in a production slow down, because lasting was a slow, tedious process in which the sole was attached to the upper part of the shoe. As a result of ten years of working in secret, he designed and perfected a machine that held the shoe on the last, pulled the leather down, drove in the nails, and delivered a finished shoe in a minute's time.

Sydney W. Winslow, who established the United Shoe Machine Company, bought Matzeliger's patent, and issued him stock in the company, rather than paying him. The machine improved working conditions for shoe factory workers, doubled wages, and decreased by fifty percent the cost of producing a pair of shoes.

Though he received five patents on his machines, between 1883 and 1891, he died before the shoe industry generated the great profits that his machine made possible. His last patent was issued two years after his untimely death.

As an inventor whose product revolutionized the shoe industry, his contribution made factory-manufactured shoes affordable for the average person. Though he never realized the profits from his machines, his invention impacted the world.

DID YOU KNOW?

- Matzeliger was so involved with his inventions, he never married.
- He died from tuberculosis.
- Because of Matzeliger's invention, the United Shoe Machine Company, which bought his patent, was able to capture ninety-eight percent of the shoe machinery trade.
- Because he received financing from two Lynn businessmen, he forfeited two-thirds of the interest in any profit resulting from his invention.
- By using his machine, the company produced seven hundred pairs of shoes in a day, compared to fifty pairs made by skilled manual lasters.
- Tuberculosis was so common among the workers it was called "the shoemaker's disease." Doctors believed it resulted from working in factories with little or no ventilation.

"I portray the type of Negro woman who has worked honestly and proudly to give our nation the Marian Andersons, Roland Hayeses and Ralph Bunches."

—Hattie McDaniel

Hattie McDaniel (1898-1952)
Actress

She became the mistress of comic rebellion in her roles as "the eternal mammy." She had the ability to dominate a scene while playing subservient characters. And, her "sass" and spirit enabled her to become the first African-American actress to win the Academy Award Oscar, when she won Best Supporting Actress for her role as Mammy in 1939's *Gone With the Wind.*

Though her fans numbered in the thousands, Hattie McDaniel was sharply criticized by black contemporaries of perpetuating a stereotype of African Americans. Some suggested that she should refuse to accept the Oscar. Known for her good nature and humor, she silenced her critics by retorting, "It's better to get seven thousand dollars a week for playing a maid than seven dollars a week for being one."

Though she was an actress and vaudeville performer, she began her professional career as a singer. As a teenager, she wrote and performed her own songs in her brother Otis' traveling vaudeville tent show. In 1915, she became the first African-American woman to sing on radio when she performed with Professor George Morrison's Negro Orchestra. And, at one point, she had her own act in Kansas City, sang at conventions, and performed in several vaudeville acts. When she was cast in the operetta *Showboat,* in 1925, her acting venue moved to theaters.

Because roles for black actresses were scarce, she found herself among the ranks of the unemployed a few years later. Like other actors and actresses, who worked other jobs between roles, she was a real-life maid at Sam Pick's Suburban Inn. She used the experience to lend authenticity to her trademark characters.

She was an immediate success in 1931 on the Los Angeles radio show *The Optimistic Donuts Show,* in the role of Hi-Hat Hattie. For the next twenty-five years, she played in a long series of movie roles. The most famous of her roles were in *Blonde Venus* (1932), *Babbie* (1934), *Music is Magic* (1935), *Gone With the Wind,* for which she earned the Academy Award in 1939, *They Died With Their Boots On* (1941), *Reap the Wild Wind* (1942), and *Since You Went Away,* (1944). Her role as Mammy, in *Showboat,* with Paul Robeson, in 1936, brought her great acclaim.

A gifted actress who had the ability to transform subservient maids into characters who seemed wiser than, and possessed more strength than, their white employers, she was type-cast in the role of Mammy, largely because she played the roles so successfully, and because she was limited in what kind of roles were offered to her.

When she played Beulah, a maid, on the radio show *The Beulah Show,* she was well-established, and in enough demand that she was able to convince the producers to allow her to change scripts that she did not like, which included not speaking in dialect. She played the role so convincingly, that mail would be addressed to Beulah McDaniel. The show was so popular that it became a television series in 1950, with Ethel Waters chosen to play the lead role. McDaniel's fans complained so loudly that actress Waters relinquished the role the following year.

Born in Wichita, Kansas, she was the thirteenth child of Henry McDaniel, a Baptist minister, and Susan Holbert McDaniel. The family moved to Denver, Colorado, where Hattie and her siblings attended the local elementary school, and East Denver High School. When she was fifteen, WCTU awarded her a gold medal for reciting *Convict Joe,* a dramatic poem. And, by the time she went on tour in 1924 and 1925, she was known as the "colored Sophie Tucker."

She married four times, and in real life, was a woman of strength. Upon her death, McDaniel became the first African-American to be buried in Los Angeles' Rosedale Cemetery.

Ronald McNair

Astronaut

NASA

". . . light a thousand torches at one torch . . . and the flame of the latter remains the same." **—Joubert**

Ronald E. McNair (1950-1986)
Astronaut, Laser Physicist

From the sweltering cotton and tobacco fields of Lake City, South Carolina, where he labored as a child to earn money, Ronald McNair soared into the ice blue skies of Florida, and into history. Though his tenure on earth was short, he fulfilled the special mission to attempt to explore the outer reaches of the universe.

As a laser physicist and astronaut, he was the second African-American to travel in space, following the success of Gion S. Bluford, Jr. Instead of lamenting the harshness of his earlier life, he stated that it served to toughen him, to enable him to endure and to persevere.

A bright child, in spite of his impoverished environment, he learned to read at three years of age. He went on to earn his B.A. degree from North Carolina State University, and his Doctorate at the Massachusetts Institute of Technology.

197

His honors were many, and included Ford Foundation Fellow, Presidential Scholar, Omega Psi Phi Scholar of the Year, and NATO Fellow. He expanded his expertise in laser physics by studying at the Ecole d'Ete Theorique de Physique in France, and served as a staff physicist with Hughes Research Laboratories. Because of his academic brilliance, and other attributes, in 1978, he was chosen for the astronaut corps. When he boarded the Challenger on his second and final flight, his immeasurable potential was cut tragically short when the space craft exploded in the calm skies of South Florida. Along with six other astronauts, McNair perished before the horrified eyes of the world.

Though the spacecraft was one of the world's most sophisticated pieces of technology, something went terribly wrong, and America was reminded of the fragility of life, and the ever-present possibility of human error.

As an astronaut, no doubt, McNair realized the risk he undertook when climbing aboard a spacecraft, but was willing to take it. It is through such courage that man is able to advance his knowledge about the universe, of which each of us is but a tiny piece.

DID YOU KNOW?

♦ The space program was twenty-five years old at the time of the Challenger disaster.
♦ The first man-made satellite SPUTNIK I, launched by the Soviet Union in 1957, ushered in the space age.

HISTORY IN A CAPSULE

In 1992, Louis Freeman, who earned his private pilot's license while in college at East Texas State University, became the first African-American to be named chief pilot of a major airline. He makes sure all operations transcend the requirements of the Federal Aviation Administration.

His career in the skies began with piloting his friends around the Dallas area. He took the United States Air Force qualifying test, and on the second attempt, passed the pilot's section, which he had on his first attempt. He completed his training and was assigned to pilot 737s in Sacramento, California.

198

"Imagination disposes of everything; it creates beauty, justice, and happiness which are everything in this world." **—Pascal**

Oscar Deveraux Micheaux (1884-1951)
Filmmaker, Author

Body and Soul, the movie in which the great Paul Robeson made his film debut, was one of approximately thirty films that Oscar Micheaux made between 1919 and 1937. Although the "race movies" he made were mostly musicals, he also included every subject from Westerns to melodramas. Brilliant in promoting his books, his films and himself, his movies were quite popular among African-Americans and a small cross-over audience of white supporters.

From a seventeen year-old pullman porter, to an industrious farmer, he went on to become one of the most prolific and successful African-American movie producers of his day. It was largely because of his box office triumphs that major studios began making movies with African-American themes.

Though his early years are clouded in mystery, he was known to have been an avid reader, and apparently taught himself to write commercially successful fiction such as *The Conquest: Story of a Negro Pioneer*. Also an entrepreneur, he published and promoted the book. In 1915, he penned *Forged Note: Romance of the Darker Races*, and in 1917, *The Homesteader*. It is believed that his melodramatic works were largely autobiographical.

His venture into film-making occurred in 1918, when the Lincoln Motion Picture Company offered to buy the rights to *The Homesteader*. The deal fell through when Micheaux insisted on directing the movie. He then left for New York, and formed his company, the Oscar Micheaux Corporation. Though his films did not deal with the social and political issues plaguing African-Americans of the day, they did not project the expected stereotypes either, and thus provided positive, though somewhat mythical role models.

He recovered from a 1928 bankruptcy, and by 1931, was producing and directing *The Exile*, and by 1932, *Veiled Aristocrats*. He wrote *Wind From Nowhere, Masquerade, Story of Dorothy Stansfield*, and *Case of Mrs. Wingate,* between 1941 and 1943. His last production was *The Betrayal* in 1948. Hard-driven, he shunned tobacco and alcohol, and was a financial success. Unfortunately, he so mishandled his profits, that by the time he died, he was destitute.

As an early film maker, Micheaux's company provided career opportunities for African-American performers, artists, and technicians. That he formed his own company to produce films for and about African-Americans, in a time when society was largely hostile toward black enterprise, is a tribute to his fortitude and vision.

Born in Metropolis, Illinois, he left home at seventeen, and made his way to Gregory County, South Dakota by 1904. While working as a farmer, he indulged his passion for writing. When he turned down the film company's offer to buy the rights to *The Homestead*, it ultimately led to one of the most successful film-producing careers of his day.

HISTORY IN A CAPSULE

The Lincoln Motion Picture Company was founded in 1915 in Los Angeles, California. It was the first African-American movie production company. Noble Johnson and Clarence Brooks were African-American actors, and James T. Smith, also an African-American, was a druggist. Harry Grant, the cameraman, was white. When they refused to allow Oscar Micheaux to direct *The Homesteader*, he struck out on his own and formed his own company.

"All my work as an actress has been done with my singing in my mind."
— Abbie Mitchell

Abbie Mitchell (1884-1960)
Singer, Actress

hen King Edward VII saw that Abbie Mitchell was missing from a birthday celebration for the Prince of Wales, he sent his private carriage to fetch her. He wished to hear her sing *Brown Baby, Mine*, the song she made famous. The year was 1903, and Miss Mitchell, a dramatic soprano cast in *In Dahomey*, was in London with the Bert Williams-George Walker company production, that was written by Jesse Shipp, after they had played in New York.

When they returned to the United States, she played at Proctor's 23rd Street Theater with the Memphis Students, a troupe that sang, acted, and danced. She also performed at Hammerstein's Victoria Theater, The Marshall Hotel, and the Roof Garden in New York.

She traveled abroad again to perform at the Schumann Circus in Berlin, and the Palace Theater in London. She also sang the lead role in *The Red Moon* in Russia, for Czar Nicholas II.

In 1904, she performed in *The Southerner*, and in 1908, appeared in another Williams and Walker production, *Bandana Land*.

During the years that a throat ailment prevented her from pursuing her singing career, she became lead actress with a Harlem theater company, the Lafayette Players. Once she recovered her singing voice, she left for Paris to study while traveling on concert tours.

She appeared in the productions *In Abraham's Bosom*, and *The House of Shadows*. She accepted the department chairmanship of the voice department at Tuskegee Institute, but continued to sing in concerts. Appearances included Town Hall in New York City in 1931, the Mecca Temple and Aeolian Opera Company in *Cavalleria Rustican* in 1934. She accepted acting roles in *Stevedore* and in Lillian Hellman's *The Little Foxes*.

Born in New York City, of a Jewish father and African-American mother, she completed her early education in Baltimore, and studied under Emilia Serrano and Harry T. Burleigh. She gained experience on stage by performing in musical comedies. Her first concert evoked critical reviews which encouraged her to continue her training in France. Though she possessed a commanding soprano voice of clarity and purity, she was never a part of the inner circles of opera because of the rigid color lines maintained by society in her day.

She married Will Marion Cook, an accomplished composer, who produced some of the musical comedies in which she starred.

Her desire to sing opera was only partly realized, and while she achieved success and acclaim as a concert singer and as a dramatic actress, she never fully gave up on her dream.

Other productions in which she delivered memorable performances include *Coquette*, in which she performed with Helen Hayes, *Clorindy, The Origin of the Cakewalk, Help Wanted* and *Madam X*.

Figure 4

"Our land is not more the recipient of the men of all countries than of their ideas."
— Bancroft

Garrett A. Morgan (1875-1963)
Inventor

T raffic in today's cities moves in a systematic and organized manner because of the invention of an African-American. In 1923, Garrett A. Morgan invented the first automatic stop signal and made driving safer all over the world. He sold the rights to the invention to General Electric for forty thousand dollars.

Born in Paris, Tennessee, he moved to Cleveland, Ohio in 1895. There, in 1901, he devised his first invention, a belt fastener for sewing machines. In 1914, he invented a smoke inhalator. In 1916, the device proved useful to a team of rescue workers trapped in a tunnel beneath Lake Erie. For his contribution, the city of Cleveland awarded Morgan a gold medal. He also won First Grand Prize for the device at the Second International Invention of Sanitation and Safety in 1914.

203

His practical inventions are a legacy to his genius and foresight in providing solutions to problems arising from life in a progressive society.

HISTORY IN A CAPSULE

The sparkling, white sugar many stir in their morning coffee is the legacy of Norbert Rillieux. In 1881, he perfected the standard system used in refining sugar, which is used by the sugar refining industry. His invention solved the problems previous inventions had by using heat properly during the evaporation process. The same technique is applied to the manufacture of glue, gelatin, and condensed milk.

Born a slave in Louisiana, he was sent to France for school, and while there, became interested in refining sugar. Though his method was not readily embraced by U.S. sugar producers, or those in Europe, renewed interest took place among Europeans with West Indian sugar plantations. Rillieux even adapted his machine to refining sugar beets.

Sugar manufacturers erected a bronze tablet in the State Museum in Louisiana in his honor. With other black inventors and scientists, he proved that creativity and inventiveness, once loosened from the shackles of bondage, could transcend society's perception of color and race.

"When whites turn on the television and see blacks the same as white people, subconsciously they are accepting this tremendous change which has come into society." — **Constance Baker Motley**

Constance Baker Motley (b. 1921)
Lawyer, Judge

A businessman named Clarence Blakeslee was so impressed with her courage and intelligence, he paid her way through college.

She attended Fisk University in Nashville, Tennessee for a time, but received her Bachelor of Arts degree from New York University in 1942 and her L.L.B. from Columbia University, in 1946. Even before she graduated, she joined the NAACP Legal Defense Team, and was one of its tacticians from 1945 to 1965. She became its principal trial attorney on all major school desegregation cases which were supported by the NAACP legal defense fund, including Brown vs. Board of Education in 1954, for which she helped write the brief.

Constance Baker Motley worked as a clerk for Thurgood Marshall during her senior year at Columbia, and won many victories during her career. Between

1960 and 1964, she won nine of ten key cases which she argued before the Supreme Court — cases which secured equal rights for black Americans. It was because of her representation, that James Meredith won the right of admission to the University of Mississippi (1962). She was chief counsel in many other similar cases, and, also, successfully handled cases involving discrimination in housing, transportation, recreation, and public accommodations.

Because of her brilliant representation of key civil rights cases, she quickly ascended the career ladder, becoming the first African-American woman to be elected to the New York Senate (1964), and the first to be elected by the New York City Council as president of the Borough of Manhattan.

Another "first" occurred in 1966, when President Lyndon Baines Johnson appointed her Federal judge to the United States District Court for Southern New York State. She became chief judge of the Federal District Court, which includes the Bronx, Manhattan, in 1982. By 1986, she was the court's senior judge.

She believes that sexism is more deeply rooted than racism, and that education is the way for minorities to gain power in society. She recognizes the Supreme Court decisions of 1954 and 1964, which declared segregation unconstitutional, as pivotal for African-Americans.

Born in New Haven, Connecticut, to parents who immigrated from Nevis, a Caribbean Island, Motley was always bright and outspoken and currently holds sixteen honorary doctorate degrees. Among her many honors and awards are the Elizabeth Blackwell Award (1968), induction into the National Women's Hall of Fame in Seneca, New York (1993), and the Equal Justice Award from the NAACP Legal Defense and Educational Fund (1997). Prior to 1968, Judge Motley received over seventy awards from various organizations.

She has written articles, and contributed to professional journals, including the *Fordham Law Review, The Harvard Blackletter Journal* and the *Yale Law Journal*. In 1991, she wrote a tribute to Thurgood Marshall for *MS* magazine.

Constance Baker Motley is now Senior United States District Judge, United States District Court, Southern District of New York.

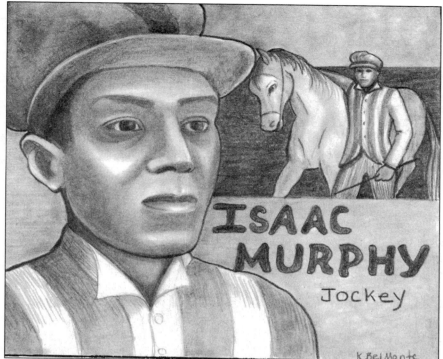

K. BelMonte

"True glory consists in doing what deserves to be written; in writing what deserves to be read; and in so living as to make the world happier and better for our living in it." **— Pliny**

Isaac "Ike" Murphy (1861-1896)
Jockey

lthough his life was short, he lived it to the glory of thundering hoofbeats. Having ridden his first race in 1875, in Louisville, Kentucky, when he was only fourteen years old, Isaac Murphy is considered by some to be the greatest jockey in United States history. In his twenty-year career, he rode in more than fourteen hundred races, and he became the first jockey, black or white, to ride winning mounts three times, and to win the Kentucky Derby two times in succession.

Born Isaac Burns, in Pleasant Green Hill, near Lexington, Kentucky, his mother was a laundress for a racing stable. Young Isaac exercised area horses and had no trouble entering racing. During his time, most United States jockeys were African-American.

He won forty-nine of fifty-one races held at Saratoga, New York, and won five Latonia Derbies, which at the time were considered more prestigious than the Kentucky Derby. Though he rode in a few races in 1875, his official career was from 1876 to 1896. His Kentucky Derby wins occurred in 1884, 1890, and 1891. In addition, he won the American Derby in Chicago in 1884, 1885, 1886, and 1888; four of the first five runnings. His record was 628 victories in 1,412 races. His forty-four percent winning average is considered phenomenal.

In spite of his impressive record, he rode relatively few mounts, having developed a weight problem that led to his retirement. He died of pneumonia at age thirty-five. Murphy was inducted into the Racetrack Hall of Fame at Pimlico, Maryland and Saratoga, New York.

DID YOU KNOW?

♦ The Kentucky Derby, one of the classic American horse races, was established in 1875.

♦ The distance the horses ran was reduced in 1896, from one and one-half miles to the present one and one-quarter miles.

♦ Colts carry 126 pounds, while fillies carry slightly less, at 121 pounds.

♦ The Kentucky Derby, the Preakness, and the Belmont races make up the United States Triple Crown, a coveted title in horse racing.

♦ Until approximately 1900, most of the trainers, handlers, grooms and jockeys in United States horse racing were African-American.

♦ In the first Kentucky Derby, fourteen of the fifteen jockeys were black.

♦ African-American jockey Oliver Lewis rode the winning horse in the first Kentucky Derby.

"Of two heroes, he is the greatest who esteems his rivals most." **—Beaumelle**

James Cleveland "Jesse" Owens
(1913-1980) Olympic Athlete

I t was 1936 in Nazi Germany, and Owens had just made myth out of Hitler's boast of Aryan superiority when he blazed his way into history books by winning four gold medals. When Jesse Owens made his way to the victory stand to receive his Olympic Gold Medals, it is said that Adolph Hitler chose to leave rather than stay to shake the hand of an African-American. Owens, however, denied that it ever happened.

He set a world record in the running broad jump, anchored the 400-meter relay team to a world record win, and won the 100 and 200-meter dashes. For his phenomenal performances, he was dubbed "the world's fastest human," and "the ebony antelope."

The youngest of thirteen children, born to a poor Alabama sharecropper, he was named James Cleveland Owens. His nickname "J.C." eventually became Jesse. He was sickly as a child, and began his track career after his health improved. Charles Riley of Cleveland's Fairmount High School, coached him and encouraged him to attend Ohio State University. There, he made history. During a Big Ten meet in May of 1935, he tied his own record in the 100-yard dash, broke records in the 200-yard dash, and in the 220-yard low hurdles, while setting the world record in the broad jump.

Owens earned his Bachelor's degree from Ohio State in 1937. After his Olympic victories, he returned to the United States to a ticker tape parade in New York City, followed by a reception at the Waldorf Astoria Hotel.

He used his celebrity as a track and field star to encourage Chicago boys, and steer them toward productive lives through involvement in sports. He worked for the Illinois Athletic Committee, and, in 1955, represented the United States Department of State, as a good-will ambassador to India. As the most outstanding track athlete of the first half of the twentieth century, he was awarded a citation by the Associated Press.

In 1984, his granddaughter, Gina Hemphill, carried the Olympic torch into the Los Angeles Coliseum in his memory.

Though there was a poignant disparity between his heroism and the racial climate in the United States, like other African-American athletic heroes of his day, Owens always displayed good sportsmanship, was a source of pride, and a role model for all Americans.

HISTORY IN A CAPSULE

The first African-American to win a national sports title was Marshall "Major" Taylor, a bicycle racer. In 1898, at the age of twenty, he won the American cycling championship. Taylor went on to win over a hundred races in the United States and abroad, and became known as "the Fastest Bicycle Rider in the World."

He was born in Indiana in 1878, and began the sport as a trick rider for a bicycle shop. He was a member of the See-Saw Club, an African-American group of cyclists. Because he was often attacked by racist whites, Taylor teamed up with two sympathetic white cyclists. He was also the American sprint champion in bicycling from 1898 through 1900.

"I am not going to move. I have paid my money." —**Rosa Parks**

Rosa Parks (b. 1913)
Civil Rights Activist

S he was a camellia beauty of uncommon strength, who became known as the "Mother of the Modern Civil Rights Movement." Her simple act of refusing to give up her seat on a Montgomery, Alabama bus forever changed the social landscape of the country.

Born in Tuskegee, Alabama, to James and Leona McCawley, her family moved to Montgomery when Rosa was eleven years old. Though her activism is generally summed up by her courageous refusal on that December day in 1955, her activism began as far back as the 1930s, when she defended the Scottsboro Boys. In 1943, she was secretary of the Montgomery NAACP and tried to register to vote. She was denied. In the same year, she refused to enter the back door of a bus, and as a result, was forced off. Tenacious in demanding her rights, she tried again to vote in 1944, and again was denied. In 1945, she finally received her certificate for voting.

She became advisor to the NAACP Youth Council in 1949. She was active in the organization when she met Reverend Martin Luther King, Jr., in 1955, the year she refused to give up her seat, because she was tired of second-class treatment. It was also the year she was arrested, fingerprinted and fined ten dollars, which she appealed, and did not have to pay.

Because of her soft-spoken act of courage, similar non-violent acts such as sit-ins, swim-ins and eat-ins sprang up all over the nation. With Reverend Martin Luther King, Jr. as spokesman, the plight of African-Americans was played out over the media before a world audience.

Her act of valor dealt a death blow to the Southern tradition of segregated public facilities. She quietly continued civil rights activism and has been honored by the Southern Christian Leadership Conference (SCLC). Shaw College (Detroit, Michigan) awarded her an honorary doctorate degree, Detroit Mayor Coleman Young named a street "Rosa Parks Boulevard" (1976), and the Progressive National Baptist Convention honored her with the Martin Luther King, Jr. Award in 1978. In the same year, the Detroit Historical District granted landmark status to the Rosa Parks Foundation, which erected a building to house her personal papers. In 1987, with Elaine Steele, she co-founded the Rosa and Raymond Parks Institute for Self-Development, to help the young realize their potential. A bust of her was also unveiled at the Smithsonian Institution in Washington, D.C. She traveled to Japan in 1994 and received an honorary doctorate degree from Soka University. In the same year, she traveled to Stockholm, Sweden, received the Rosa Parks Peace Prize, and lit the Peace Candle.

Rosa Parks: My Story (New York: Dial Books), her first book, was published in 1992. In her book *Quiet Strength* (1995), she states that she wants to be remembered for standing up to injustice and as someone who wants a better world for youth.

DID YOU KNOW?

- The Montgomery bus boycott lasted for 381 days.
- The custom of the pre-civil rights era was for African-Americans to pay at the front door, get off the bus, and re-enter through the back door to find a seat.
- Some of Rosa Parks papers have been donated to the Walter P. Reuther Library of Urban Affairs, and Wayne State University.
- She moved from Montgomery to Detroit, to escape the harassment following the bus protest.

Bill
Pickett

Rodeo
Star

K.BelMonte

"The man who succeeds above his fellows is the one who, early in life, clearly discerns his object, and toward that object, habitually directs his powers."

— Bulwer

Bill Pickett (1860-1932)
Cowboy, Wild West Showman

The saying, "When a man bites a dog, it's news," is a bit of what made Bill Pickett one of the most dazzling showmen of his day. He introduced the sport of "bulldogging" by watching a bulldog control an unruly steer by biting its lip. Pickett tried exactly that — he bit the lip of a steer, grasped it by the horns and twisted its head until it fell to the ground. It did not take long for the daring stunt, which he is generally credited for creating, to become popular.

Because of it, and other daredevil stunts, he was signed to perform in Millers 101 Ranch Wild West Show, near Ponca City, Oklahoma, where he was head-lined as the "Champion Bulldogger," for many years. He became one of rodeo's most popular performers in history. His other daredevil tricks included jumping from a running horse onto the back of a steer.

213

The sport of bulldogging today is one of eight major events in rodeo competition. Though cowboys no longer bite a steer's lip, a "hazer" keeps the animal running on a straight path so that the contestant can jump from his horse onto the steer's back, grab the horns and wrestle it to the ground.

Born in Texas, and reared on open range country, Pickett learned to ride almost as soon as he learned to walk. Having also worked on ranches in South America, he was so experienced, by the time he became a young adult, horseback riding was second nature to him. This enabled him to perform many of his spectacular riding tricks on his horse, Spradley. Because of his popularity, he performed in England before George V and Queen Mary, in 1914.

In 1932, on his Oklahoma ranch, at the age of 72, Pickett was roping a bronco and was kicked in the head. He died of a fractured skull nearly two weeks later. In 1971, he became the first African-American to be inducted into the Cowboy Hall of Fame.

HISTORY IN A CAPSULE

Another of the "other" cowboys that Zane Grey overlooked in his tales about the Old West figured prominently in author J. Evetts Haley's recounting of Charles Goodnight's life as a cowboy.

Bose Ikard, born a slave in Mississippi, was taken to Texas when he was five years old, where he learned roping, fighting and riding. After the Civil War, he participated in the cattle drives of Charles Goodnight and Oliver Loving, as they pushed cattle through Texas and New Mexico, winding northward. Although he also rode with John Slaughter and John Chisum, both famous cowboys, he and Goodnight were constant companions.

Ikard took care of his money, acted as detective and took over whenever Goodnight became too exhausted to continue. He also saved his life on at least two occasions. A tough frontiersman who was capable of handling the perils of the cattle drive, Ikard was described in Haley's book as a friend, as well as a hired man, to Goodnight, who added warmth and life to the long, exhausting drives that were a cowboy's lot.

"If a man has any brains at all, let him hold on to his calling, and, in the grand sweep of things, his turn will come at last."   — **W. McCune**

Sidney Poitier (b. 1927)
Actor

hen the winner of the Oscar for Best Actor was announced in 1963, Sidney Poitier stepped forward to receive it for his performance in *Lilies of the Field*. It was the first time in history that a black actor had been afforded the highest honor in the motion picture industry. He then became one of America's most sought after performers. He is unique in his success not only for his portrayals, but in the fact that he does not sing or dance, but relies solely on his skill as a dramatic actor.

Born in the West Indies, he did not begin his education until he was eleven years old. When he was fifteen, however, he dropped out of school. His family sent him to Miami, Florida, where he lived with relatives, and earned a living as a dishwasher, longshoreman, and construction worker. He volunteered for the Army, and after spending four years in the service, went to New York. The turning point in his life occurred in 1945 when he answered an ad for the American

Negro Theater. Because his heavy West Indian accent was nearly unintelligible to his listeners, his audition for a role was a horrible failure. He was determined to become an actor and taught himself proper diction by imitating the speech patterns of television and radio actors. When he returned for a second audition , he was awarded small parts on and off-Broadway. Because he could not afford to pay for acting lessons, he agreed to work as a handyman at the theater in exchange for instruction.

He earned his first major role in *Lysistrata* (1946). He starred in *Anna Lucasta* (1947) and then shifted his focus from stage to motion pictures, appearing in *Cry The Beloved Country* (1952). He starred in *The Blackboard Jungle* (1955) and, in the same year, received the Sylvania TV Award for his performance in *A Man is 10 Feet Tall*. In 1957, he co-starred in *The Edge of the City*, and in *The Defiant Ones*, for which he was nominated for an Oscar. In the same year, he starred in the stage version of *A Raisin in the Sun,* which enjoyed a nineteen-month success on Broadway, while also playing the lead in the movie adaptation. He played the title role in the stage version of *Porgy and Bess* (1959).

A pioneering actor, whose resume generally includes no stereotyped roles, he both starred in and directed 1965's *A Patch of Blue*, and 1967's *In the Heat of the Night,* which later became a television series. He also directed *Stir Crazy* in 1980, which was one of the most successful films made by an African-American.

Though he faced great adversities, Sidney Poitier's dream of becoming an accomplished actor was achieved through conscientious study, and belief in himself. The humiliation of his first failure in an audition did not deter him from his goal. His perseverance, skill and handsome looks made him the first straight dramatic African-American actor to achieve Hollywood stardom.

HISTORY IN A CAPSULE

It was the release of the D.W. Griffith's *Birth of a Nation,* in 1915, that spurred the NAACP to launch its first national black social protest. Because the film depicted African-Americans as either servile or insolent villains, it was considered offensive by blacks. Their protest involved legislative lobbying, picketing, nationwide mail campaigns and combined efforts with sympathetic white organizations.

To counter the stereotypical propaganda depicted in the movie, African-Americans formed their own performance companies, including the Lincoln Film Company and the Ebony Company of Chicago.

"At Cornell, I was the only black student. UCLA, the same. So I don't think you always need models. What you have is a vision of what you want to be."
— **Alvin Poussaint, M.D.**

Alvin Poussaint (b. 1934)
Psychiatrist

Of the many titles that he has — author, educator, psychiatrist — the one of which he is most proud is that of being a parent. He believes that it is necessary to have both good fathers and mothers as well as a strong extended family of uncles, aunts, and grandparents who support both the parents and the child. Because of this philosophy, he advocates mandatory parenting classes for all school-aged persons. Providing networks that provide direction, tutoring, and mentoring, he believes, will produce children who are physically, spiritually and emotionally healthy.

Alvin Poussaint was born in New York's East Harlem. His father was a printer, his mother, a housewife. His ancestors immigrated to the United States from Haiti in the nineteenth century. He is the seventh of eight children. A bout with rheumatic fever, when he was nine years old, resulted in hospitalization for six months. While convalescing, he developed a passion for reading, which resulted in his excelling in school. At the same time, he saw many of his peers, including his brother, descend into the heroin culture of the 1950s.

Because he showed aptitude in science and mathematics while in junior high school, he competed for, and won, a place in Peter Stuyvesant High School, one of New York's most respected institutions. The intellectual stimulation and challenges contrasted sharply with the ills of his own community, instilling in him a passion to succeed. Poussaint graduated from Peter Stuyvesant and enrolled at Columbia University in New York, where he earned his B.A. degree in 1956. Although he was excluded from certain events, due to the tacit rules of segregation, while he was at Columbia, he remained focused on his goal to become a medical doctor, specializing in psychiatry. In 1960, he earned his M.D. degree from Cornell University, and completed his internship at UCLA in 1964. In his final year, he became chief resident and head of the intern training program.

He has completed research on the effects of racism on African-Americans, and identified six different personality types in oppressed black communities. He is certified by the American Board of Psychiatry and Neurology (1970), and is a specialist in child psychiatry. His many academic appointments include senior clinical instructor at Tufts University Medical School in Boston, Massachusetts (1965-1966); dean of student affairs, Harvard Medical School (1969 - present); associate professor of psychiatry at Harvard Medical School (1965 - 1993); and director of the Media Center for Children, Judge Baker Children's Center in Boston (1994-present). In addition to lecturing and teaching, he has been production consultant for *The Cosby Show*. He has also served as consultant to the FBI, the State Department, and the White House (1979 - present).

He worked with Dr. Martin Luther King, Jr., Reverend Jesse Jackson, and others, as Southern Field Director of the Medical Committee for Human Rights, in Jackson, Mississippi, during the Civil Rights Era. His many awards include the Martin Luther King, Jr. Memorial Drum Major Award in Education (The Southern Christian Leadership Conference, 1981). He serves on many editorial and advisory boards, and is a member of the American Academy of Child and Adolescent Psychiatry. He is also a founding Fellow of the Black Academy of Arts and Letters.

Poussaint is the author of *Why Blacks Kill Blacks* (1972), and he co-authored *Black Child Care* (1975) and *Raising Black Children* (1992), with Dr. James P. Comer. He was also one of several authors who contributed articles to the eighty-fifth anniversary issue of the NAACP's *Crisis* magazine. He has written the introduction and epilogue to many publications, including *The Souls of Black Folk* (W.E.B. DuBois, 1969), and is listed in *Who's Who in America* (1969), *Living Legends in Black* (1975), as well as many other publications.

COLIN POWELL
Four-Star General

". . . in our nation, people can rise as far as their talent, their capacity, their ideas, and their discipline will carry them." — **President William Jefferson (Bill) Clinton**

Colin L. Powell (b. 1937)
Four Star General, U.S. Army

He graduated in 1958 from City College of New York with a Bachelor's degree in geology. Because he was active in the ROTC during his college career, he also graduated with the rank of cadet colonel. The strong calling to be a soldier propelled him to join the Army, which he entered as a second lieutenant. He rose steadily through the ranks and served as commander in Germany, Korea and the United States. In 1962, he was military advisor in South Vietnam.

In 1983, he served as military assistant to the secretary of defense and held various positions in the National Security Council. He was appointed by President Ronald Reagan as National Security Advisor, heading the National Security Council (1987-1989). In 1989, President George Bush appointed Powell to the highest military position in the United States — that of chairman of the Joint Chiefs of Staff. He was the first African-American, and at age fifty-two, the youngest man ever to hold the position. He became one of the chief draftsmen of the 1991 Persian Gulf War.

He was born in Harlem, in New York City, to West Indian immigrant parents and grew up in the South Bronx. As a lifelong soldier of stellar character and accomplishments, Powell has received many honors. In 1963, he was awarded the Purple Heart and the Bronze Star, and, in 1969 and 1971, he received the Legion of Merit Award. In 1988, he received the Soldier's Medal, the Secretary's Award and the Distinguished Service Medal.

Of his long career as a soldier, Powell has stated, "I've never wanted to be anything else...and I thank the nation for having given me the opportunity to serve in the proud armed forces of the United States." He has been mentioned as both a presidential and vice-presidential candidate on the Republican ticket. Though he declined both after serious consideration, he remains a popular figure.

Powell retired from the military in 1993, after thirty-five years as an officer.

DID YOU KNOW?

◆ Powell attended the National War College.
◆ He was brigade commander of the 101st Airborne Division.
◆ Powell directed the United States invasion of Panama, to arrest its leader, Manuel Noriega, on drug trafficking charges.

HISTORY IN A CAPSULE

Dubbed "Buffalo Soldiers," for their bravery in battle, by the Native Americans who fought them, they were the first all-black regular Army regiment, and the first all-black regiment commissioned during peace-time. Their duty was to guard settlers in the hostile, unsettled West.

Though they suffered discrimination in places such as San Angelo, Texas, and in procuring necessities such as equipment, rations and horses, they had the highest re-enlistment and the lowest desertion rate in the military. Unfortunately, they received little acknowledgment in military and historical accounts.

In 1992, General Colin Powell addressed the audience attending the dedication of a monument in their honor at Fort Leavenworth.

"Music is the art of the prophets . . . one of the most magnificent and delightful presents God has given us."   — *Luther*

Leontyne Price (b. 1927)
Opera Singer

T he year was 1966, when the Metropolitan Opera, for the first time ever, opened its season with an African-American vocalist, dramatic soprano, Leontyne Price, in the role of Cleopatra.

Like many other great African-American singers, she began by singing in her church's choir.   When she graduated from high school in 1948, Dr. Anna Terry and President Charles Wesley, both of Central State University, in Wilberforce, Ohio, encouraged her to enroll in New York Julliard School of Music. At the prestigious school, while still a student, she won a role in *Four Saints in Three* and studied with Florence Page Kimball.

As star of the opera *Porgy and Bess*, she toured Europe from 1952 through 1954. One of the most celebrated sopranos of our time, she has also appeared in operas around the world, including *Don Giovanni, Madame Butterfly,* and *Il Trovatore.* While she excelled in all roles, her most acclaimed was in Verdi's

221

Aida. It was with this electrifying performance that she ended her Metropolitan Opera career in 1985.

Born Mary Leontyne Price, in Laurel, Mississippi, she became an international star after singing at the La Scala Opera in Milan, in 1960.

She has played leading roles in NBC-TV productions of opera since 1957, including *The Magic Flute,* and Poulenc's *Dialogues of the Carmelites.* Other engagements include the Arena di Verona, the Vienna Staatsoper, and London's Covent Garden. She made her debut with the Chicago Lyric Opera in 1959.

In the role of Cleopatra, in the opera *Antony and Cleopatra*, she opened the 1966 season in the Metropolitan Opera House's new location, at the Lincoln Center for the Performing Arts. She has also performed as the guest solosit with some of the most prestigious orchestras in the world.

Among her awards are the Sprigarn Medal for High Achievement (1965) and the first National Medal of Arts, which she was presented in 1985 by President Ronald Reagan.

Leontyne Price has excelled in a field which was traditionally believed to be beyond the African-American artist's ability. The excellence of her performances has brought her international fame.

HISTORY IN A CAPSULE

Because they were largely excluded from performing in major opera companies, African-Americans formed their own companies. Established in 1873, the Colored Opera Company, whose participants were all amateurs, was the first of these companies. The Drury, established in 1900, followed. Primarily a touring company, it made appearances in Philadelphia, Boston, Providence, and New York. Companies such as the Harlem Opera Workshop and the American Negro Opera Company had their roots in the black church, but were sadly under funded.

To ensure their own survival, and to provide assistance to other aspiring black opera singers, the National Association of Negro Musicians was formed in 1919. They raised money for scholarships, and for students who needed financial assistance in pursuing careers as professional musicians.

"A great man is he who chooses the right with invincible resolution . . . and whose reliance on truth, on virtue, and on God, is most unfaltering." — *Channing*

Asa Philip Randolph (1889-1979)
Labor Leader, Civil Rights Advocate

efore the historic March on Washington in 1963, there was a threat by Asa Philip Randolph to bring one hundred thousand marchers to Washington D.C. to protest the United States government's refusal to use African-American labor in the war effort. The purpose of the threatened march was to persuade the government to cancel contracts with companies practicing segregation among their workers. President Franklin D. Roosevelt, who supported the movement, created the Fair Employment Practices Commission, which resulted in thousands of African-Americans having wider job opportunities.

Asa Philip Randolph, principal leader of the protest, was an anti-establishment protester who was born in Crescent City, Florida, and who was educated at Bethune-Cookman College in Daytona Beach, Florida.

His efforts to organize for the benefit of black labor began around 1920 when, with the assistance of African-American Chandler Owen, and white radical friends, he tried to establish the National Association for the Promotion of Labor Unionism Among Negroes. Initially they tried to organize black laundry workers, but the effort failed.

Along with Owen, who was a law student at Columbia, he set up The Brotherhood, an employment bureau that was to provide training to Southern blacks arriving in the North, with no skills. The small agency was commissioned to publish *The Hotel Messenger*. After running an article publicizing the plight of black head waiters, who were being cheated by those who worked over them, Randolph lost his client, but kept the publication. It eventually became one of New York's most militant newspapers.

By the mid-twenties, he was so well-known in his crusade to promote black labor, he was contacted by Ashley L. Totten, when he was fired by the Pullman Company for attempting to organize a union. Having organized The Brotherhood of Sleeping Car Porters, he was elected their president. After twelve years, the union was recognized as the bargaining agent for the group. Although as many as eight hundred porters were fired in the interim, they took other employment and remained active in the union to keep it viable. The union won its struggle in 1935, after Randolph refused to accept ten thousand dollars from the railroad company to withdraw from the case.

It was largely through Randolph's leadership in the Committee Against Discrimination in the Armed Forces that President Harry Truman was convinced to outlaw segregation among United States troops. In 1958, Randolph organized the youth March on Washington, to support the execution of the 1954 school desegregation decision. Still active in the struggle in 1963, he helped to organize the March on Washington, to urge the passage of the Civil Rights Bill. In 1966, he was honorary chairman of the White House Conference on Civil Rights, and helped formulate methods of enforcing the 1964 and 1965 Civil Rights Acts.

Asa Philip Randolph never wavered in his belief in equal rights for all .

DID YOU KNOW?

- In 1947, Asa Philip Randolph founded the League for Nonviolent Civil Disobedience in the Armed Forces.
- He became vice president of the AFL-CIO in 1957.
- In 1960, he founded the Negro-American Labor Council.

"Prototypes break stereotypes." — **Bishop Harold Calvin Ray**

Harold Calvin Ray (b. 1955)
Evangelist, Businessman

 s one of the new generation of pastors, Bishop Harold Calvin Ray states that he sees no conflict between entrepreneurial enterprises and preaching the word of God, and believes wealth, that is the result of hard work, to be a blessing. Through Redemptive Life Fellowship (RLF), a complex which sits on a six-acre site in West Palm Beach, Florida, Bishop Ray's programs show the relationship between spiritual, educational, and economic empowerment, and extend across racial, cultural and social lines. As part of RLF's strategy, it supports the education and spiritual nurturing of each member. Focusing on disadvantaged youth, Ray established Youth Enterprises and Services, which includes the Restoration and Education Center, the Winner World Tour Program, the Family Life Institute, the University and Senior Wisdom Council and the Cultural and Performing Arts Institute. Redemptive Ranch, which Ray also established, provides positive role models through mentoring, for inner city youths.

Because the programs are all non-profit, Bishop Ray established a number of RLF-run businesses, including Kingdom Video, Redemptive Pointe Bookstore, Restoration Travel and Winners Royal Lineage Fashions, located in the Palm Beach Mall.

Ray left a lucrative law practice to pursue his vision of establishing RLF, investing his total savings, and raising the remaining amount needed through private, philanthropic and charitable gifts.

Born in Arkansas to William and Earlene Ray, young Harold benefited from a positive male role model in his father, a chemical engineer. His mother, a store clerk, instilled in him Christian values. He earned his A.A. degree at Joliet Junior College in Illinois (1975), his B.A. at Oral Roberts University (1978), and his J.D. degree at Notre Dame Law School (1981), where he graduated with honors.

He practiced law in Texas from 1981 to 1990, during which time he received the vision for RLF. He served as Regent at Oral Roberts from 1976 to 1987, was vice-chairman of the Palm Beach County Juvenile Delinquency Commission from 1984 to 1985, served on the board of directors of the University of Notre Dame Law Association from 1988 to present, and is currently a continuing education instructor at the National Institute of Trial Advocacy. Ray is chairman and chief executive officer of W.I.N., West Palm Beach, Inc., a community development corporation. He hosts several telecasts, including *Feedback*, which is aired weekly on Trinity Broadcast Network (TBN), and *Living the Redemptive Life*, a daily program on Christian Broadcast Network (CBN).

His many honors include the Presiding Bishops Medallion, the highest civilian award of the Church of God in Christ, The Florida Governor's Letters of Commendation (1994 and 1995), and The African-American Achievement Award from JM Family Enterprises (1996).

Ray's professional memberships include the Texas State Bar, the Federal Bar, The Association of Trial Lawyers of American, and the National Institute of Trial Advocacy. In September, 1996, he was commissioned to the office of Bishop of the Kingdom Dominion Network of Interdependent Churches and Ministries. His role includes coordinating, overseeing, and developing an apostolic network of churches throughout the United States, as well as abroad.

Garth
Reeves

Publisher
Activist

"It makes a great difference in the face of a sentence whether a man be behind it
or no." — **Emerson**

Garth C. Reeves, Sr. (b. 1919)
Newspaper Editor, Community Activist

e has been a bank president, and a Pulitzer Prize juror, and was the first African-American to have served on the governing boards of Miami-Dade Community College and Barry University, and the first to become a member of the Greater Miami Chamber of Commerce and the United Way of Dade County. Garth Reeves' newspaper, the seventy-five year-old *Miami Times*, is the most widely circulated African-American weekly in the state of Florida. The publisher emeritus has used his newspaper as the voice of the African-American community in stinging editorials which have questioned police brutality, inequities in municipal services and funding of school facilities.

As president of the Black Cosmopolitan Golf Club, he initiated the first civil rights discrimination lawsuit, Rice *v.* City of Miami, 1956. It challenged the custom of allowing African-Americans the use of the golf course only on Mondays, when the course was being maintained. Seven years later, the United States

Supreme Court declared the law unconstitutional.

In 1959, Reeves, Reverend Theodore Gibson, and Dr. John O. Brown, led a group of African-Americans to a landmark confrontation with the Dade County Commissioners. Armed with their tax bills, they protested the county's segregationist policies on Miami's Grandon Park Beach. Ignoring a line of armed police officers, Reeves and Oscar Range, another community activist, went swimming; African-Americans have been swimming on county beaches ever since.

He was organizing chairman of the board for National Industrial Bank, served as its president in 1971, and became vice-chairman in 1976 when it merged to become Capital Bank of Miami. He was also a juror for the Pulitzer Prize in Journalism in 1977 and 1978.

Reeves was president of Amalgamated Publishers of New York City (1984 - 1994), which represented one hundred and ten black newspapers throughout the country. He served two terms as president of the National Newspaper Publishers Association, is a member of the Board of Trustees of Florida Memorial College, Chairman of the Dade County Educational Facilities Authority and vice-president of the Black Archives Research Foundation. He is a life member of the NAACP, Sigma Pi Phi, and Omega Psi Phi fraternities. In addition, Reeves is a founding member of the Episcopal Church of the Incarnation, and is currently chairman of the board of the Peoples National Bank, the only black-owned bank in Florida.

Born in Nassau, in the Bahamas, his father was a master printer and publisher of *The Nassau Guardian*, and his mother was a housewife. His family moved to Miami with his three sisters when Garth was four months old. He graduated from the city's Booker T. Washington High School in 1936, and earned his B.A. degree in printing from Florida A&M University in 1940.

Reeves was also a technical sergeant in the United States Army, serving with the 372nd Infantry Regiment in the European and Pacific theaters from 1942 to 1945, during World War II. After the war, he returned to Miami to work with his father at the *Miami Times,* serving as its reporter, columnist, managing editor, editor and publisher. He also managed the commercial printing department of the newspaper.

Florida A&M University established the Garth C. Reeves Eminent Scholars Chair in Journalism and Graphic Arts (1986). Other honors include the receipt of the Greater Miami Chapter of the American Jewish Committee's Human Relations Award, the *Miami Herald's* Charles Whited Spirit of Excellence Award and the National Business League's Top Ten Award. He received the National Newspaper Publishers' Publisher of the Year Award (1977, 1982, 1988), was winner of the Christian Family Association's Presidential Excalibur Award (1985), and was the Juvenile Diabetes Father of the Year in 1996. He has also been awarded several honorary degrees.

"In my music, my plays, my films, I want to carry always this central idea: to be African . . ." — **Paul Robeson**

Paul Robeson (1898-1976)
Actor

When Paul Robeson was born twelve days before the Spanish-American War, it was as though a playwright had crafted his life for the stage, foreshadowing the trials to come.

Alienating himself from the American government, and certain factions of black society, by idealizing the Soviet Union during the 1930s through 1960s, he declared, after visiting Soviet Russia in 1935, "The Soviet Union is the friend of the African and West Indian peoples." Having resided there periodically from the 1940s through the mid 1960s, he has been described as the first American artist who used his artistry to protest the horrible treatment of black people in America. He performed in concert halls throughout the United States and Europe, incorporating black folk songs, black dialect, and Negro spirituals in his artistry. "To be African," he felt, "is a cause worth dying for."

Though his professional career began in 1922, when he made his debut in *Taboo*, his interest in acting started in an amateur production at the Harlem branch of the YMCA, in *Simeon the Cyrenian*. A baritone soloist, in addition to touring Europe, he also sang in Ziegfeld's *Showboat*.

In 1925, he appeared in a revival of *The Emperor Jones*, and *All God's Chillun*, both plays by Eugene O'Neill. He instituted the use of African-American culture in the struggle of the black man in America when he performed in a concert featuring all black music, complete with dialect songs. The purpose of these "protest" performances was to illuminate the African-American struggle, and hold it up to the eyes of the world.

He spent most of the period of 1927 through 1939 in Europe. He tried to form a nexus between American blacks and working-class nonblack people whose oppression he felt was similar to that of the African-American. In 1949, he spoke at the World Congress of the Defenders of Peace in Paris, saying it was "unthinkable" that African-Americans would go to war against Russia.

With W.E.B. Du Bois, he co-founded the Council of African Affairs, and for a while, the two served as co-chairmen. The purpose of the Council was to assist those of African descent in their struggle, and to make sure that accurate information regarding Africa and Africans was distributed. The council also sought to unite whites and blacks with all oppressed people, regardless of race or nationality, in their common struggle for liberty and peace.

Educated at Rutgers College (1919), he received his law degree from Columbia University. He was an honor student who also excelled in athletics.

For his political views, he suffered greatly. At one point, he was denied a passport by the United States government. Despite the pressures of being an expatriate and a pariah, by segments of both white and black society, his great talent places him among the eminent performers of the twentieth century.

"Self trust is the essence of heroism." —Emerson

Jack Roosevelt "Jackie" Robinson
Baseball Player

B efore there was Brown v. The Board of Education, a Montgomery bus boycott, swim-ins, sit-ins or eat-ins, there was Jackie Robinson. In 1947, Robinson became the first African-American of the twentieth century to break the color barrier and play major league baseball. Not only was this a great personal victory for Robinson, it gave other persons of African ancestry the hope that someday they may break through in other areas of society.

In 1946, Robinson began his professional baseball career as second baseman of the Montreal Royals, a Dodger's farm club. In 1947, Branch Rickey, general manager of the Brooklyn Dodgers, decided to experiment with hiring an African-American as a major league player. Robinson was the man of choice. That same year, the Dodgers won the pennant and the Baseball Writers Association of America selected Robinson as its first Rookie of the Year. With Robinson, who was named the National League's Most Valuable Player of 1949, the Dodgers went on to win five more pennants in the five years following their 1947 win.

Born on a sharecropper's farm near Cairo, Georgia, Jack Roosevelt Robinson was raised by his mother, who moved to Pasadena, California, after his father deserted the family, when Jackie was six months old. Robinson attended Muir Technical High School, where he excelled in sports, including baseball, track, football and basketball. He went on to attend Pasadena Junior College and UCLA.

In 1941, Robinson was drafted into the Army, and served as morale officer, after attending officer's candidate school. He was discharged early in 1945, and coached at Sam Houston College in Texas. Later that year, he left to play for the Kansas City Monarchs, in the Negro Baseball League, eventually signing with Branch Rickey to play in the Minor League Royals, in Montreal.

The many racist insults he endured served to magnify his quiet dignity and remarkable abilities. As a bellwether to social revolution, he demonstrated non-violence before it became a trademark of the early civil rights movement of the 1950s and 1960s. His tremendous skills, even under the pressure of hazing and racial attacks, earned him a place in the Baseball Hall of Fame in 1962.

When Jackie Robinson retired from baseball at the age of thirty-eight, he served as vice-president and personnel director for the Chock Full o' Nuts Corporation. He was also co-chairman of the Freedom National Bank in Harlem, and aide to Governor Nelson Rockefeller, of New York. In 1974, two years after his death, a New York City junior high school in East Harlem, was named in his memory.

For his great courage in facing the many difficulties of pioneering such a momentous social change, baseball chose the entire year of 1997 to honor him. He remains to this day the prototype of an American hero.

DID YOU KNOW?

- ◆ He once played professional football.
- ◆ In 1982, the United States Postal Service issued a Jackie Robinson Commemorative postage stamp.
- ◆ Of the four sports in which Jackie excelled, baseball was considered his weakest.
- ◆ Three other African-American players were hired in the major leagues in 1947 — Larry Doby (Cleveland Indians), Hank Thompson and Williard Brown (St. Louis Browns).
- ◆ He was the first African-American elected to the Baseball Hall of Fame.

"He who has a firm will molds the world to himself." — **Goethe**

Luther (Bill)"Bojangles" Robinson
(1878-1949) Dancer, Actor

Accidentally spilling hot oyster stew down a customer's back resulted in an association that made "Bojangles" Robinson world famous!

As an out-of-work dancer, Robinson was working waiting tables when the mishap occured. Instead of being reprimanded by an angry customer, he ended up meeting Morty Farkins of the Western Vaudeville Managers Association, the man who managed Robinson for the balance of his career.

In the 1930s and 1940s, he appeared in fourteen films. His most popular movies though, were with Shirley Temple in *Rebecca of Sunnybrook Farm* (1937), *The Little Colonel*, and *The Littlest Rebel* (1935). He also starred in the movie such as *Stormy Weather* (1943) with Lena Horne, and in the Broadway shows *Blackbirds of 1928*, and *Brown Buddies* (1930).

Hailed as America's first great tap dancer and as a pantomimic dancer of genius, he held the world's record for running backwards, and was known to

233

dance one hour and fifteen minutes without repeating a step. In his famous trademark "stair dance," he tapped, completely relaxed, up and down a flight of stairs.

Luther Robinson started as a shoeshine boy. When business was slow, he tap-danced in barbershops, taverns, and even on sidewalks. People tossed more coins for his dancing than he earned from his shoeshine business and other odd jobs combined. Later, he performed with Eddie Leonard, a minstrel, for five dollars a week, and traveled with other shows. He enhanced his image by using his brother's name, becoming known as Bill "Bojangles" Robinson.

He once gave up dancing and worked as a stable boy, until Vaudeville veteran Eddie Leonard spotted his fancy footwork in a dance hall. He hired him to appear in *The South Before the War* (1892). After the show closed, Robinson teamed with George Cooper, but stopped performing when Cooper died of cancer. It was then that he took the job as a waiter and Farkins as his manager.

Born in Richmond, Virginia, Robinson was orphaned in infancy, and raised by his grandmother, who cared for him, as well as his older brother and sister. Extreme poverty dictated that the children work to help support the family.

Though he suffered many humiliations, as did all African-American entertainers of his era, he eventually became the highest paid tap dancer in the world, reaching the height of his popularity during the Depression. Fred Astaire honored him in a movie, with a dance called *Bojangles of Harlem*. Affable and ingenuous, he was even cast as the likeable lackey. His directors criticized his "faithful servant" roles in productions such as *In Old Kentucky, Rebecca of Sunnybrook Farm, The Littlest Rebel* and *Road Demon*. His performances, they said, reinforced the stereotyped notion of the Negro, and did little to dispel misconceptions that were socially and psychologically damaging. The one exception was his role in *One Mile From Heaven* (1937), in which he played a character with dignity.

Though he was unequaled in his tap dancing, like other black performers of the era, he was a victim of the times. His great talents were limited by the parameters surrounding him.

DID YOU KNOW?

- ◆ During the formative years of African-American theater, it was common practice for white rowdies to jeer and assault black performers.
- ◆ Of the great fortune that Robinson earned, he gave away huge sums to charities and to other less fortunate actors.
- ◆ He celebrated his sixty-second birthday by dancing sixty-two blocks down Broadway.

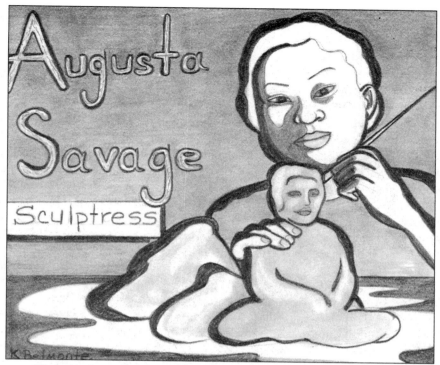

"Never judge a work of art by its defects." — **Washington Allston**

Augusta Savage (1900-1962)
Sculptor

Her accomplishments were many, as were her trials. Her highest achievement was *The Harp*, a sixteen-foot high sculpture that stood in the court of the Contemporary Arts Building, on the grounds of the 1939 World's Fair. The work depicted a choir, supported by the arm and the hand of the Creator, with a kneeling figure holding the text of James Weldon Johnson's *Lift Every Voice And Sing*.

August Savage was one of only four women artists, and the only African-American to whom the Fair Corporation awarded a commission to execute a work which reflected the African-American's contribution to music. The sculpture received wide acclaim and was a popular subject among black Americans. Unfortunately, because there were no funds to cast the work, it was destroyed at the end of the World's Fair.

One of the best recognized artists of the Harlem Renaissance, she was also a political and social activist, whose special interests focused on causes affecting opportunities for African-American artists. Because of her concern that they have opportunities to study fine arts, she established the Harlem Community Art Center. It was a trend setter that became a model for other urban areas.

Spirited and ambitious, she fought racism, sexism, and other forms of discrimination. She even fought her father's disapproval of her career choice. A Baptist minister, he disdained her fashioning "graven images." She overcame this conflict as well as the early deaths of her first two husbands, and a third marriage which ended in divorce. Throughout it all, she managed to continue producing art.

She was primarily interested in portrait sculpture, and at one time, tried to support herself by creating busts of famous African-Americans. The reception to her work was lukewarm, and the venture was not commercially successful. She studied under George Brewster at Cooper Union Art Institute in New York, at Florida A&M College, and under Felix Beauneteaux at the Grand Chaumiere in Paris (1934-1935). Fellowships from the Rosenwald Fund and the Carnegie Foundation enabled her to study abroad.

She lost a scholarship to study at Foutainbleau, near Paris, France, in 1923 when two young Alabama white women, who were also recipients, complained that they did not wish to room or to travel with a "colored girl." The scholarship was withdrawn on that basis, but not without controversy. The president of the Sculpture Society, to his credit, renounced the committee's decision, and invited Savage to study privately at his College Park, New York studio that summer.

She exhibited her work at the Societe de Artistes Francais Beau Arts, the Salon d'Automne, the Grand Palais, and at the Salon Printemps. She also traveled to Germany and Belgium on a Carnegie Foundation grant.

With the help of a Carnegie grant, she opened her own school, The Savage Studio of Arts and Crafts, in Harlem, New York, which was associated with the State University of New York. It was the largest New York school of its kind. The Federal Art Project of the Works Progress Administration (WPA), and the Carnegie Foundation supported her studio.

Savage was an ardent advocate of struggling African-American artists, and in 1936, became an assistant supervisor for the WPA Federal Art Project. In 1937 she was named the first director of the Harlem Community Art Center, in addition to directing the first black-owned corporation, to open a gallery exclusively for black artists' work. Named the Salon of Contemporary Negro Art, it opened in 1939, but closed after a few months due to the lack of funds needed to keep it viable.

Considered a pioneering African-American artist, she helped to influence the course of African-American art by becoming one of the first artists to use black physical types in her work, and portraying them with sensitivity and dignity.

"Let me have music dying, and I seek no more delight."   **— Keats**

Philippa Duke Schuyler (1932-1969)
Musician

B
ecause she had an I.Q. of 185, her parents planned early for educational programs to suit her needs. A child prodigy, she played the piano, composed music, and had written poetry by the age of three. By the time she was ten, Philippa had completed the eighth grade at Sacred Heart Annunciation Girl's School. She did not enroll in college after finishing Father Young's High School. She was, instead, performing at concerts, while being tutored in history, languages, psychology, and other subjects.

When she competed in the young composer's contest at Grinnell Foundation in Detroit, her *Manhattan Nocturne*, and the scherzo *Rumpelstiltskin* won both first and second prizes. Her score for a one hundred-piece symphony orchestra, *Manhattan Nocturne* has been performed by the Chicago and San Francisco symphony orchestras, and by the New York Philharmonic symphony orchestra. She made her Town Hall debut in 1953, and continued in her career as a concert pianist, touring around the world.

She spoke Spanish, Italian, and French, was poisoned in West Africa, kidnaped in Nigeria, and was in the Congo when the 1960 revolution took place. All of these adventures are recounted in her book *Adventures in Black and White*.

She also performed for royalty in Africa, Asia, and Europe. A vocalist as well as a musician, she was guest soloist with some of the nations most respected symphony orchestras. Some of her most memorable works include *Sleepy Hollow Sketches, Six Little Pieces*, and *Eight Little Pieces for the Piano*.

Tragically, the world lost out on seeing the full scope of Phillipa's talents realized when she died in an airplane crash in 1969.

HISTORY IN A CAPSULE

An earlier child prodigy, Thomas Greene "Blind Tom" Bethune was born a slave. He began composing and playing the piano at the age of five. Inspired by the sounds of a storm, he composed *Rain Storm*. Though he was born without sight, he mastered the piano quickly, and toured America and Europe. He possessed a phenomenal memory, absolute pitch, and an unfailing ear. He had over seven hundred pieces in his repertoire that he learned by listening to others play.

He was of pure African ancestry, and was born in Columbus, Georgia. He was purchased by Colonel Bethune, who encouraged his musical talents. He made his debut in Savannah, Georgia in 1858, and continued in a career that spanned forty years. His audiences were always amazed by his total recall as well as his skill. His works include *Battle of Manassas, Delta Kapa Epsilon, Grand March de Concert, Guitar* and *Cascade*. He also won acclaim for his interpretations of Beethoven's *Pathetique Sonata* and Mendelssohn's *Andante*.

"It is not so important to know everything as to know the exact value of everything, to appreciate what we learn, and to arrange what we know." — **H. More**

Eric O. Simpson (1914-1994)
Newspaper Publisher

ithout the money to do so, he stated, "I want to start a newspaper." It was tough at first, with only his wife's salary as an elementary school teacher, and a dream to sustain him. He attained his goal though, by perseverance and by reporting news of concern to blacks in the *Florida Star,* which he nurtured into becoming the state's second largest African-American newspaper. Established in 1951, the weekly tabloid covered desegregation, and championed civil rights and equal opportunities for African-Americans in education, employment, and other areas in society. It also chronicled historical events, significant to African-Americans, which were ignored by daily papers.

Simpson believed that the best way to solve problems was to expose and confront them. Sometimes characterized as militant and radical, because of his independent nature and blunt writing style, he never sacrificed publishing the truth for the sake of appeasing his critics.

Born in British Guiana, South America, Simpson was sent to the United States as a boy to further his education, in the Episcopal schools of New York City. He studied journalism at New York University. During his lifetime he was employed as a journalist, photographer, disc jockey and newscaster. He was also a personal pal of boxing great Joe Louis, and for a while, dabbled in fight promotion. In addition to all this, he served in the merchant marines, and in the Army Corps of Engineers as a statistician.

He was active in voter registration drives for African-Americans in the 1950s, and attacked police brutality, segregated public facilities, and job discrimination. When "white" papers blacked out coverage of a boycott of the Jacksonville Woolworth store, Simpson was there, alerting his community about the demonstrations, via *The Florida Star.*

Described as charming, witty, and straightforward, Simpson was a voracious reader who spoke on many topics. As the champion of the "little guy," he treated everyone with dignity, no matter what their rank.

He ran unsuccessfully for several political seats, and finally decided with characteristic humor that "newspaper men should not run for political office." Though he lost his races, *Jet* magazine noted that his 1960 bid for a seat on the Duval County Civil Service Board drew nearly sixteen thousand votes, which was more than any other black candidate in Florida's history.

In April, 1994, three months after his death, the Florida Senate honored him with Resolution Number 3162, which recognized his contributions to civil rights, his efforts in pioneering the black press in Florida, and his dedicated service to his community.

Simpson was so esteemed by both whites and African-Americans that Jacksonville's largest newspaper, *The Florida Times Union*, determined his death to be front page news. His influence will be felt for many years to come, as the changes he made live on.

Naomi
Sims
Fashion Model
Business Woman

K·B.

"The atmosphere of expectancy is the breeding ground for miracles." **—Parsley**

Naomi Sims (b. 1949)
Fashion Model

I n a commercial for AT&T, she became the first African-American model to appear in a television advertisement. Naomi Sims was also the first African-American woman to appear on the cover of a major women's magazine when *Ladies Home Journal* featured her. A *Vogue* magazine spread made her the first of her race to be featured in a multi-color ad, and she was a repeat feature in *Harper's Bazaar* magazine, in the late 1960s through the 1970s.

When she was a girl, Naomi knew that she wanted to be a model, or involved in some way, with the fashion industry. Her parents, however, did not understand that modeling could be a lucrative career for a black girl, and encouraged her, instead, to go to college.

Born in Oxford, Mississippi, in extreme poverty, her family sent her to live with foster parents in Pittsburgh, Pennsylvania when she was nine years old. She attended Westinghouse High School, and was raised in the city's East End. A bright student, she graduated in 1967 with a "B+" average, and was awarded three scholarships. At New York University, she studied psychology, and concentrated on modeling at the Fashion Institute of Technology. A third scholarship, for subsistence, enabled her to explore the world of modeling, to establish her career.

She got her first big break in an interview with Gosta Peterson, a photographer who found her to be so impressive, he thought she had more experience than she actually had. Immediately, she became one of the most sought-after models, earning seventy-five dollars an hour. Because of her success, she left New York University and began modeling full-time.

She considered her selection to appear on the cover of *Life* magazine, her biggest single break. Because of her phenomenal success, she was selected by International Mannequins as Model of the Year in 1969 and 1970, and was repeatedly on the International Best Dressed list. As an author, she was a columnist for *Essence* magazine. She also wrote a children's book entitled *The Gum Tree Monster*, and a beauty book titled *The Beautiful Black Woman*.

She developed the "Naomi" line of cosmetics, which was formulated from earth tones she discovered while conversing with a Brazilian painter.

She has also raised funds for sickle cell anemia and cancer research. In 1970, the New York Board of Education presented her with an award for her volunteer work in teaching underprivileged children in Bedford Stuyvesant, and in 1971, she received an award for working with the New York Drug Rehabilitation Program in Harlem.

As a pioneer in the field of modeling, Naomi Sims paved the way for other aspiring African-Americans to enter a lucrative glamour field from which they were absent.

DID YOU KNOW?

♦ Photographer Gosta Peterson's wife was the fashion editor of *The New York Times.*
♦ Naomi was referred to as the "space-age nubian princess."
♦ Her sister, Betty, was also a model, as well as an airline hostess.
♦ She tested for the movie role of *Cleopatra Jones*, but lost out to Tamara Dobson.

"Old ideas are prejudices and new ones, caprices." — **Dondan**

Benjamin "Pap" Singleton (1809-1892)
Colonizationist

H e advocated the "Exodus of 1879," after terrorist organizations such as the Ku Klux Klan destroyed the political gains of African-Americans through violence and intimidation. A fugitive slave who resided in Canada, Benjamin Singleton returned to the United States after the Emancipation Proclamation. He led the black separatist movement because he didn't believe it possible for the Negro to advance while in competition with hostile whites.

His vision was to set up a separate state in which only African-Americans lived. He traveled throughout the South promoting Kansas as a refuge from economic and political oppression. Weary of the battle, thousands of blacks migrated to Kansas and the Missouri area. He founded Singleton's Colony, a town of about three hundred blacks, in Cherokee Count, Missouri, in 1873.

Though leaders such as Richard T. Greener, dean of law at Howard University, agreed that conditions in the South justified emigration, abolitionist and orator Frederick Douglass, and other educated blacks, denounced it.

243

Southerners accused Northern Republicans of luring blacks away to boost voter rolls. A congressional committee investigated the charge in 1881, with both Singleton and his friend, Henry Adams, testifying.

A mulatto, who was born a slave in Tennessee, Singleton, though barely literate, was innately intelligent, and a skilled speaker, who had the power to persuade. Though he incurred much hostility from many educated blacks, he persisted in his notion that colonization was the only answer to the wave of terror that had seized African-Americans in both the North and the South. His movement attracted approximately fifty thousand blacks within a few months, making it the largest exodus of African-Americans, from the South, in United States history. Adams, an influential supporter and friend, who shared Singleton's dream, recruited nearly one hundred thousand blacks from Mississippi, Texas, Alabama, and Louisiana.

Though white Southerners, as a whole, deeply resented blacks, they took measures to prevent them from leaving. Transportation companies refused to sell them tickets, and anyone advocating migration was whipped and driven from town. Vagrancy laws were enforced to justify the arrest of black travelers.

Instead of finding utopia in Kansas, most met with hostilities similar to those from which they had fled. Still, they arrived by the thousands, with groups spreading into Iowa and Nebraska. Though some were able to acquire land under the Homestead Act, most endured grinding poverty, with assistance only from the Freedman's Relief Association, and a few sympathetic Northerners.

Even so, few returned to the South, and interest in immigration waned. The word gradually spread back home that there was no Utopia in Kansas.

Because of his vision of a better life for his people, thousands regard him as a hero. Though his plan was largely a failure, the spirit in which it was formed gained him much support.

DID YOU KNOW?

- ◆ Singleton chose Kansas because militant white Abolitionist John Brown settled there in 1855, to assist anti-slavery forces located there.
- ◆ The Freedman's Bureau was the popular name for the United States Bureau of Refugees, Freedman, and Abandoned Lands.
- ◆ The Bureau was established in 1865 during the Reconstruction period, following the United States Civil War, to provide help for newly emancipated blacks in their transition from slavery to freedom.
- ◆ Impoverished whites, as well as African-Americans, were assisted by the Bureau.

Moneta Sleet

Pulitzer Prize-Winning Photographer

K. BelMonte

"Memory tempers prosperity, mitigates adversity, controls youth, and delights old age." **— Lactantius**

Moneta Sleet, Jr. (b. 1926)
Photographer

rozen in time, Coretta Scott King's youthful face, veiled in black, is upturned, even in her grief. The tableau, one of the Civil Rights movement's most poignant scenes, is etched in the nation's collective memory as friends and admirers of Dr. Martin Luther King, Jr., gathered in final tribute to him. The moment, captured by Moneta Sleet, Jr., a photojournalist, whose career has been largely with Johnson Publishing Company, is known the world over. In 1969, the picture made Sleet the first African-American to be awarded the Pulitzer Prize in photography.

No African-Americans, Sleet recalls, were initially included in the pool of photographers and journalists covering King's funeral. Only white reporters from mainstream publications such as *Life* and *Time* magazines, and high profile newspapers were invited. Only Coretta King's threat that there would be no pool unless the black media were present ensured Sleet and other African-American representatives a spot in the pack.

Born in Owensboro, Kentucky, he attended its segregated schools. His infatuation with pictures began as a boy, with a gift of a box camera from his parents. His love continued through high school. While attending Kentucky State College, he finally had the opportunity to formally study photography.

Sleet left college for the military during World War II, and upon discharge, returned to earn his degree in business education (1947). By then, his love for photography had blossomed into his career choice. In 1948, when his mentor and instructor, John Williams, transferred to Maryland State College, he asked Sleet to follow him, to set up a department of photography. Sleet did, but remained for only a short time before moving to New York, where he studied at the School of Modern Photography. He earned his Master of Arts degree in journalism from New York University in 1950.

Sleet's career included a brief stint with the *Amsterdam News*, where he was a sportswriter, and a staff position at a popular African-American picture magazine, *Our World*, where remained for five years. In 1953, under publisher John Davis' exacting standards, he covered a series on Superior, West Virginia, a coal mining town. It became one of his most memorable stories.

Sleet then moved to Johnson Publishing Company, where he was employed as staff photographer for *Ebony*, an illustrated monthly magazine about African-Americans. Publisher John J. Johnson's assignments sent Sleet to cover international stories and also to photograph events of the growing Civil Rights movements for *Ebony* and *Jet* magazines. It was during this period that he met Martin Luther King, Jr., a young Atlanta, Georgia, based minister, who would emerge as the undisputed leader of the movement. Sleet photographed crucial moments in King's life, including his receiving the Nobel Peace Prize in Sweden (1964), the Selma to Montgomery march (1965), and the events surrounding his 1968 assassination.

Sleet was present to cover periods of transition in Africa's struggle for independence, when self-governing nations emerged from colonial domination. He covered vice-president Richard Nixon's trip through Africa in 1957 and photographed Kwame Nkrumah at Ghana's independence, as well as events in the Sudan, Libya, and Liberia. He has traveled as a journalist to the West Indies, Europe, Russia and South America.

Along with the Pulitzer Prize, he was awarded an Overseas Press Club citation in 1957, a National Urban League Award (1969), and the National Association of Black Journalists Award (1978). He has exhibited his photographs at the Metropolitan Museum of Art and the Studio Museum in Harlem. The New York Public Library arranged a solo exhibit (1986), which toured nationally through 1989. His photographs chronicle some of the most important events in African-American history.

Mabel Keaton
Staupers

Nurse

"Every human being has a work to carry on within . . . which no conscience but his own can teach." — **Channing**

Mabel Keaton Staupers (1890-1989)
Nurse, Activist

Her 1961 book entitled *No Time for Prejudice: A Story of the Integration of Negroes in the United States*, summed up the long, bitter fight of African-American nurses for respect and equality.

Mabel Keaton Staupers launched a battle against mainstream American nursing to ensure that black nurses were accepted as professional equals. Her fight was most intense during the Great Depression and World War II. She is remembered for her unrelenting struggle which triggered desegregation of the United States Army Nurse Corps, during the war years. The shortage of nurses created the opportunity for her to voice the dilemma of black nurses and take the issue to the national level. The Army agreed to accept a quota of fifty-six African-American nurses. When the Navy refused to admit any into the Nurse Corps, she made their denial public, and solicited help from black leaders, who met with government officials. The impact of their protests against discrimination was more keenly felt shortly before the end of the war

247

2222

2222

when they proved victorious against second-class treatment and quotas in both military and non-military employment.

She was born in Barbados, West Indies, to Thomas and Pauline Doyle. In 1903, they came to New York City and settled in Harlem, where she completed her early education. She enrolled in the Freedmen's Hospital School of Nursing, now Howard University College of Nursing, in Washington, D.C., in 1914, graduating with honors in 1917. In 1931, she became the first African-American to earn a Masters degree in nursing.

Staupers, reflecting the lot of nearly all black nurses, found positions and opportunities in hospital staff and public health nursing virtually closed to her. She began her career as a private duty nurse. Shortly after, along with James Wilson and Louis T. Wright, both African-American physicians, she was instrumental in organizing the Booker T. Washington Sanitarium, which was the first facility to offer in-patient care for black tuberculosis patients in Harlem.

She shed light on the depth and breath of segregation and discriminatory policies that plagued blacks seeking adequate medical care. She also witnessed the crude treatment and lack of respect for black professionals by both college personnel and white physicians.

As a result of surveying the health needs of African-Americans in Harlem, in 1922, the Harlem Committee of the New York Tuberculosis and Health Association was established, with Staupers serving as executive secretary for twelve years.

She became executive secretary of the National Association of Colored Graduate Nurses (NACGN) in 1934. Along with Estelle Massey Osborne, the group's president, Staupers labored to ensure the acceptance and full integration of African-Americans into the main tributary of American nursing.

Staupers co-founded the National Council of Negro Women along with Mary McLeod Bethune in 1935, organized a national bi-racial advisory council to broaden the support of NACGN in 1938, and was elected president of NACGN in 1949. After having pressured the American Nurses' Association (ANA) to integrate since 1934, she won her battle, and at the 1949 convention, the members agreed that NACGN had accomplished its purposes and was no longer needed. Its members were absorbed into the ANA.

Her many honors include the NAACP's 1951 Sprigarn Medal, a 1967 citation of appreciation by New York Mayor John V. Lindsay, and, in 1970, the Howard University Alumni Award.

A true fighter for justice and equality for African-American nurses, she also contributed her time and organizational skills to ensure superior health care for black citizens. She believed in the dignity of all human beings, and her heroic efforts created a high standard to which African-American youth may aspire.

"Boldness is ever blind, for it sees not dangers and inconveniences." —**Bacon**

Bessie B. Stringfield (1911-1993)
WWII Motorcycle Courier, Stunt Rider

arely five feet tall, she owned twenty-seven Harley Davidson motorcycles in her lifetime. Not only did she own them, she rode them like a pro around the walls of a motordrome, sidesaddle, lying down, hoisted from one side to the other, and standing on one foot-peg.

In a time of overt racism, when most women — both African-American and white — were chasing mops, brooms and unruly toddlers, Bessie Stringfield was packing her money belt and what clothes she could stuff into a saddlebag, and hitting the roads. Not only was her adventurous nature considered unladylike, it was almost unheard of for a black woman.

Born of a white Dutch mother, who died when she was a baby, and a Jamaican father of African descent, who abandoned her when she was only five years old, Bessie was raised by adoptive white parents of Irish heritage. She married and bore three children. Unfortunately, each became ill and died. Bessie, who never recovered from the devastating loss, spent the remainder of her life stunt riding and traveling the roads, only finding a sense of belonging in motorcycle clubs.

She purchased her first bike, a 1928 Indian Scout, at sixteen years of age, taught herself to ride, and was soon performing daredevil stunts. She purchased a Harley in 1930, and when wanderlust overtook her, her adoptive parents supported her decision. At nineteen years of age, she set out on her first cross-country adventure.

Because it was a time in the United States, when African-Americans were not welcome at hotels and motels, she slept on her Harley, at filling stations, or if she encountered a sympathetic black family, she boarded with them.

During World War II, she wanted to serve her country, but shunned the traditional female groups such as the Women's Army Corps (WACS) and the Women Accepted for Volunteer Emergency Service (WAVES). Her choice had to have more intrigue, so she joined the motorcycle dispatch unit and braved the back roads of the country, her saddlebags laden with top secret documents. She served from 1941 to 1945. There were six other African-American dispatchers in the unit; Stringfield was the only woman.

She became a nurse in the late 1950s, and started the Iron Horse Motor Club in Opa Locka, Florida, a suburb of Miami, winning trophies from the American Motorcycle Association (AMA). When she could not afford to replace her 1978 FLH, that was damaged in a robbery attempt in the late 1980s, she rented Harley bikes.

She was honored at the Heritage Museum in Ohio by the AMA in 1990. She logged in sixty-three riding years and crossed the country alone, eight times.

Fearless and independent, Bessie Stringfield used her unusual bent for adventure in the service of her country, while indulging her passion for Harley bikes and daredevil stunts. Her life is one of the subjects in Ann Ferrar's *Hear Me Roar*, a book whose subject is women and their bikes.

"Painting is silent poetry, and poetry is a speaking picture."   **— Simonides**

Henry Ossawa Tanner (1859-1937)
Artist

His family encouraged him to continue its ministerial tradition and sent him to Atlanta, Georgia, where his brother was pastor of a prominent church. But Henry Tanner had his own dream. He wanted to be a painter. In a time when art was not regarded as a career for black Americans, he became one of the country's finest painters, and one of history's most famous African-American artists.

He was born to Benjamin Tucker Tanner, an African Methodist Episcopal (AME) bishop, who discouraged Henry from pursuing a career in art. Though he graduated from the Pennsylvania Academy of Fine Arts, his father, no doubt, felt that sending him to Atlanta would steer his son into the ministry. Henry obeyed and went to Atlanta, where he taught art at Clark College, trying to supplement his income by selling paintings. There, he met Bishop Hartzell, who arranged an art exhibit for him. When it failed to generate any sales, the bishop purchased the entire collection himself. He further tried to help Tanner raise the money needed to study in Europe by asking his friends to help.

In 1892, Henry traveled to Paris, enrolled in the Academie Julian, and studied under Benjamin Constant and Paul Laurens. Four years later, he began to pique the interest of art lovers with his *Young Sabot-Maker* and *Music Lesson*. No doubt influenced by his religious upbringing, he painted *The Resurrection of Lazarus*, and earned critical recognition for its masterful rendering. It's impact was so powerful, it was purchased by the French Government for the Luxembourg Gallery.

Inspired by a visit to Palestine, he developed a series of paintings on biblical themes, which established him firmly as an accomplished artist, and earned him worldwide recognition and commercial success.

Though America provided a profitable market for his work, he preferred to live abroad in the Near East and in France, where more attention was paid to his work than to his race.

He received the 1900 Lippincott Prize, a gold medal at the San Francisco Exposition, a silver medal at the Paris Exposition, and the prestigious French Legion of Honor award.

His famous biblical themes, including *The Annunciation, The Five Virgins, Christ and Nicodemus on the House-Top* and *Christ on the Road to Bethany*, are presently exhibited in prominent museums all over America.

Tanner was an artist who reached the height of mastery, setting a standard for other African-American painters. Through his accomplishments, he gave them the hope necessary to proceed.

DID YOU KNOW?

♦ Earlier black artists, shunned by established galleries, exhibited their work in places such as public schools, YMCA buildings, churches, and public libraries.

♦ Tanner was one of the painters who ushered in the new era for African-American artists.

♦ He was the only one of the earlier black artists to gain international fame.

♦ He also marketed his photographs.

"We always have the ability to change and grow and create our own possibilities."
— Susan Taylor

Susan L. Taylor (b. 1946)
Editor

T he intelligence, talent, and spirit of this former actress and cosmetologist radiate from her now-famous "In the Spirit" column, which appears in *Essence* magazine, a monthly that debuted in May, 1970. Also in 1970, Susan L. Taylor had given birth to a daughter, and felt she needed to rechannel her efforts. So, she created Nequai Cosmetics, naming the company for her daughter, Shana Nequai. Her expertise in cosmetology caught the attention of the editors of *Essence*, who gave her freelance writing assignments the same year. She progressed quickly, and in 1971, was named the magazine's beauty editor. The following year, her duties expanded to include fashion.

After her first marriage ended, Susan found herself a single parent, with the sole responsibility of providing for her daughter and herself. It compelled her to live her life with purpose, work and discipline. Because of this, she was able to accomplish most of what she wanted for herself and her daughter, whom she calls her anchor.

She ascended to editor-in-chief of the country's top selling magazine for African-American women in 1981. She has guided *Essence* through phenomenal growth, to a monthly readership of over seven million. Once dealing with only women's concerns and issues, the magazine has expanded to include an annual issue on men and a monthly column, "Brothers," written by males.

Taylor hosted *Essence*, the nation's first nationally syndicated black-oriented magazine show, which ran for four seasons in more than sixty markets in the United States, and in several African and Caribbean countries. She helped to bring new, positive images of African-American women and men to the television audience.

In March, 1986, she became vice-president of Essence Communications, and was named senior vice-president in 1993.

She has authored several books, including *In the Spirit: The Inspirational Writings of Susan L. Taylor*, in which she shares experiences in risk-taking, and in honoring one's own abilities and achievements. Her latest book, *Lessons in Living*, shares her insights into the universal quest for faith and spirituality as one faces life's challenges.

She is a member of the National Association of Black Journalists, the American Society of Magazine Editors, and Women in Communication.

Taylor supports the Edwin Gould Services for Children, a foster care-adoption agency, and a number of other community-based organizations. She has a personal commitment to help empower the poor, to work with teenage mothers and disadvantaged women, and enable them to realize their strengths in order to take charge of their lives.

Lincoln University, the first black college, Spelman College, and Delaware State University have awarded her honorary Doctorate degrees.

She balances her successes as editor and media personality with parenting and community involvement. She seeks always to project a positive image of the black woman. She advises women to believe in their own attributes. "You were born for this hour, born to win in life, not to lose," she states.

Mary Church
Terrell

Civic Leader

"There is a transcendent power in example. We reform others unconsciously, when we walk uprightly." **— Swetchine**

Mary Church Terrell (1863-1954)
Civil Rights Advocate

At the age of 91, she was still a soldier in what she called "the righteous war" of the civil rights struggle. Fluent in French, Italian and German, she addressed the International Congress of Women in fluent German when they met in Berlin in 1904, making her the only American delegate who spoke in a language other than her native tongue. Having inherited the light complexion of her white grandfather, she often "crossed the color line" and patronized white establishments. After being served, she would then inquire why others of her race were not allowed there.

Born in Memphis, Tennessee, Mary Church's parents were former slaves and were relatively prosperous by the time of her birth. Her father worked for his white river boat captain father, and her mother owned a hairdressing salon.

She attended Oberlin College in 1880, and majored in classical languages. She became a teacher at Wilberforce University in Xenia, Ohio upon graduating in 1884. She left teaching to continue studying in Europe, and earned her Master's degree when she returned to the United States, enrolling again at Oberlin College.

In 1891, she married high school principal Robert Terrell. After giving birth to two daughters, Mary still felt compelled to fight the discrimination she saw and experienced, and to fight for equal rights for women. Educator Booker T. Washington, a good friend of hers, admired her ability to capture large audiences.

She was instrumental in helping to organize the Colored Women's League of Washington in 1892, later urging its merger with other women's groups in 1896. The new group was the National Association of Colored Women, and, for two terms, she was elected its president. With "lifting as they climb," as their motto, they sought to help less fortunate African-Americans, to lobby for adequate day care and kindergarten facilities, and to advocate equality in education.

She was also a columnist for *Women's Era* magazine, using it as a forum to advocate for women's concerns, including the right to vote.

The Board of Education appointed her to serve in 1895, making her the first woman of African heritage to do so. She served for two terms. During her tenure, she ensured that African-American children received quality education, even though she was not able to end segregation in schools.

She assisted W.E.B. Du Bois in his sociological study of black churches in 1903, and spoke at the Atlanta University Conference. She published an article on lynching in *The North American Review*. Other, more polemical articles, were published in England. Mrs. Terrell was tireless in her fight for equal rights, and was a charter member of the NAACP. She reduced her political activity after her husband became the first African-American municipal judge of Washington, D.C.

She published *A Colored Woman in a White World*, her autobiography, in 1937. Well into her eighties, she was still active in the civil rights struggle. She was chairman of the coordinating committee of Washington, D.C., and, along with its members, picketed restaurants which refused to serve African-Americans. She brought suit against one restaurant, which refused her service. She won in 1953, when the United States Supreme Court ruled in her favor.

Because of her courage in challenging unjust laws and traditions, Mary Church Terrell assured a better life for all Americans of African heritage.

"I would like to . . . use my celebrity status to try to help people learn to live together in harmony and to respect each other's differences . . . to help people see that these differences can be assets to us all if we are willing to work together." — **Debi Thomas**

Debi Thomas (b. 1967)
Olympic Figure Skating Champion

In 1986, nineteen-year-old Stanford University freshman engineering major, Debi Thomas, completed an extraordinary feat of five triple jumps, on the ice, to win theUnited States Women's Championship over Tiffany Chin. From there, she traveled to Switzerland where she vanquished Katerina Witt, who had held the World Title since 1984.

She was born in Poughkeepsie, New York, but grew up in San Jose, California. She graduated from San Mateo High School in San Mateo, California.

At five years of age, she first laced on skates, after being impressed by Mr. Frick, the Ice Follies comedian. During her training, her mother totaled three thousand miles a month driving Debi to the closest skating rink, where she honed the skills she needed to become one of the elite skaters of the world.

She competed in the National Championships in 1980, when she was only thirteen years of age, is a two-time United States National Figure Skating Champion (1986, 1988), the 1986 World Figure Skating Champion, and a three-time World Professional Figure Skating Champion (1988, 1989, 1991). She toured with Stars on Ice for four years following her Olympic success, and starred as the Sugar Plum Fairy in an NBC production of *Nutcracker on Ice* (1997). She retired from competitive skating in 1992 to pursue her dream of becoming a doctor.

Her awards include Figure Skater of the Year (1985), Amateur Female Athlete of the Year (1986), and the Wide World of Sports Athlete of the Year (1986).

She was named by *People Weekly* as one of "The 25 Most Intriguing People of 1986," and was profiled by the magazine in 1996. Though she endorses products for Campbell's Soups, Raytheon, and Champion Sportswear, as a black Olympian, she felt she did not receive as many endorsements as her white counterparts. She remains philosophical, however, and has stated that the experience served to toughen rather than to embitter her.

She was an expert figure skating analyst for WBBM-TV in Chicago during the 1994 Winter Olympic Games, was a celebrity guest on *American Gladiators* for Samuel Goldwin Television (1995), and is spokesperson for a number of causes, including the MacMillan Reading Program, the Women's Sports Foundation, the U.S. Postal Service (1995-1996), Sears Skate on State (1996), and the American Dry Bean Board (1996-1997). She promotes charitable causes including Make-A-Wish, Grant-A-Wish, Cystic Fibrosis, Loyola University Medical Auxiliary, Chicago Inner-City Games, the Ara Parseghian Medical Research Foundation, the Boys and Girls Club of Indianapolis, and the Moraine Girl Scout Council.

She is also a member of Athletes Against Drugs (1995 to present), and was appointed by astronaut Jim Lovell to the advisory board for Mission HOME (Harvesting Opportunities for Mother Earth), in 1996.

DID YOU KNOW?

♦ Studying Russian is one of Debi's hobbies.
♦ Her long term goal is to apply to the NASA astronaut program.
♦ She plans to use her engineering background to develop prosthetics and in the space life sciences.
♦ She supports issues regarding children, adolescents, and people with handicaps.

"The way of a superior man is three-fold: virtuous, he is free from anxieties; wise, he is free from perplexities; bold, he is free from fear." — **Confucius**

Adah Belle Samuels Thoms
(c. 1870-1943) Nursing Pioneer

A t the outbreak of World War I, there was a sharp increase in the need for nurses. Though there were too few whites, the surgeon general of the army refused to allow black nurses to participate in the war effort. The American Red Cross initially ignored their applications, but later decided to accept a limited number of African-Americans; by the time a decision was made to allow them to participate, the war was over. Eighteen fully qualified black nurses were then appointed to the Army Nurse Corps, with full pay and rank in December, 1918.

It was largely through the urging of Adah Belle Thoms that the nurses enrolled in the Red Cross Nursing Services, even though it was too late for service in World War I.

Not one to participate in only one effort, Adah Thoms shifted her interest to helping organize the Blue Circle Nurses, a new order of black war nurses, in 1917. They were recruited by the Circle for Negro War Relief, and paid to help in poor communities, by instructing black people in the importance of hygiene, proper clothing, and a balanced diet.

Thoms was appointed to serve on the Women's Advisory Council of Venereal Diseases of the United States Public Health Service, by the assistant surgeon general in 1921.

Born in Richmond, Virginia, around 1870, she was the daughter of Harry and Melvina Samuels. Thoms moved to New York to study public speaking and elocution at Cooper Union. Before long though, she left to work at the Woman's Infirmary and School of Therapeutic Massage. She graduated in 1900, the only African-American in a class of thirty.

She worked as a private duty nurse in New York City, later becoming head nurse on the staff at St. Agnes Hospital in Raleigh, North Carolina. After only one year in the position, she returned to New York, to upgrade her training.

By then, Lincoln Hospital had opened a new school of nursing. Thoms entered, becoming head nurse on a surgical ward in only her second year. After graduating, in 1905, she was offered full-time employment at Lincoln University.

Obviously bright and efficient, she became assistant superintendent in 1905, eventually holding the position for eighteen years. She instituted a six month postgraduate course for registered nurses in 1913, and began a course in public health nursing in 1917. Though fully qualified to fulfill the duties of superintendent, the strict racial policies of the day prohibited her promotion. She still managed to improve nurses' training.

As a member of the Lincoln Nurses' Alumnae, she encouraged the group to sponsor the initial meeting of what would become the National Association of Colored Graduate Nurses (NACGN). She was elected treasurer, and later served as president from 1916 to 1923. The organization was necessary, because of the refusal of the American Nurses' Association (ANA) to allow African-American nurses to become members.

She fought valiantly to improve employment opportunities for black nurses, and to improve their training. She worked with the National Association for the Advancement of Colored People and the National Urban League in 1916, in an effort to improve the state of training institutions and hospitals for blacks. She also worked to institute state and local nursing associations for African-Americans, and to increase membership in NACGN.

In 1923, she retired from Lincoln, but remained active in a number of organizations. She wrote *Pathfinders: A History of the Progress of Colored Graduate Nurses* (1929), which chronicled the struggles of African-American nurses in their fight for equality and professional recognition by mainstream America. For her efforts, she received the first Mary Mahoney Award in 1936, and was elected posthumously to nursing's Hall of Fame in 1976.

"A reputation for good judgment, fair dealing, truth and rectitude, is itself a fortune." — **H.W. Beecher**

Channing H. Tobias (1882-1961)
Interracial Relations Leader, Clergyman

His experience working in the Young Men's Christian Association prepared Channing H. Tobias to apply Christian values to the encouragement of positive relationships between whites and African-Americans. His long career with the organization included his service as student secretary in 1911, and in 1923, as the senior secretary of the department for colored men.

He was born an orphan in Augusta, Georgia. Later, the president of the city's Paine College, in Augusta, Georgia, befriended him, and assisted him in obtaining a higher education. Tobias also attended Drew Theological Seminary in Madison, New Jersey, earning his degree in 1905. From that time, through 1911, he taught biblical literature at Paine College. He then began an association with the YMCA that lasted for the remainder of his life. He believed in cooperation between races, and in the 1930s and 1940s, he was an outstanding liaison between the groups. Blacks across economic, social, educational, and regional lines admired him, and considered him a leader. Governmental agencies also sought his counsel because of his popularity in various groups.

When the World Conference of the YMCA met in 1937, he was both chairman and delegate of the committee on race relations. He was Chairman of the Board of the National Association for the Advancement of Colored People (NAACP), directed the Phelps-Stokes Fund, served on the board of directors for the Jessie Smith Noyes Foundation, the American Bible Society, the Marshall Field Foundation, the Stittinius Associates of Liberia, and the Modern Industrial Bank of New York City.

During World War II, he was associate administrator of the War Finance Committee of New York State, and because of his strong leadership abilities, was also appointed to the Committee on Welfare and Recreation, and the Advisory Committee on Selective Service. Though he was a political independent, President Harry Truman appointed him to the Committee on Civil Rights in 1946.

For his service in religious matters, he received the Harmon Award and Sprigarn Medal, both in 1928.

Though he received several honorary degrees, the most outstanding was the Doctor of Laws. Given in 1950, it was the first time that New York University had bestowed the honor on a person of African ancestry.

Channing Tobias sought common ground between people, and sought cooperation and reconciliation.

HISTORY IN A CAPSULE

The YMCA originated in 1844 in London, England, led by George Williams. Though a Christian organization, it is nonsectarian, and is not politically affiliated. Its purposes are to provide group activities such as camping, sports, education, and counseling to help young men to develop positive character traits, and to help them to become good citizens.

By 1851, the organization had spread to North America, with the first group being formed in Montreal, and the second in Boston, Massachusetts. In addition to its programs, the group sponsors cafeterias, hotels, and residence halls. During the Civil War, the YMCA began services to the military, and in 1929, by the Geneva Convention, was directed to promote certain facilities and programs in many prisoner of war camps. The World Alliance of YMCAs has its headquarters in Geneva, and was established in 1855.

"... if race prejudice and persecution and public discrimination for mere color was to spread up from the South and result in a fixed caste of color ... every American would really be a civil outcast, forever an alien, in public life."
— **William Monroe Trotter**

William Monroe Trotter (1872-1934)
Journalist, Civil Rights Leader

He graduated from Hyde Park High School in 1890, as an honor student, and held Bachelor of Arts (1875), and Master of Arts (1896) degrees from Harvard University, where he graduated Magna cum laude (1895). He was also the first African-American member of Phi Beta Kappa, the national scholarship fraternity. Unfortunately, in the end, William Monroe Trotter, a driven man, was almost penniless, having invested nearly all of his physical energy and finances into his dream of equal rights for African-Americans.

From 1897 to 1906, he was a Boston insurance and mortgage broker, with a secret dream of editing a militant newspaper. In 1901, *The Guardian* was the fulfillment of that dream. He remained its head until his death. So important was it to him that even its symbolism was carefully planned. It was housed in the

263

same building that abolitionist William Lloyd Garrison used to publish *The Liberator*. It was also where *Uncle Tom's Cabin*, the Harriet Beecher Stowe novel, that was cited as having contributed toward the outbreak of the Civil War, was printed. He edited centennial volumes on abolitionists John Greenleaf Whittier, Charles Sumner, and William Lloyd Garrison. The paper was his uncompromising forum to denounce discrimination against black citizens. Chief on his list of compromisers was educator Booker T. Washington, who, he felt, monopolized the publicity on the state of the Negro. So strongly did he disagree with Washington, that he and his supporters heckled Washington when he was the featured speaker in Boston, at the Columbus Avenue African Zion Church, on July 30, 1903. So great was the extent of the interruptions, that Trotter and his associates were arrested, and jailed for thirty days. He later explained that he felt it was the only way to call attention to his views on civil rights. They conflicted so completely with Washington's, that he threw his support behind the more militant W.E.B. Du Bois and the concept of the Niagara Movement. He collaborated with DuBois in organizing the group in 1905.

No person or institution was beyond his critical eye. He challenged President Theodore Roosevelt in 1906, when three companies of the 25th United States Infantry Regiment were discharged because of a Brownsville, Texas incident. When *The Clansman* (1910), an anti-black play, was performed in Boston, he launched a successful demonstration against it. Similarly, he picketed the movie *Birth of a Nation* (1915), for which he was again arrested, but later acquitted.

His dislike of President Woodrow Wilson's policies led to his 1913 protest against discrimination aimed at black workers in government offices. But his greatest coup occurred when he applied for a passport to place the plight of the black man before the Allied statesmen at the Paris Peace Conference (1919). When he was denied, he learned to cook, applied for, and was hiredto work in the kitchen on a transatlantic steamer. Once in Paris, to the surprise of all, there he was — a delegate of the National Equal Rights League and Secretary of the Race Petitioners to the Peace Conference. Even though Wilson and the other heads of state refused to outlaw racial discrimination as part of the Covenant of the League of Nations, Trotter continued the struggle until his death. Although he was never to see the fruits of his personal labors, his courage in speaking out against inequities inspired others to continue his fight.

Sojourner
Truth

Speaking
Tonight

Congregational
Church

Abolitionist

K. Belmonte

"Hateful is the power, and pitiable is the life, of those who wish to be feared rather than to be loved."   — *Cornelius Nepos*

Sojourner Truth (1797-1883)
Abolitionist, Civil War Heroine

Because she believed that the Lord ordained her to declare truth to the people, she changed her name to Sojourner Truth, and began her journey in 1843.

Born Isabella, a slave, in Hurley, Ulster County, New York, she was a powerful speaker for the abolitionist cause, and had the talent to persuade her listeners. Though she had no formal education, she had innate wisdom and insight into the human condition.

Once a married woman with five children, she was separated from her husband before the state of New York outlawed slavery in 1827. Once freed, she left her former owner, and began walking, eventually ending up in New York City. She worked for a deeply religious man named Pierson, but left him when she became disillusioned with his group.

She was unpredictable in her rhetoric, and would speak out whenever she felt the urge, and when the opportunity presented itself. She was also a champion for women's rights, and attended the second National Women's Suffrage Convention in Akron, Ohio, in 1852. She objected to the fawning excessiveness of speakers concerning the male intellect.

She spoke with President Abraham Lincoln and urged him to allow free Northern blacks to take up arms and to fight for their freedom. She helped to care for newly freed slaves and soldiers during the Civil War, and advocated education, and the ownership and development of land, by freed men.

With the help of friends, she purchased a small home in Battle Creek, Michigan, where crippled and quite elderly, she died at the age of 96, having pricked the conscience and chided the duplicity of America.

HISTORY IN A CAPSULE

Mary Elizabeth Bowser, whose mistress, Elizabeth Van Lew, was a leader of the Union Army supporters in Richmond, Virginia, was placed in Jefferson Davis' Confederate White House to perform espionage. She feigned illiteracy, but in reality had been educated in Philadelphia. She would read orders and dispatches while dusting and cleaning. She would then relay the information to Van Lew, through another spy who traveled between the Van Lew plantation and the Confederate White House daily, delivering farm produce. When Bowser overheard dinner conversations between Jefferson Davis and others, she would pass on their army plans to Van Lew, who in turn, would inform General Grant. In spite of the danger involved in her activities, Bowser served as a Union spy without detection for the duration of the Civil War.

Many other African-American women served in the Civil War, such as Susie K. Taylor, who was a teacher, nurse, and laundress. Some also served as scouts and spies, Harriet Tubman being the most famous of these intrepid ladies.

"Go down, Moses 'Way down in Egypt Land, Tell Ole Pharoah to Let My People Go." — **Negro Spiritual**

Harriet Tubman (1823-1913)
Underground Railroad Conductor

She was called "The Moses of her People," and is believed to have traveled south nineteen times in her rescue of over three hundred slaves. Though she suffered from sleep seizures, resulting from a blow on the head by an overseer, when she was a young girl, Harriet Tubman became one of the toughest trail bosses of the Underground Railroad. Known to pack a pistol, she would hold it to the head of the fainthearted and threaten, "You go on, or you die." She even carried drugs to quiet crying babies.

She freed her two children, her sister, and her elderly parents. To raise the capital for her expeditions, she worked as a maid. Usually starting her rescue trips on Saturday nights, she and her escapees would have a head start by Monday. Her exploits so embarrassed and angered slave-owners, that rewards totaling forty-thousand dollars were offered for her capture.

Born on a slave-breeding plantation in Dorchester County, Maryland, she was one of eleven children born to Benjamin Ross and Harriet Greene. She worked as a field hand until her head injury rendered he incapable of being a "breeder."

She married John Tubman, a free black around 1844. She, however, remained a slave. In 1849, the master of her plantation died, and the rumor among the slaves was that they would all be sold to the Deep South. Along with two of her brothers, Harriet made her first escape. Her brothers were so afraid of being recaptured, they returned to the plantation; Harriet chose instead to follow the North Star.

She traveled by night, hiding during the day. She eventually found her way to Philadelphia. By the time she returned to Maryland two years later, however, her husband had remarried.

Though disappointed at the turn of events, she continued her rescue efforts. By 1850, she had already rescued a brother and sister, and a year later, led eleven slaves into Canada to freedom. So proud was she of her success, she was known to brag that she never ran her train off the track and never lost a passenger.

The anti-slavery workers of New York and New England helped her to raise enough money to purchase a home for herself and her aged parents in Auburn, New York, after she rescued them in 1857. William Seward, an abolitionist, sold her a home and tried to get Congress to award her a government pension for her courage, as well as for her service as scout, cook, and spy during the Civil War. She is said to have credited her courage to fervent prayer.

Though she never learned to read or write, she demonstrated the savvy of a trained general with her ingenious management of fleeing slaves. At her death, she was buried with full military honors, for her many contributions to the cause of freedom. On June 12, 1914, a tablet commemorating her deeds was unveiled in Auburn.

HISTORY IN A CAPSULE

Because women were less likely to be suspected as spies, Lucy Carter was issued a pass which entitled her to pass through lines at her pleasure. As a spy for the 16th New York Cavalry, stationed at Vienna, Virginia, Lucy moved from one plantation to another. She passed on information such as troop locations and strength to superiors such as Lieutenant George S. Hollister, who issued the pass.

"I did not set out to establish an internationally known performance group. I simply wanted to share the joy of music with African-American children."

— Dr. Walter Turnbull

Walter Turnbull (b. 1943)
Choirmaster, Vocalist

cCall's magazine named him "One of the Fifteen Greatest Men on Earth." President Clinton awarded him the National Medal of the Arts. As an artist, educator, master teacher, and founder-director of the Boys Choir of Harlem, he has been extensively profiled by the media. A hero by every right, Dr. Walter Turnbull invested in, and dedicated his life to, the most important of pursuits: that of drawing the best from disadvantaged youths, enabling them to realize their potential.

What began as the Ephesus Choir, in the basement of the church, with twenty boys, in 1968, grew to an institution serving approximately five hundred and fifty boys and girls, ages eight through eighteen. It addresses the educational, social, and emotional needs of inner city youths, in areas where the drop-out rate is seventy-six percent.

Under Dr. Turnbull's direction, over one hundred fifty thousand witness live performances annually by the choir, and millions more through television. The group gives annual recitals at Merkin Hall in New York City.

The Choir Academy of Harlem is an on-site school that is in partnership with the New York Board of Education and Community School District 5. The school boasts a ninety-eight percent college enrollment from its high school graduates.

Embodying the old African proverb, "It takes a village to raise a child," Dr. Turnbull seeks to bond with the children and their families. He further wishes to establish a sense of stability and security in their lives, as he presents an alternative to life on the streets and negative peer pressure.

Born in Greenville, Mississippi, he attended local schools, and was an honor graduate of Tougaloo College. He received his Masters in Music and Doctor of Musical Arts degrees from the Manhattan School of Music. He is also a graduate of the Columbia University School of Business Institute for Non-Profit Management. He holds honorary degrees from Tougaloo College, which also named a scholarship in his honor for Boys Choir of Harlem graduates, as well as Queens College, Mannes College of Music, California State University, Skidmore College, Hofstra University, and Muhlenberg College. In addition, he is listed in *Who's Who in American Colleges and Universities.*

A vocalist as well as an educator, he made his operatic debut in Scott Joplin's *Treemonisha*, which he also performed on Broadway, with the Houston Grand Opera. Other performances include appearances as a tenor soloist with the Philadelphia Orchestra and the New York Philharmonic. With Opera South, he has appeared in *Turandot* and *Carmen*. He has also had roles in *La Traviata, Die Zauberflote,* and *Carnima Burana*, with the Alvin Ailey Dance Theater.

In addition to receiving several distinguished alumnus awards, he is the recipient of the Edwin Berry National Business Award, the Eleanor Roosevelt Service Award, the National Association of Negro Musicians Award, the President's Action Award, and numerous others.

Under his direction, the choir has traveled worldwide, and has two Grammy albums. In addition, their voices are heard on soundtracks from the movies *Glory, Jungle Fever* and *Malcolm X*. The group has also performed with famed tenor Luciano Pavarotti.

Media profiles include *Nightline, 20/20, 60 Minutes, The Today Show*, and *Amazing Grace with Bill Moyers.*

His autobiography, *Lift Every Voice and Sing,* not only tells of his humble beginnings in a segregated, rural Mississippi town, it illuminates how, with love and support from his family and educators, he gained the confidence to dare for something greater. He now communicates the same positive thinking to his students.

K. BelMonte

"Do you see a man who excels in his work? He will stand up before kings. . ."
— Proverbs 22:29, NKJV

Madame C.J. Walker (1869-1919)
Businesswoman

auper Becomes Princess" would have been a fitting headline to describe Madame C.J. Walker.

Born Sarah Breedlove, in a sharecropper's cabin in Delta, Louisiana, as a daughter of ex-slaves, she was orphaned at six years of age. When she was only fourteen years old, she married C.J. Walker. Unfortunately, by the time she was twenty, she was a widow eking out a living by taking in laundry.

Sarah possessed a spirit of adventure, and was interested in embellishing her good looks. She experimented with different concoctions that softened her hair, but did not relax the tight curl. Desiring to do this, she developed a metal comb that, when heated and used with her special emollients, relaxed her hair and gave her more styling freedom. At last, black women had the answer, to what many considered a major cosmetic problem.

At a time when cosmetics designed for women of color were virtually non-existent, the "Walker System" caught on like the proverbial wildfire. After becoming wealthy, from selling door-todoor, she established her own schools in Denver and Pittsburgh. Agents purchased franchises and she supplied them with the products needed. She also profited from her large factory in Indianapolis, and from the manufacture of other beauty products.

Her annual payroll totaled more than two hundred thousand dollars — no small amount in her day. Every African-American oriented publication carried Walker's ads, as well as stories about her active and high profile social life.

Walker built a mansion in New York, at Irving-on-the-Hudson, at a cost of more than two hundred thousand dollars. Her furnishings were the finest that money could buy. In spite of her great wealth, she remained sensitive to the poverty of the majority of black people, and contributed generously to charities concerned with their welfare.

Her resourcefulness and business savvy made her the first black American woman to become a self-made millionaire. She was also one of the prominent social leaders of her day. Her system was the foundation for later cosmetics and hair products for African-American women.

DID YOU KNOW?

♦ Madame Walker furthered her education by attending night school after moving to St. Louis, Missouri.
♦ In 1913, she established Lelia College in New York, to train her agents in the Walker Beauty System.

HISTORY IN A CAPSULE

The National Negro Business League was established in 1900 by Booker T. Washington, in order to promote capitalism among African-Americans. He believed that, through industrial and practical education, blacks could achieve some level of economic success.

"The true aim of everyone who aspires to be a teacher should be not to impart his own opinions, but to kindle minds." — **F.W. Robertson**

Booker T. Washington (1856-1915)
Educator

His philosophy was that of practical education, in which, blacks were offered industrial courses, which would prepare them to be domestics, farmers, mechanics and the like. These were trades that Booker T. Washington felt African-Americans would be offered and allowed to practice. The study of science, mathematics, and history he thought impractical.

The underlying rationale was that through industry, and financial success through hard work, the resistance of whites to black Americans would eventually wear down. As a former slave, his attitude toward racism was that of conciliation. His hopes were that, if African-Americans performed needed and practical jobs within society, and did not antagonize the power structure, they stood a better chance of succeeding. Industrial development, he believed, would "prepare the Negro...to...enter the all-powerful business and commercial world."

Though he had many wealthy and powerful friends, some of his harshest critics were members of the black intelligentsia, who felt that Washington's ideas kept blacks from progressing, by discouraging them from the "arts and profession." W.E.B. Du Bois, a highly intelligent young black man, who earned his Ph.D. degree from Harvard University, and was editor of the NAACP's official magazine, saw Washington as compromising. But because he had become so powerful, no black editor dared to challenge him in print.

Booker T. Washington established the Tuskegee Institute in Alabama, because he was so hungry for an education when he was younger. He walked nearly two hundred miles to enroll in Hampton Institute in 1872. He taught at Malden, West Virginia, and entered Wayland Seminary in Washington, D.C. He eventually returned to Hampton, intending to teach Indian boys. Because the Tuskegee Institute needed a principal, he went there instead. At the time, the school was comprised of thirty students and two small buildings.

Under his guidance, the institute grew and became known the world over. President Theodore Roosevelt and William Howard Taft consulted with him when they needed information about the status of the Negro in the United States. He was invited to speak for his race at the Atlanta Expo in 1895.

Also a businessman, Washington organized the National Negro Business League in 1900. In 1910, he helped to organize the General Education Board, and in 1911, the Stokes Fund.

Patience, with practical jobs and realistic expectations, was the crux of his advice for the Negro. He knew that improvements would come slowly, but, he felt in time, white prejudice and indifference toward African-Americans would eventually dissipate.

In spite of his conciliatory attitude towards whites and racism, he was known to have contributed his own personal finances toward early anti-segregation cases.

He denied that his philosophy limited African-Americans, believing that his generation should seek to reach loftier goals by first, "laying the foundation in the little things of life that lie immediately at one's door."

In spite of his network of powerful white friends, he was unable to persuade any of them to work toward stopping the wave of lynchings, beatings, and burnings of black businesses, which was sweeping over the nation at the time.

Although his philosophy had some failings, he accomplished many positive things for African-Americans and is considered by many as one of the nation's great educators and leaders.

"Poetry is the art of substantiating shadows, and of lending existence to nothing."
— Burke

Phyllis Wheatley (c. 1753-1784)
Poet

A s a little African-born girl of about seven years of age, she stood on the docks of Boston, as she was sold to the highest bidder. Years later General George Washington would write her a letter of commendation for her poetry.

Born in Senegal, Phyllis was brought to the shores of America in 1761. John Wheatley, a tailor, bought the youngster. The Wheatleys gave Phyllis the family name, and taught her how to read and write. The Bible was the first book she learned to read, and it instilled a deep faith and a love of poetry in the young girl.

Because the Wheatleys were cultivated people, they treated Phyllis like a member of the family. Proud of the poems the teenager produced, Mrs. Wheatley showed them to her friends. Soon, the cultured element was requesting Phyllis' poem, *On the Death of the Reverend Mr. George Whitefield,* which was written in

1770 to commemorate his death. The gentleman had been chaplain to the Countess of Huntington in England. Three years later, Phillis, whose health had always been fragile, was sent to England in hopes that she would improve. While there, the Countess presented her to society by introducing her to members of the nobility.

Before she left to return to America, her collection of thirty-nine poems made her the first African-American woman to publish a book.

Phyllis' book was so well received, it was reprinted several times. When Mrs. Wheatley died in 1774, followed by her husband in 1778, Phyllis was free. She married John Peters, a black man. The coming of the Revolutionary War made the desire to read poems and money to spend on such scarce. Unable to support herself through writing, she earned her way by working in a boarding house. She gave birth to three children, who all died in infancy. Tragically, she developed complications during her third pregnancy; she and her baby died only a few hours apart.

Though her life was brief, and her end tragic, her accomplishments demonstrate what people can achieve when allowed the freedom to develop and express their talents. A symbol to anti-slavery advocates, and a contradiction to the pro-slavery supporters, Wheatley's work has survived. The last edition of her poems was printed in 1966.

DID YOU KNOW?

♦ The full title of her first collection was *Poems on Various Subjects, Religious and Moral.*
♦ Her poems were influenced by Alexander Pope, the English poet.
♦ She had some knowledge of Latin.

Isaac White
Civil War Soldier

86th U.S. Colored Infantry

"The glory of ancestors sheds a light around posterity; it allows neither their good nor bad qualities to remain in obscurity." **— Sallust**

Isaac "Bogue" White (1840-1936)
And The 86th Colored Infantry

As members of the 86th Colored Infantry, Company E, Isaac White and his compatriots waded through icy streams, and endured bone-chilling cold on long treks to confront the enemy — the Confederate army.

Born a slave in the Marianna-Cottondale area of northwest Florida, in the 1840s, "Bogue" White escaped from bondage and made his way to Barrancas, a city in west Florida, in what is now the Pensacola area. He left behind his wife of Indian ancestry and a son, and signed up with the 86th. His company's roll lists him as having "enlisted under President's call of July 6, 1864," with an "advance bounty of one hundred dollars due."

Organized from the 14th Corps de Afrique Infantry, on April 4, 1864, the 86th served at Barrancas until March, 1865. Isaac White and his fellow infantry-men marched from Pensacola, Florida to Blakely, Alabama, between March 20 and April 1, 1865. They assaulted and captured Fort Blakely on April 9, and occupied Mobile, Alabama on April 12. The unit marched to Montgomery, between April 13 and 25th, and had duty there and at Mobile through May 19. At some point, Isaac White served in Knoxville, Tennessee, but the circumstances of his stay are not clear.

His granddaughter, now ninety-six years of age, remembers his stories about slavery and the Civil War. Tales of him walking in his sleep raise speculation that perhaps he pretended to be sleep-walking when he escaped from slavery.

White and the 86th were part of more than 186,000 African-Americans in combat troops who fought in the Union Army. Nearly a third of that number were killed in battle. Only snippets of White's military service remain preserved in documents. Those who remember him recall that, after the war, he became a prosperous citizen with servants living in his house. At some point, he learned to read and write. Thousands of others of his era were not so fortunate. Yet their deeds, if not their names, must not be forgotten.

HISTORY IN A CAPSULE

Prior to the Civil War, marriages between African-Americans were performed in local churches where records of such unions were kept. After the War, the State of Florida passed legislation requiring married "persons of color" to appear before a magistrate and state that they mutually wished to continue in the relationship. If each agreed to do so, they were "joined together in bonds of Matrimony...in pursuance of an act of the General Assembly of the State aforesaid approved January 11, 1866."

Isaac White and his wife, Sarah, were re-married on June 17, 1866. At that point, the union was put into the county records.

"True statesmanship is the art of changing a nation from what it is into what it ought to be." **—W.R. Alger**

Lawrence Douglas Wilder (b. 1931)
Civil Rights Activist, Politician

nder the barrage of enemy fire on Korea's Pork Chop Hill, he carried wounded comrades to safety. Again and again, he returned for the injured, risking his own life under hostile shelling. For his valor in battle, Douglas Wilder received the Bronze Star. He used the clout it gave him to complain that not enough African-Americans were receiving promotions for feats that deserved them. To their credit, the command responded and began decorating, albeit belatedly, black soldiers for courage in the service of their country.

Born in Richmond, Virginia, he was educated in the city's segregated schools. After graduating from Virginia Union University, with a Bachelor's degree (1951), he served in the Korean War, and returned to enter Howard University Law School. He earned his J.D. degree in 1959, and was soon admitted to the Virginia Bar. Initially, his parents feared that he would be unable to succeed in Richmond, with its historically strict color line, and its white judges and juries. The war veteran

279

began winning cases and achieving what he had set out to do. He won his parent's support and calmed their fears that he would be broken by a system they did not feel he could change.

He participated in the Civil Rights Movement of the 1950s and 1960s, though as a disciple of nonviolence rather than a militant. He was director of the Richmond branch of the National Urban League, and a member of the National Association for the Advancement of Colored People (NAACP). He handled cases without fee as a member of the association's legal defense fund.

Wilder first entered politics in 1969, when he ran for a state senate seat. He felt that he had to run as a liaison that could bring the races together. Even though he delivered a campaign speech criticizing *Carry Me Back to Old Virginny*, the state's song, which he felt glorified slavery, he won the race. He became the first African-American elected to the Virginia senate since the era of Reconstruction.

In 1985, he became the first American of African ancestry to win as lieutenant governor. On January 13, 1990, he was sworn in as governor of the state of Virginia. It was the first time that a member having African ancestry had ever been elected governor in the history of the United States.

Wilder began his campaign for the presidency in 1991, but later withdrew from the race. His political daring and achievements, however, demonstrate that the United States truly is a country where anyone may grow up to be President.

DID YOU KNOW?

◆ Wilder was once considered a fun-loving free spirit and a prankster.
◆ He and tennis great Arthur Ashe grew up in the same neighborhood.
◆ Wilder attended college on the G.I. Bill.

HISTORY IN A CAPSULE

In 1994, Beverly Joyce Bailey Harvard became the first African-American female chief of police, of Atlanta, Georgia, a major metropolitan area. Born in Macon, Georgia, in 1950, she received her B.A. degree from Morris Brown College (1972), her M.S. degree from Georgia State University (1980), and her certification at the Federal Bureau of Investigation (FBI) Academy.

Roy
Wilkins

Civil Rights
Activist

NAACP
Official

"Rebellion against tyrants is obedience to God." **— Franklin**

Roy Wilkins (1901-1981)
Civil Rights Leader

He was the last survivor of the time of the giants. Those who dominated the Civil Rights movement of the 1950s and 1960s — Martin Luther King, Jr., Malcolm X, A. Philip Randolph and Whitney Young — were all dead. Toward the end, though, those who followed Roy Wilkins, and who indeed reaped the benefits of his leadership and dedication to the improvement of the lot of African-Americans — did not understand him. He had become to them an anachronism.

Because he disdained the term "black," because he was not prone to rash actions, it caused a faction within the NAACP — the organization he so dearly loved — to consider new leadership. In the face of much criticism, like an old soldier bound to his cause, he stayed on until his declining health forced him to retire in 1977.

Born in St. Louis, Missouri, he was reared by an uncle and aunt who lived in St. Paul. Although he attended integrated schools, and grew up in racially diverse circumstances, he witnessed the worst days of segregation.

After graduating and joining *The Kansas City Call*, a leading black newspaper, he got his first real taste of the bitterness of a segregated society. He stepped up his activities in the NAACP, which he joined while in college at the University of Minnesota, where he received his Bachelor's degree (1923). With majors in journalism and sociology, he worked as night editor of the school newspaper, *The Minnesota Daily*. He was also editor of the black weekly, *The St. Paul Appeal*.

He left *The Kansas City Call* in 1931, and began a long career in the NAACP, as executive secretary under Walter White. In 1931, he proved discrimination charges on a federally financed flood control project in Mississippi, and played a leading role in getting Congress to monitor and curb the practice.

His first arrest came in 1934, when he picketed in Washington, D.C., hoping to encourage the Attorney General to add anti-lynching to an agenda at a conference on crime.

He succeeded W.E.B. Du Bois, who edited *The Crisis*, the NAACP's official magazine. He was also an advisor in the War Department, and in 1945, during a United Nations conference in San Francisco, he served as consultant to the American delegation.

When Walter White took a year's leave of absence, in 1949, Wilkins became the NAACP's acting executive secretary. He also chaired the National Emergency Civil Rights Mobilization group, which lobbied Washington for legislation guaranteeing civil rights and fair employment.

In 1955, the year that Walter White died, Wilkins became executive secretary of the NAACP. He was an articulate leader in his own right, conferring with presidents, testifying before congressional hearings and using his journalistic skills and training as he wrote for numerous publications. He was instrumental in the passage of the 1964 Civil Rights Act. Though the NAACP and Wilkins became more radical in the 1970s, they were more moderate than their counterparts in the Nation of Islam and other militant groups. Though he and the group were attacked as being too soft, Wilkins always believed in using lawful means to bring about change.

He also chaired the Leadership Conference on Civil Rights, was a trustee of the Eleanor Roosevelt Foundation, the Estes Kefauver Memorial Foundation, and the Kennedy Memorial Library Foundation. He received the Alpha Phi Psi fraternity's Outstanding Citizen Award, the American Jewish Congress' Civil Rights Award, the Anti-Defamation League's American Democratic Legacy Award, the Sprigarn Medal in 1964, and a number of other honors.

Upon his death in 1981, President Ronald Reagan ordered all flags on governmental installations and buildings to fly half-staff, in appreciation for Wilkins' contributions.

K. BelMonte

Daniel
Hale
Williams
Surgeon

"He who wishes to fulfill his mission in the world must be a man of one idea . . . one great overmastering purpose, overshadowing all his aims, and guiding and controlling his entire life." — **Bate**

Daniel Hale Williams (1856-1931)
Surgeon

Before the fame of heart surgeons DeBakey and Barnard, there was the fame of Dr. Daniel Hale Williams. The year was 1893. The patient was one James Cornish, who, as a street ruffian, had sustained a knife wound to an artery a fraction of an inch from his heart. The patient's life was saved as a result of a procedure formerly thought impossible; Dr. Williams opened the patient's chest, and repaired the wound. His fame became worldwide, as he became the first physician to perform surgery on the human heart.

He was the founder of Provident Hospital in Chicago, which became the first interracial hospital in the United States. It was a training facility for African-American nurses and interns. He later established a nursing school at Freedman's Hospital in Washington, D.C., and surgical clinics at Meharry Medical College in Nashville, Tennessee.

In 1894, he founded the Freedman's Hospital of Howard University, and organized a staff of twenty specialists. He also organized medical departments. In 1898, he returned to Chicago, and became St. Luke Hospital's only black staff member. He was elected a Fellow of the American College of Surgeons which was founded in 1913, and was the only black original member of the organization.

Born in Pennsylvania, he left home and supported himself with odd jobs. He eventually learned barbering, and in 1873, operated his own shop in Wisconsin. He also worked as assistant to Dr. Henry Palmer, the state's surgeon general, who was so impressed with the quality of William's work, he encouraged him to study, allowed him to use his medical books. The doctor also sponsored William's admission to Chicago Medical College, where he graduated in 1883.

His contributions to medicine, and to the furthering of opportunities for African-American doctors and nurses are numerous, and immeasurable in value.

HISTORY IN A CAPSULE

Although James Derham was born a slave in 1762, he became a successful physician, specializing in disorders of the throat. He gleaned his knowledge from three masters, each a medical doctor. Through the encouragement of a Dr. Robert Love, his third owner, Derham purchased his freedom in 1783, with money he earned as a medical assistant and apothecary. He established his practice in New Orleans, thus becoming the nation's first African-American physician.

He met Dr. Benjamin Rush during a trip to Philadelphia, and was convinced to move his practice there. He became an esteemed professional among his colleagues, and was regarded as an expert on the relationship between climate and disease.

"Architecture is the printing press of all ages, and gives a history of the state of the society in which the structure was erected." — **Morgan**

Paul R. Williams (1894-1980)
Architect

C alifornia is filled with structures designed by Paul R. Williams, an African-American pioneer in the field of architecture. His clients included executives, movie stars and hotel and government agencies.

The homes he designed were planned a round their environment. While working with accomplished architect Reginald D. Johnson, he won his first big contract — to design a one hundred thousand dollar home. He went on to become chief designer for commercial building specialist, John C. Austin.

Some of Williams' projects include the Chamber of Commerce building, many area schools, the Los Angeles Shrine Auditorium, and the First Methodist Church. After three years of working with Austin, he launched out on his own.

Williams was born in Los Angeles, California, and educated at Polytechnic High School in the same city. He worked his way through the University of

California, where he earned his B.A. degree. He taught art in Los Angeles, and in 1915, became a certified architect. He also studied at the Beaux Arts Institute of Design, and the Los Angeles Art Commission. He became one of the most successful architects of the early twentieth century, designing more than three thousand buildings and over four hundred homes during his career. As a boy, he was discouraged from pursuing his dream of becoming an architect. There was no chance, he was told, that an African-American could succeed in a field dominated almost exclusively by whites.

Paul R. Williams held on to his dream and proved them wrong. His lavish designs for movie stars' mansions won him worldwide recognition. In 1953, he was awarded the NAACP Sprigarn Medal. He received honorary degrees from Lincoln, Howard and Atlanta Universities, and Hampton Institute. He was a hero ahead of his time.

HISTORY IN A CAPSULE

The first African-American woman to become a licensed architect was Norma Sklarek in 1954. She graduated from the Columbia University School of Architecture in 1950. In 1955, she moved to Los Angeles after Skidmore, Owings and Merrill, one of the country's largest architectural firms, hired her. She earned her California license in 1962. For twenty years, she worked for Gruen Associates, another large firm. It was there that she became director of architecture, and was involved with impressive projects, including the Pacific Design Center in West Hollywood, and the U.S. Embassy in Tokyo, Japan. In 1980, she was the first woman to become vice-president of Welton Becket Associates, and in the same year, became the first black woman to become a Fellow in the American Institute of Architects. Sklarek was also project director of Terminal One at Los Angeles International Airport.

"I was raised to believe that excellence is the best deterrent to racism and sexism. And that's how I operate my life." — **Oprah Winfrey**

Oprah Winfrey (b. 1954)
Talk Show Host

She is not only the first African-American woman to host a nationally syndicated weekly talk show, she is also the first black woman to own her own television and film production company, Harpo Studios, Inc., based in Chicago, Illinois.

Born in Kosciusko, Mississippi, to Vernon Winfrey and Vernita Lee, she moved to Nashville at around eight years of age, to live with her father and stepmother. She was required to read five books every two weeks, learn lists of words, and study about successful black people. She grew up with a strong self image, and the assurance that allowed her to try anything of interest to her.

As a novice actress, with a leading role in *The Color Purple* (1985), she was nominated for both the Oscar and the Golden Globe Award. She also starred in *Native Son* (1986), *Throw Momma From the Train* (1988), and *The Women of*

Brewster Place (1989), which she produced. She was also producer of the ABC Movie of the Week, *Overexposed* (1992).

Though her success is largely due to her talent and personal warmth, she admits that sacrifices made by other pioneers opened the doors of opportunity, allowing her phenomenal success.

She graduated from Tennessee State University with a Bachelor of Arts degree in speech and performing arts, and began her media career as a news reporter on WVOL Radio, Nashville, Tennessee (1975-1976). She was a news anchor on WTVF-TV, also in Nashville (1973-1976), and hosted television shows in Baltimore and Chicago. *A.M. Chicago* was the lowest rated of the city's morning talk shows in 1984 when she became host. Soon after, the ratings skyrocketed, and, in 1985, it was renamed *The Oprah Winfrey Show*, which premiered on the largest number of stations ever, of any syndicated program. In 1986, her show was syndicated on one hundred twenty-eight stations across the country.

Oprah Winfrey strongly believes that education and the ability to communicate with people is power. Because she was highly intelligent and never felt limited by her race, she did not have the requisite anger that made one a popular figure on campus during her college years. She was largely ostracized for not being a militant, but has explained her lack of anger as simply not understanding the basis for it. She deals with inequities and stereotypes by demonstrating excellence in her work.

One of the wealthiest entertainers in America, she has won a number of awards and honors, including the Woman of Achievement Award (NOW, 1986), Emmy awards for Best Daytime Talk Show Host (1987, 1991, 1992), NAACP Entertainer of the Year Award (1989), and Broadcaster of the Year by the International Radio and Television Society (1988).

She uses the power she has in the industry to help others, and to inspire them to develop their potential. She also uses her power and success to provide the types of superior programs that enlighten, encourage, and uplift.

DID YOU KNOW?

◆ Her birth name, Orpha, was misspelled Oprah on her birth certificate.

◆ She spent her early years living with her grandmother on a Mississippi pig farm.

◆ She hosted a Baltimore talk show called *People Are Talking.*

◆ She also had movie roles in *Native Son, There Are No Children Here,* and *Listen Up: The Lives of Qunicy Jones.*

"My goal is to obviously be the best."   **— Tiger Woods**

Eldrick "Tiger" Woods (b. 1975)
Golf Champion

The smouldering embers of slavery's legacy of exclusion were all but snuffed out at the Augusta National Golf Club. Twenty-one year old Eldrick "Tiger" Woods is the first man of African descent, and the youngest ever, to win the Masters Championship.

His shots, referred to as "silken beauty," by one sportscaster, were straighter, higher, and went farther, than all the other competitors. Not since Willie Smith won the U.S. Open in 1899, has a golfer won by a larger margin of victory.

With his career earnings already at $1,757,594.00, professional golfers predict that the young player will eventually capture every title.

Considered one of the traditionally "white" sports, the celebration of Woods' victory on Sunday, April 13, 1997, saw more racial diversity than ever before at the conservative Augusta National Golf Club, where the tournament took place.

In an atmosphere where racism is subtle, where blacks "know their place," and where historically, they were restricted to jobs as waiters, trash collectors and caddies, Woods' victory was doubly sweet. Not only did he break the color barrier of the winner's circle, he changed the future and the face of professional golf forever.

Because he would like to see golf become a common choice for African-Americans and other minorities, Woods established a foundation to promote their participation in the game. He sees the opening of opportunities as the true fruit of his winning.

In a culture where the media tend to focus on the worst elements in black communities, Woods provides an effective counter-balance and has become a role model for others who wish to enter golf as a career.

His phenomenal win, called "almost surreal," by a journalist, prompted a congratulatory call from President Bill Clinton.

He is decidedly unconcerned about the politics of race, believing that young minorities should concentrate on what victory does for their sense of self, rather than focusing on their anger.

Born on December 30, 1975, in Cypress, California, to a Thai mother and a father of African descent, Woods is bothered by being described as African-American. Like a growing number of persons of mixed racial ancestry, he prefers to be accepted simply as a human being. As a child, he invented the term "cablinasian" to encompass his Caucasian, Black, Indian and Asian ancestry.

Woods attended Stanford University for two years before deciding to focus full time on his career as a professional golfer. He held many amateur titles before he claimed the green jacket of the Master's Championship.

His wins include the 1994, 1995 and 1996 U.S. Amateur Championships, and the 1996 NCAA Championship. From 1991 to 1993, he was also the U.S. Junior Amateur Champion.

He realizes that others such as Lee Elder, Calvin Peete, Charlie Sifford and Ted Rhodes paved the way for him. He considers Elder as his hero, and thanked him for making it possible for him to pursue, and realize, his dream in a profession dominated by whites.

His win prompted golfing great Jack Nicklaus to state, "There is no room for an elitist attitude. The game has passed that time by."

"Thoughts are mightier than armies." **— Paxton**

Granville T. Woods (1856-1910)
Inventor

His patents were sold to some of the biggest names in American industry, including General Electric Company, Westinghouse Air Brake Company, the American Engineering Company and American Bell Telephone Company. Part of his genius lay in the fact that he worked in a machine shop by day, and studied privately, attending evening classes. As early as 1872, at age sixteen, while he worked as an engineer and fireman on a Missouri railroad, he continued studying electrical and mechanical engineering.

His imagination was fueled through experience gained by working for two years on a British steamship, and later, in 1880, as an engineer on the Danville and Southern Railroad. He believed that he could improve the current crude communication and transportation devices the railroad employed.

He opened a factory and manufactured telegraph, electrical, and telephone equipment after settling in Cincinnati. In 1884, he introduced a steam boiler furnace. He also produced an incubator in 1900, a telegraphic device for transmitting messages between moving trains, over fifteen devices for electrical railways, and the automatic air brake in 1902.

His most important invention of the thirty-five he patented during his lifetime was the "induction telegraph," which enabled moving trains to communicate between one another, thus avoiding collisions and accidents. His Synchronous Multiplex Railway Telegraph was challenged by the Edison and Phelps Company, because it was working to develop a similar mechanism. The case of Woods vs. Phelps was decided in Woods' favor.

Born in Columbus, Ohio, his inventions have made modern life easier and safer. His genius and industriousness provide incentive for inventors who believe in their ideas, and who are willing to work to make them a reality.

HISTORY IN A CAPSULE

Born in Chelsea, Massachusetts, in 1948, Lewis Latimer was an immensely talented man and the only black member of the famous "Edison Pioneers." After the Civil War, Latimer went to work for some patent lawyers. He became the company's chief draftsman, and made the illustrations for Alexander Graham Bell's application for the patent of his telephone. Bright and inventive, he began working on his own, and, in 1881, invented, and patented, a carbon filament incandescent light bulb. As engineer for the Edison Company, he supervised the installing of electrical lighting systems in Philadelphia, New York City, London, and Montreal. The first textbook on the lighting system, *Incandescent Electrical Lighting, A Practical Description of the Edison System,* was authored by Latimer. He was also an expert court witness in defending the patents, and a published poet, artist, and musician.

"People never improve unless they look to some standard or example higher and better than themselves." — ***Tryon Edwards***

Carter G. Woodson (1875-1950)
Educator, Historian

Although he did not start school until the age of twenty, he is known as "The Father of African-American History." Having started school late didn't stop him. He had educated himself over the years and finished work for his diploma in less than two years.

Born in New Canton, Ohio, the importance of an education for the African-American was always stressed in his home by his parents. As former slaves, they wanted something better for their son. Because of the family's poverty, he was compelled to work during his early years.

He attended Berea College in Kentucky, where he earned his Litt.B. in 1903. He earned his Bachelor of Arts degree from the University of Chicago in 1907, and his Master of Arts from the same institution the following year. He also studied at the Sorbonne in Paris, and in Asia.

He organized the Association for the Study of Negro Life and History in 1915, and incorporated it in 1916. He became the founding editor of the *Journal of Negro History* in 1916. It was published from 1918 to 1922. He also organized the Associated Publishers, in 1921, to ensure that books about African-Americans were made available.

He organized and instituted the observation of Negro History Week to elevate self-esteem in African-American students, and he organized and promoted the *Negro History Bulletin* in 1930, to enlighten the public, as well as students and teachers. Because he believed that the contributions made by African-Americans in helping to build this nation deserved to be recognized, he collected, compiled, and edited information that recorded their deeds and accomplishments.

Among his many writings are, *The Disruption of Virginia* (his Ph.D. dissertation, 1912), *The Education of the Negro Prior to 1861* (1915), *A Century of Negro Migration* (1918), *Negro Makers of History and African Myths* (1928), and *African Heroes and Heroines* (1939).

For his many innovations in education, he was awarded the Sprigarn Medal (1926) for contributions to the advancement of the Negro.

HISTORY IN A CAPSULE

The Niagara Movement was organized in 1905 by W.E.B. Du Bois and other intellectuals. The twenty-nine original black members met secretly in Niagara Falls, Ontario, and formulated a manifesto that would ensure full civil liberties for black citizens, recognize human brotherhood and abolish racial discrimination. The group met annually, but suffered from a lack of funds and other weaknesses. It had no permanent headquarters or staff. Though it won some local victories, it never attracted the support of the masses. In 1910, it disbanded and merged with another group to form the NAACP.

Louis T. Wright

Physician

"He who has no inclination to learn more will be very apt to think that he knows enough." — **Powell**

Louis T. Wright (1886 - ?)
Physician, Activist

While he was a student in obstetrics at Harvard University, he was told that he could not deliver babies in the Boston Lying-In-Hospital; he had to deliver infants in an area separate from the rest of the class. As a fee-paying student, he courageously demanded the same opportunities as white students. As a result of his challenge, the policy was abandoned.

In 1919, he became the first African-American to be appointed to a municipal hospital in New York City. He designed a brace for fractures of the cervical vertebrae, and devised a blade plate for the surgical treatment of fractures of the knee. The first tests of Aureomycin on human beings were made under his supervision, and he devised an intradermal smallpox vaccination.

One of the most militant of African-American physicians, Wright did not hesitate to picket as a form of protest. He was chairman of the board of the

National Association for the Advancement of Colored People (NAACP), and also established a board of health committee.

He fought against racial discrimination in the American College of Surgeons, and against the color line at Harlem Hospital, and picketed D.W. Griffith's movie, *The Birth of a Nation* for three weeks outside a Boston Theater, and demanded that the movie be withdrawn.

Born in La Grange, Georgia, he left to study medicine at Harvard Medical School, graduating with honors in 1915. In the same year, he returned to Georgia to practice medicine.

He joined the Army medical corps at the outbreak of World War II, and was ranked as a lieutenant. He was sent to France, and served in the Vosges sector. Prior to the launching of offensives, his duty was to make medical surveys of the areas. While serving in France, he was gassed and hospitalized. Upon recovering, he continued in service, and attained the rank of captain.

Regarded as one of the nation's distinguished surgeons, he practiced at Harlem Hospital for more than thirty years. He believed in the delivery of excellent services, and that all citizens deserved to be treated with equality and respect.

Under a grant from the Damon Runyon Fund, he engaged in cancer research. Because of his excellence in his field, he was admitted to fellowship in the American College of Surgeons in 1934. He was awarded the Sprigarn Medal in 1940.

For all of his brilliance and achievements, Dr. Wright realized that, without equality in society, many of the opportunities enjoyed by whites would be little more than a dream for those of African descent. Therefore, he fought discrimination through lawful protest, to make the way easier for the coming generation.

DID YOU KNOW?

♦ Dr. Wright became police surgeon of New York City in 1928.
♦ He lectured all over the United States.
♦ Wright invented the brace used in handling and transporting patients with neck injuries.
♦ In 1945, he was the only African-American in the twelve thousand member American College of Surgeons.

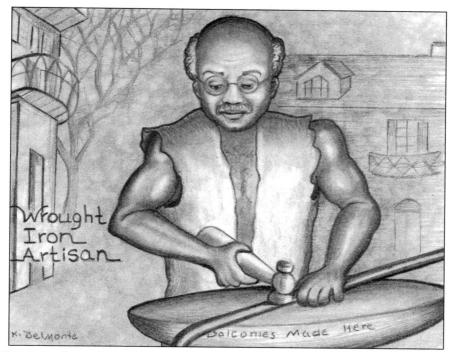

"There is always hope in a man who actually and earnestly works — in idleness alone is there perpetual despair." — **Carlyle**

The Wrought Iron Men
Artisans

heir names and their faces are like the fog and the mist, existing only in the mind's eye, shadows without substance. Their works are undated, unsigned. Only through the permanence of the iron from which they wrought their craft does the world know of their existence.

The famous old wrought iron balconies that grace New Orleans houses are now items prized by antique dealers, connoisseurs, and collectors. The best of these, with their charming grilles and lunettes, were formed before the War of 1812, when blacks held a monopoly on skilled crafts and trades.

They received the best of apprenticeship training, because a talented young blacksmith could be loaned out to others, while his master derived additional income from his labor. It is believed that the smithies of exceptional skill rendered their products from engravings and pictures provided them by their white patrons. It was not unusual to see a charming blend of styles in their workman-ship, such as Rococo and Gothic, with curves, junctions, and perpendiculars to which the nature of iron readily bends.

Because of the artistry required to render some designs, patrons sought the skill of the locksmith or armorer, who wrought their designs largely by using the saw and file, applying heat only at the beginning stages of their work.

In order to make a profit from working in wrought iron, the artisan had to be able to work quickly, while the iron was white-hot. This resulted in bold designs with the charm of irregularities, which occur when work is rendered freehand, rather than beaten around a model.

The era when African-American artisans dominated the craft of wrought iron ended somewhere around 1830. After this period, German tradesmen flooded the New Orleans area, bringing with them foundries and other labor-saving mecha-nisms which eventually replaced the smithies who worked largely by eye and hand.

Heavy iron bars bent, shaved, sawed, and filed into sensitive and delicate works are the legacy of skilled artisans whose identities we will never know. They took Spanish and French motifs and expressed them in designs uniquely their own.

Today, we enjoy them, and give honor to the skilled craftsmen that will be forever known only as The Wrought Iron Men.

HISTORY IN A CAPSULE

James A. Porter produced the first book on the history of African-American art. Entitled *Modern Negro Art* (1943, 1969), it was the first comprehensive study of its kind. He was born in Baltimore, Maryland in 1904. In 1927, he graduated from Howard University, having also studied at the Art Students League and Columbia University in New York City. A grant made it possible for Porter to travel to study collec-tions of arts and crafts produced by Africans. He earned his Master of Arts degree in art history from New York University, and taught the sub-ject for forty years at Howard University (Washington, D.C.). His book is considered a standard reference work.

". . . change, indeed, is painful, yet ever needful; and if memory have its force and worth, so also has hope." **—Carlyle**

Malcom X (1925-1965)
Nationalist

Much of Malcolm X's earlier self-destructive behavior and anti-white views no doubt resulted from a childhood in which he witnessed the fire-bombing of his home by whites, the horrible death of his father that he attributed to Ku Klux Klan activity, and the committing of his mother to a mental institution following his father's "murder."

Though his father was a Baptist minister, he was also an activist who supported the black separatist concepts of Marcus Garvey and others which generated vengeful white backlash.

Malcolm (El-Hajj Malik El-Shabazz) dropped out of school in the eighth grade and left his home in Michigan for New York, where he worked as a waiter in a Harlem restaurant. It was during this period that he began using and selling illegal drugs and committing burglaries, for which he was given a ten-year prison sentence in 1946. While incarcerated, he converted to the Muslim faith, and it was while he was in prison that he developed the voracious appetite for reading and learning about the history of the black man. He was paroled in 1952, a vessel in which a new fire blazed. He became a vocal advocate of the Nation of Islam beliefs, one of which was the branding of whites as "devils," and declaring the white Christian world evil. He gave unflagging support to the leader of the faith, Elijah Muhammad. He became white America's "bete noir" with his black separatist statements and inflammatory accusations and remarks which also included his disdain for "Uncle Tom" blacks.

His advocating vengeance, and espousing of self-defense, against white violence, frightened whites, moderates, and conservative blacks. However, his "eye-for-an-eye" policy appealed greatly to the militant element of the Civil Rights movement. Largely due to his fiery speeches, the Nation of Islam became a feared and hated sect, that, for the first time in the modern era, told white society it did not desire its acceptance, and rejected its institutions.

After the assassination of John F. Kennedy, Elijah Muhammad suspended Malcolm for describing the murder as "chickens coming home to roost." Malcolm became increasingly dissatisfied with the black Muslim's teachings, and formed his own group, the Organization of Afro-American Unity and the Muslim Mosque Inc. He visited Mecca, Islam's holy city, in 1964. For the first time, he witnessed "brotherly love" between blacks and whites. He took the Muslim name El-Hajj Malik El-Shabazz. Death threats followed his changed views. His home was fire-bombed, though he and his family escaped harm. In the span of a week, however, he was assassinated while planning to speak at the Audubon Ballroom in Harlem.

Malcolm X deviated from traditional black leaders. The masses, if not the elite, saw him as a kind of "street prophet," who spoke the language of the people, and neither solicited establishment approval, nor compromised his beliefs.

Following the posthumous publication of *The Autobiography of Malcom X*, written with Alex Haley, both white and black America re-evaluated Malcolm's life. Many have come to see his reversal as his desire to seek brotherhood between all people.

One of the most controversial figures of the twentieth century, he was born Malcolm Little in Omaha, Nebraska. His family moved to Lansing, Michigan, in an attempt to escape the frequent harassment his father's militant views generated. By paradox, as Malcolm fled from violence, violence chased him down. As he courted the white man's hatred, he discovered the transforming power of brotherly love. Ironically, it was this brotherly love, which he wished to preach to his followers, which cost him his life.